Exploring
San Luis
Obispo County
and nearby coastal areas

By
Ron Stob

Central Coast Press
San Luis Obispo, California

Publisher:

Central Coast Press
P.O. Box 3654
San Luis Obispo, CA 93403

Second Printing

ISBN: 0-9658776-2-0

All photographs are by Ron Stob

DEDICATION

About the time I began writing for the *Telegram Tribune* in 1984, I met my wife Eva. The first gift I gave her was unabashedly self-serving; I gave her a pair of Nike hiking boots. I wanted a partner who would walk with me. Those little size 5 hiking boots have gone nearly everywhere I have, sometimes grudgingly, but some of our best times together have been on wilderness trails and in primitive campsites near running streams.

I didn't realize at the time that my hiker/wife would also become my copy editor. Now I wouldn't think of sending a story off to an editor without Eva's discerning eye. Where I'm florid, she's economical. Where I dance around the truth and decorate it and embellish it to so the reader doesn't know where I began, or where I'm going (as illustrated here), she cuts to the chase and makes the literary rough places plain. When I doubt my own ability to tell a story and I'm sure my writer's mind has turned into turnips, she lifts me up and tells me she likes turnips.

I feel like Brahms, she thinks like Bach; if together we have created something that is readable or even beautiful, I'm the first one to recognize that music without meter is nothing...a writer without a good copy editor is a noisy gong or a clanging cymbal.

Thanks, Eva.

AUTHOR'S NOTE

I want this book to be what it has meant for me, afternoons of delight and an escape from the tedium of business, office and committments. When I don't give myself time to be outdoors in nature, my disposition sours and my perspective dims.

These stories are my personal psalm.

You visit the earth with water from heaven
You fill the furrows
and settle the ridges
You soften the earth with showers
and make things grow

The pastures of the wilderness are green with life
the hills are wrapped in happiness
The meadows clothe themselves with flocks
the valleys are decked with grain
They shout and sing together
for joy.

Psalm 65

Ron Stob

A TRIBUTE TO A FRIEND

If a guy has to walk the trail by himself, he soon begins talking to himself. My friend, Ben Horner, keeps me from being lonely, frequently accompanying me on hikes. As a hike leader in our Methodist Church, he gathered the believers together and provided the ideal format for writing stories about the outdoors. Invariably, those good folks did things or said something that provided the theme for the story; unfortunately, it was those same good folks that bore the brunt of Ben's athleticism and poor judgment regarding the difficulty of a hike. We congratulated ourselves on getting everybody back alive, but it was sometimes seriously in doubt.

Ben is a triathlete kind of guy with a lean heart, long legs and the endurance of an iron man; but he was always a gentleman, guardian, path finder and friend. He walked as slowly as the oldest person and he would be the first to stop if someone's blister needed bandaging. It was comfortable being with him because we knew that if we got lost in the woods, he'd be out there looking for us (see the Villa Creek story). Thanks Ben, you're a gentleman and a hiker and my best friend.

And my gratitude to the people of the First United Methodist Church in Arroyo Grande. We didn't intend our hikes to be deep religious experiences, but when steep mountain trails disappeared into shale fields, or the hike that was supposed to be seven miles turned into 17, and when the walk around the last prominence at Point Sal Beach turned out to be a deep hole 8 feet deep that swallowed you up and you had to swim ashore...it turned out to be a life turning event for all of us and our worship on Sunday never had more depth and meaning because we had seen the Lord. Thanks for being good sports.

CONTENTS

SAN LUIS OBISPO COUNTY

And

Nearby Coastal Communities

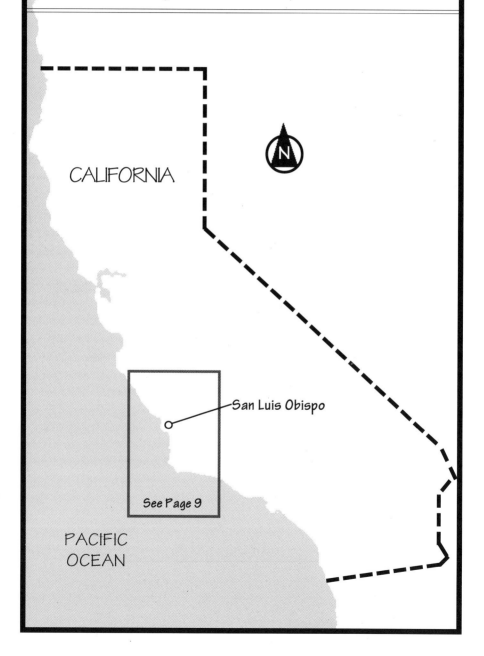

CALIFORNIA

San Luis Obispo

See Page 9

PACIFIC
OCEAN

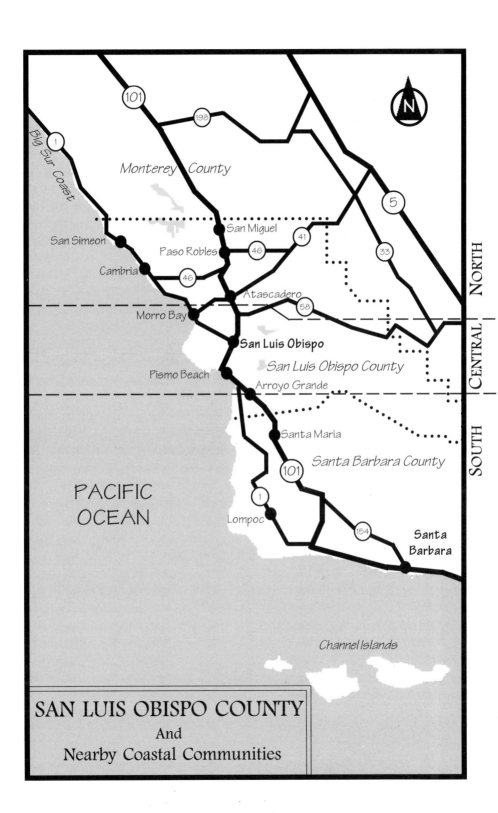

SAN LUIS OBISPO COUNTY
And
Nearby Coastal Communities

THERE'S NOTHING LIKE A HUNDRED MILES...

(Back Roads and Destinations within 100 Miles of San Luis Obispo)

There's nothing like a hundred miles between me and trouble in my mind
There's nothing like a hundred miles
Show me the yellow line
There's nothing like a hundred miles when I'm only passing through
There's nothing like a hundred miles
to make me forget about you.

Now, I realize James Taylor is singing about some lovesick guy, probably himself, but forgetting about you, could be your crummy job, the pressures of work, the tedium of life, the dirt and endless chores around the house or simply the need to get out of the house and go somewhere.

I know scads of visitors who think the Central Coast has some of the most interesting scenery in America, and I've learned that some of you haven't been anywhere in a long while. It may be time to saddle ol' paint and hit the trail. So here goes - a dozen ideas for getting wild in the great outdoors.

A) GOING NORTH-NORTHWEST ALONG THE COAST ON HIGHWAY ONE

I'd skip the mystery of Morro Bay, the expanse of Atascadero State Beach and the romance of seaside walks along Moonstone Beach in Cambria. I'd even pass up the intrigue of gift shops, and basket shops and fresh-baked-everything shops in Cambria and head right up to Ragged Point. Maybe I'd stop at San Simeon where Hearst's zebras feed in the fields at the base of his castle, but only when the fields turn blue with lupine and they look like carpets of flowers in scenes from **The Sound Of Music**. The flower show at San Simeon goes until May, so if the fields aren't quite ripe when you go through, go back later.

But I would certainly stop at the elephant seal beaches south of the Piedras Blancas Lighthouse. They've become our county's fastest growing tourist attraction and we haven't seen the best yet as seal populations increase and work their way down the coast.

After you drive past the lighthouse, wend your way to Ragged Point, a distance of 9 miles. Pull in at the drive-in or the Union 76 station and walk past the coffee shop to the trailhead of the descending path down the north facing slope. The trail is well maintained, and at the bottom it traverses a tributary of San Carpoforo Creek, which runs good in spring. The stream cascades over rocks and sluices through chutes and drops in several impressive falls before it enters the sea. You can walk all the way to the black sand beach; but be careful. The savage strength of the waves and currents of the point can be treacherous.

If you're out of shape or unable to hike, at least stop, Get out of the car and walk the level path to the point. If you decide to stay the night, you'll probably blame me for a romantic evening swaying to the sound of the surf. Ragged Point is the beginning of the rugged Big Sur coastline and you shall not miss it. Heah?

Salmon Creek

Water falls with tremendous thunder and might after spring rains at Salmon Creek. The hike is short and not steeply ascending, and if you bear left, staying close to the creek you will be able to squirm between VW size boulders. Before you know it you will be under the influence of the falls. A rush of cool-wet wind will turn you mossy green in minutes. It's a good place to have lunch, kiss your sweetheart or throw the kids in the pools. Dogs go a little nuts with all this excitement of rushing waters and clear running pools, so don't hang onto them or you'll be in the drink too.

There is a steep trail up the hill which will take you to Spruce Creek, Estrella Campground and the headwaters of the falls. You can't get to the trail from the base of the falls, so backtrack and find the fork in the trail that ascends. Along the way are many good sitting rocks for lunch that have great vistas of the ocean.

To get there: Salmon Creek is a few miles inside Monterey County. The highway makes a big sweep into and out of Salmon Creek gorge. Park alongside the road before passing the Forest Service buildings. The trail begins on the right (south) side of the creek. There are no signs along the road to indicate Salmon Creek and the falls; in fact, there aren't signs to any of the coast's fascinating features, except for state parks and beaches, so pay attention. The distance from San Luis Obispo To Salmon Creek is about 60 miles.

Sand Dollar Beach

Sand Dollar Beach is a great place to have lunch and to take out your little pail and shovel for some serious beach play. This is one of the prettiest all-white crescent beaches along the coast; and NO ONE IS THERE (well, hardly anyone). You can camp at nearby Plaskett Creek Campground if you're planning an overnight. You are 71 miles from San Luis Obispo.

Mill Creek

The rampaging creek unearths beautiful jade stones in the spring of the year, and the scene at the beach is the sound and sight of rolling stones. The stream brings jade down from the hills and the surf rolls them over and over again until they're smooth and polished. Every stone is a winner in my book - common or precious. I'll bet you'll pick, gather, hold and fondle a bucket of gems even if they are not jade. Take a pail and small shovel, and wear your old raggedy clothes because you'll end up wet. You're 76 miles from San Luis Obispo at Mill creek.

McWay Creek and Julia Pfeiffer Burns State Park

There's an anomaly of nature here - McWay Creek rides atop a saddle of land and then cascades as a waterfall into the sea. There aren't many places along the whole Pacific Coast where this happens. Pull in at Julia Pfeiffer Burns State Park and park your car. Follow the trail toward the ocean, passing under the highway in a 7 foot high culvert, then taking the right fork in the trail to the lookout. On the way back take the left trail to a walk above the falls. Before returning to your car, meander down the short trail to the Pelton wheel exhibit, it's a bit of mechanical history that's fascinating. You're 93 miles from San Luis Obispo at Julia Pfeiffer Burns State Park.

Partington Cove and Tanbark Trail

North of Julia Pfeiffer Burns State Park a few miles is the pull-off for Partington Cove (unmarked). Walk through the gate to the broad trail that winds down toward the ocean. Take the left fork in the trail over a wooden bridge to the hole in the wall that leads to the cove. The trail straight ahead goes to the beach.

In the 1880s John Partington cut 50 feet through the sheer rock cliff to make a six-foot high, eight-foot wide beam-supported tunnel to the picturesque cove on the other side. A boom that unloaded ships is still intact. Partington shipped out tanbark, redwood and lime. Tanbark was the source of tannic acid used for tanning hides and as a dye and astringent. On the up side (east) of the highway is the Tanbark Trail, one of the few places along the coast where you can explore the redwood groves flourishing along the streams that flow to the sea. The trail ambles to the Babcock grove, and over a wooden bridge to the McLaughlin grove. This is one of my favorite walks and ought not be missed. Continue for several hours on the trail if you wish to go to the Tin House, and return on the firebreak road back to the highway, close to where your car is. You're 95 miles from San Luis Obispo at Partington Creek.

Deetjen's Big Sur Inn

Deetjen's is a wonderfully cozy overnight inn and restaurant at Castro Canyon. If you don't stay overnight at least stop for a meal. It's an unforgettable experience. Get out of your car and walk the old coast highway around the horseshoe-shaped canyon to get an idea of the views from the rooms. You could call Deetjen's *Bohemian glitch* or *super funk*. It ain't anything like Holiday Inn. You're 100 miles from San Luis.

Ventana Inn

When you arrive at Ventana Inn you will probably feel like you have reached Mecca. Okay, so it's mammon, but it's good mammon. It's how most of us want to live - coddling indulgent service, orderliness and beauty, exquisite food and a pleasuring ground for carnal appetites.

Ventana is a harmonious blend of indigenous California architecture and landscape. The 60 units are built into the hills like tree houses. Huge timbers rise from the ground, buttressed by bold cross-members supporting houses wearing the weathered skin of rough-hewn cedar. There is no offense of man on the environment and the use of indigenous plantings along curving walkways and between buildings produces a synergy of natural landscapes and architectural forms. Seldom are native and synthetic used so creatively to produce a unified image with the natural woodlands and upland meadows.

A fascinating lighted walk of 15 minutes leads the cliff dwellers to the restaurant on the far hill. The path skirts a woodland of oak and bay laurel, traverses a ravine of coastal redwood and tanbark trees and emerges into the bright light of a grassy meadow near the restaurant. The views from their four star restaurant are seaward with huge windows and outdoor seating that worship the ocean and woods. Everywhere nature is adored and man-made environments are designed to accentuate the natural beauty of Big Sur.

Ventana is a couples place. The environment has a sensuous quality; the rooms are spacious and quiet, each of them having breathtaking views, yet are never seen from other windows. Our room had a high vaulted ceiling and a king size bed with an eight foot curved headboard. Tree stumps served as end tables for two large pottery lamps. A cache of wood next to the fireplace guarantees the romantic glow of flickering flames late into the night. The sharp angular lines and dull natural wood cedar siding of the interiors are comforted with soft cushions and subdued colors. Hard plays against soft, visually and tactically, and the result is wonderful.

Television, VCR, wet bar and a stocked liquor cabinet are all provided. Movies to rent are also available. After dinner there was time for the Japanese hot baths, men on one side, women on the other. We each entered the 4 foot deep hot baths from our respective changing rooms and showers, and slipped through the labyrinth of quiet pools until we were together in the common area under open skies and steamy night air. In the morning it was breakfast in the library, a peaceful place in a garden setting overlooking the ocean. The table was set for a king amidst heavy wooden furniture. Couples clustered in private corners and others took the bright sun and sharp breezes on the porch facing the ocean. Classical music played and everyone hummed, and for a moment there was peace on earth. You're 102 miles from San Luis Obispo and you won't want to go back. Call Ventana Big Sur Country Inn Resort for information and reservations: (408) 667-2331 or (408) 624-4812.

Alternative housing in the Big Sur might include the lodge and campgrounds at Pfeiffer Big Sur State Park (408) 667-2171 two miles north of Ventana; Deetjens, a miles south (408) 667-2377; the cabins at Lucia, 22 miles south (408) 667-2403; Post Ranch, across the road from Ventana, phone 800/527-2200, or 408/667-2200.

B)   ROADS NORTH—INTO THE JOLON VALLEY

Begin by taking Highway 101 to Paso Robles then jump on State Route J14 through the countryside to Lockwood and on to Jolon following Mission Road to Mission San Antonio. The Hearst Ranch headquarters, designed by Julia Morgan, were leased to Hunter Liggett Military Reservation, who have in turn transformed it into an overnight country inn called Milpitas Rancho. What was at one time cowboy headquarters is now a yuppy haven and worth a night or two. There are cowboy cells for cheap, or garden rooms, tower rooms and even a deluxe suite. Call 408/386-2511 for information.

Two trips worth your time: Jump on Del Venturi Road by Mission San Antonio and proceed over Hunter Liggett Military Reservation territory to the Indian Ranger station along Arroyo Seco Road. Proceed a half mile beyond the ranger station to a pull off on the right side of the road. There are numerous trails to the Arroyo Seco Gorge, an extensive area of sculpted sandstone formations. There are many grottoes, caves and enchanting water holes. Sycamores and alders overhang the pools and kingfishers sit on the limbs overhead.

The area of Nacimiento Road is always a good place for spring wildflowers. Take Del Venturi Road from Jolon a short way to Nacimiento road and travel to the foothills of the Santa Lucia coastal mountains. Nacimiento is a good return route from the coast if you decided to go up north along the coast. Jolon is 75 miles from San Luis Obispo.

C) DESTINATIONS EAST INTO THE CARISSA PLAINS

Take state highway 58 out of Santa Margarita to Shell Creek Road, a prime wildflower area. The Sinton family of the Avenales ranch has set aside a ten-mile section (north) along Shell Creek Road for wildflower viewing, and this area is probably one of the most colorful spring floral shows around. Proceed on highway 58 into the Carissa Plains for more wildflower viewing and a visit to Painted Rock. Turn right onto Simmler-Soda Lake Road about six miles beyond the service station and fire house to the entrance to Painted Cave. Distance from San Luis Obispo is about 75 miles.

D) DESTINATIONS SOUTH.

An Amtrak train trip to Santa Barbara from San Luis Obispo is the only way to see much of the coastline on Vandenburg Air Force Base and the roadless expanses near Point Conception. The steep grades of the Santa Ynez Mountains forbade the railroads from following highway routes through the passes so the rails were laid on seaside terraces from Casmalia to the Santa Barbara Channel, with one rail hanging over the surf and the other one nailed to the ground. The views are scenes motorists never see - dunes resplendent with coreopsis (in March), marshes, desolate beaches, and the old lighthouse at Point Conception.

Trains leave San Luis Obispo (Call 541-5028 for reservations) at 7:00 a.m. (the San Diegan, day trip train to San Diego), and 2:47 p.m. (the Coast Starlight, long distance train from Seattle to San Diego) for Santa Barbara each day. The San Diegan would allow you to take the Coach Starlight back the same day if the train ride was the only thing you were interested in. But if you chose to stay overnight in Santa Barbara, either train would be suitable. What are you going to do in Santa Barbara? Everything! This is a wonderful little city to visit overnight and if you book yourself into someplace romantic, like the Upham Hotel, or the Villa Rosa, you'll have an unforgettable time.

Walk from the station to the Villa Rosa or take a cab or city bus from the train station on Chapala to the Upham and begin an unforgettable evening. The Arlington Theater is nearby and you might tie in your visit with a live show, or catch a movie at the Arlington and hear the giant 1928 Robert-Morton pipe organ shiver the timbers. It plays almost every night during the 7 p.m. intermission. The Upham is a very special place in Santa Barbara and the oldest established continuously operating hotel in southern California. The decor and feeling of the Upham is more of New England than California, and on the rainy, cool night we were there fires crackled in the fireplaces and the dark walled interior and white trimmed windows and French doors made it a cozy den.

The Upham is an 1871 Italianate style hotel built like an adorned cube. Its 15th and 16th century Italian details of eave brackets, window pediments and roof cupola stand apart from the predominant mission architecture of the city.

Amassa and Abigail Lincoln, relatives of President Abraham Lincoln, came from Boston in the 1860s and saw the need for a rooming house in Santa Barbara and opened for business in 1873. Cyrus Upham acquired the hotel in 1898 and maintained it in his family for generations.

We sat before the fire in the lobby until nearly midnight, while Bob, the house cat, snoozed contentedly. The clock on the mantle always reads 10:15 and guests find themselves transfixed by flickering flames and the comfort of big wing-back chairs until someone realizes the hands on the clock aren't moving.

Part of the appeal of the Upham is its fine restaurant. No need to scour the town for great food, just walk to the front of the hotel and enter Louie's, a fine, little establishment that serves up things like parmesan crusted halibut with a tomato-caper-pecan sauce; or the grilled sea scallops with spinach fettuccine, roasted egg plant and tomatoes in a wine sauce.

Our room was in the Rose cottage, a short stroll from the main house among roses, hibiscus and azaleas. Each room in the cottages has a fireplace, downy comforters and period furniture. The carriage house, the cottages and the main buildings have been totally renovated and reflect the quality of this first-rate hotel. The Upham is at 1404 De la Vina Street, Santa Barbara. Call 962-0058 for information and reservations. The Villa Rosa is within walking distance of the train at 15 Chapala Street, ph. 966 0851.

E)   HIGHWAY STOPS GOING SOUTH TO SANTA BARBARA

Let's say you want to drive down instead. Here are several must- see stops along the highway that are special in springtime. About 4.5 miles south of Buellton on Highway 101 (4.5 miles from the Highway 246 junction) is a sign to Nojoqui Falls. I know you've seen the sign and wondered if you should stop, and the answer in the spring is, yes. We were there after heavy winter rains and it was spectacular. Take the short trip off the highway along the old coast highway a few miles to the park. Follow the signs once you exit. It's a ten minute walk from the parking lot to the falls along a well-maintained trail that parallels the boulder-strewn stream bed, crossing over it many times on wooden bridges. The falls are an impressive free wall of water down a marbleized rock face formed by mineralization as the water falls and evaporates. The sculpted surface is akin to the formations of Yellowstone National Park's mineral formations.

A few miles further south along Highway 101, where it intersects with Highway One, is Gaviota Hot Springs State Park, a primitive back country hot springs. Fortunately this one is only a half mile from the parking area alongside the highway. According to tritium testing this 115 degree water fell 38 years ago and is now coming out of the bowels of the earth at a depth of 3,280 feet and a rate of 25 gallons a minute into two pools. No doubt native peoples used these natural hot springs for thousands of years.

These are not neat tiled pools with showers and towel service; these are like all back country hot springs – clay tubs formed from use at a place where water under pressure gurgles to the surface. The pools are human excavations around the vent so the shape and contour of the pool changes according to human use. The water is tepid if there has been some runoff, or if the weather has been cool. Swim suits are required according to state law, but if you're in

You need an umbrella to stay dry at Nojoqui Falls in spring

the raw I can't imagine a ranger ordering you out of the pool to get dressed.

To get there take the Highway One exit going south and turn left at the top of the ramp, going over Highway 101 in an eastern direction. Turn right immediately, on the frontage road (going south) and drive to the end. Park and walk. In a quarter mile a jeep trail will go to the right (which is a fascinating trail that circles Gaviota Peak and comes out again by the hot springs). Stay with the main road-trail which veers left and go another quarter mile to another road-trail junction. Go right and proceed a hundred yards until you see a palm tree growing alongside the pools.

F) DESTINATIONS SOUTHEAST ALONG FOXEN CANYON ROAD AND SAN MARCOS PASS ROAD.

The quick way to Santa Barbara is Highway 101 south to Highway 154 and the San Marcos Pass and over the top, but a more interesting way is to get off in Santa Maria on Betteravia Road (State route 176) and go east to Garey and Sisquoc, where 176 ends. A block from town is the Blochman School with its collection of bells from outlying historic school houses that were consolidated to form the present school. More than 135 years ago visiting priests from the Santa Ynez Missions came to the Sisquoc to marry young couples and baptize babies under the shade of the poplar trees behind the school.

Pick up Foxen Canyon Road in Sisquoc and drive this historic stage coach route to Los Olivos. This was the principle route between Santa Maria and Santa Barbara before 1900. In two miles you'll come to the Ramone-Goodchild Adobe. It's on the right side of the road, situated on a bench beyond a row of eucalyptus which were planted on the boundary line around 1870.

After you pass Paragon Vineyards you will come into view of the 1875 San Ramone Chapel and cemetery which bears the remains of Benjamin Foxen, Juan Pacifico and many other famous names in Santa Maria history.

If you're interested in a picturesque back country winery, take the private road at the chapel a few miles to Rancho Sisquoc Winery, a pleasant hideaway winery among country vernacular frame farm buildings and wisteria-garlanded cottages. Continue on Foxen Canyon Road past the Frederick Wickenden Adobe, a large white frame house on the right side across from a red barn of Rancho Tinaquaic, to Zaca Mesa Winery and over a ridge to Zaca Station Road. Turn left to go to Zaca Lake, a fun place to see and visit. Grab a bite here or see if you want to make reservations to stay sometime. It's a wonderful retreat in the foothills of the Sierra Madre Mountains. If you take a right on Zaca Station Road you'll be in the neighborhood of Firestone Vineyards. Foxen Canyon road continues until it bisects route 154 (San Marcos Pass Road) near Los Olivos.

Beyond Los Olivos on Highway 154 is the road into the Figueroa Mountain area. There are many places to walk and picnic, and if you continue straight through you can exit on Happy Canyon Road, a pleasant circuit into the mountains of about 30 miles. Figueroa Mountain is about 100 miles from San Luis Obispo.

Aren't you glad you live here? Within 100 miles of home you can discover romantic getaways and enough outdoor activities to last a lifetime of weekends and mini-vacations.

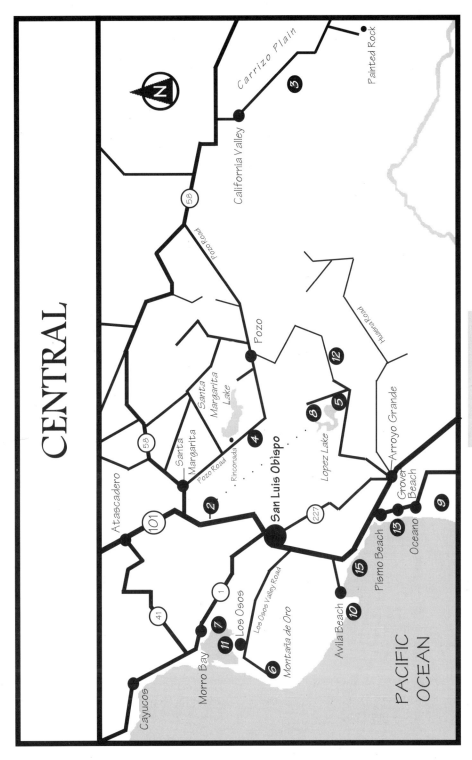

EASY AS PIE SEVEN MILE HIKE DOWNHILL

(Cuesta Grade To The Creeks Behind Lopez Lake)

I've learned not to believe certain triathletes when it comes to distances and levels of difficulty for hikes and runs.

When my friend Ben (who has just qualified for the Boston Marathon which I think means that he will run to Boston from California, run around the city and then run back to California) the hike down the wilderness trail from the top of Cuesta Grade into the Upper Lopez Canyon near Big and Little Falls, was said to be 7 miles. He had RUN this distance a year ago, so he should know.

"Seven miles?" I said in disbelief. "I can't believe that it is only seven miles from Cuesta Grade into the creeks behind Lopez, Ben."

"Yep, once you get on the trail after walking five miles on the East Cuesta Ridge Road it's only two miles and you're down in Lopez Canyon by Big Falls."

"Well let's do it, Ben. That should be just about right for our church group."

So we assembled a group of believers from our Methodist Church on a Saturday morning (in the first week of March when only 4.68 inches of rain had fallen), a troupe full of hope and promise, the kind of people that believe. They take you at your word. "It'll be an easy hike." I said to them in church. "It's all down hill. The wind will be at our back and we should be back at the church by three in the afternoon."

Our group consisted of four 12 year olds, a couple of teenagers, a bunch of 50 year olds and Helen, whose age I would never disclose but I'll tell you this much - when she was born Ford Motor Company paid its workers $2.40 for a nine hour day. We assembled at the church at 8 am.

When we arrived at the top of the grade and got onto the East Cuesta Road (also called Mt. Lowe Road) Ben and I looked at each other and said "This is really great isn't it?" You know, it's sometimes difficult getting out and onto the trails but once you're out here you find such exhilaration in the beauty of the land and in the sweetness of the air. Thoughts of war and drought and all earthly troubles fell away and the world looked bright and beautiful. We walked along with a lilt in our steps knowing that we only had seven miles to go...more or less.

From our perch above the city we looked out to the Chorro and Los Osos Valleys that were still filled with fleecy clouds. The details of the city were just coming into focus through the veil of clouds that covered the sleeping village. A Southern Pacific train was winding its way along the tracks on the slopes opposite us. The terraced slopes of Cuesta Grade are a written record of transportation in this area. The rails were laid in 1897, the old stage coach road was built in 1873 and at the bottom of the Cuesta Canyon is the old Padre trail dating back to 1772. Interspersed throughout are remnants of the first auto highway built in 1911, 1920 and 1947; and running with the fall line in utter indifference to the grade is the present highway built in 1967.

While the morning was fresh and moist the upland slopes looked barren. Seedlings of spring flowers were absent on the sunny slopes and perennial plants looked exhausted but a bit refreshed from recent rains.

But some species have done splendidly. Moors of new chamise have grown out of the ashes of past fires, and numerous pine tree saplings have found root and grow robustly despite the strangling grip of drought, looking none the worse for the tardiness of winter rains. Our group was excited to see the manzanita blooming, the rounded forms ablush with hanging urn-shaped flowers.

In an hour of walking we approached the Mt. Lowe Repeater where electronic signals are relayed. This area was badly burned in the fires of 1985 and '91, and grotesque forms of burnt trees litter the landscape.

After a steep uphill climb, (which Ben RAN UP a year ago. I suppose he never noticed it), we walked an even stretch to the trailhead to Lopez Canyon. It was at this five mile point that the truth was revealed. The trailhead sign clearly indicated that the distance from this point (5 miles from our cars at the Cuesta Grade) to Big Falls is 7 miles and another 2 miles farther to Little Falls. My pickup truck which was to take us back to Arroyo Grande was near Little Falls.

What was billed as "AN EASY AS PIE 7 MILE DOWNHILL WALK WITH THE WIND AT YOUR BACK" was now beginning to look like 12 or maybe 14 miles. There was a little swooning and fainting and sighing like people do when some awful truth has just been told them.

Not to worry. Ben could run that in about an hour and a half. But what about the rest of us? Bill Paulsen passed out pistachios to everyone and we all filled our molars with nuts, girded our loins, shifted our packs, drew a deep breath and headed down the trail.

The twelve year olds sprang out in front like arrows for a target, while the rest of us kept up an even pace, wending downhill in long sweeps, then descending precipitously into the Lopez watershed.

Sooner than we realized we heard water running. A small stream ran along side the trail in small waterfalls forming pretty little pools. The air was cool and

CENTRAL

moist and ferns and moss grew on weeping walls. The soil beneath our feet was dark and damp and spongy with humus. The volume of water in Lopez Creek that flows into Lopez Lake was beyond our imaginations.

Frank Parkes lends a hand to Helen Rader across one of many creeks

CENTRAL

Anemones bloomed by the side of the trail and I began to see the early forms of spring flowers in the damp understory. Overhead, huge oaks that have survived fires and storms gave the canyon the stable look of an ancient forest.

Soon the trail crossed the meandering creek. The creek became bigger and the trail crossings more frequent. We counted ten crossings, then thirty. Each crossing became more interesting and challenging. In a spring with abundant rainfall you have to swim across, but following our dry winter, we only had to jump or stone step or walk wet logs that rolled under our feet when we were in the middle of the creek.

Everyone did splendidly, even Helen, whose age I would never disclose but I can tell you that when she was three years old, the first telephone conversation took place from New York to San Francisco. We looked out for Helen, but she's not one to lean on someone. Bill found a nice walking stick which he used as an extension of his hand in getting her through the muddy holes and the creeks with deep water.

I've observed that the disposition of a group of hikers changes from excitement at the beginning of a hike, to mellowness in the middle, to fatigue and introspection later in the hike, sliding into sullenness when the hike goes on beyond the reasonable limits of a person's body. We were getting there. Creek crossing 43 came up. A colony of lady bugs congregated in the cool wet of the canyon, covering just about everything. There were hundreds of thousands.

At 2:35 we hit the road and Ben and I decided to run ahead to the truck so we could pick up our group along the way. Two fellows in a Jeep gave us a ride and a thousand yards from the truck we caught up with the twelve-year-olds of our group. They had outdistanced us by about an hour, the equivalent of 3 miles.

By the time we were ready to leave the creeks behind Lopez Lake, we had crossed Lopez Creek 71 times and had walked about 17 miles. Needless to say we made Ben walk home. He said he'd prefer to run.

On the way home most of us were dead tired, except Helen, whose age I would never disclose, who kept up a banter of conversation that made us all look at her and think - "I hope I have the energy and stamina of this lady when I'm..." When we tumbled our aching bodies out of the vehicles at church Courtney spotted the sermon title and shouted "Ron, look!" The title read SOME THINGS ARE WORSE.

Note:
Hikers should exercise caution because Lopez Creek rises quickly following heavy rains. At the time of our hike, only 4 inches had fallen in San Luis Obispo since the beginning of the rainy season.

THE EAST COUNTY NOBODY TALKS ABOUT

When I came to California in the winter of '81 I headed over the frozen plains, crossed the mountains and deserts and stood on the edge of the San Joaquin Valley at Tehachapi. I looked into the valley, already into a new growing season, and thought to myself, "This is the promised land."

I coasted into Bakersfield and studied the map for the last leg of the trip to San Luis Obispo. I was already on Highway 58 so staying on it from Bakersfield into San Luis Obispo looked like a logical choice.

I recall a roller coaster section of Highway 58 across an expansive plain, then a portion that was wild and uninhabited. "Where were all the people?" I asked myself, "This is California. Everyone's moving to California." (They were then.) The winding road of blue oaks and chaparral ended abruptly and I was in a small town (Santa Margarita), which led to the highway into San Luis Obispo.

That was a fine introduction to the coast. Nearly the entire ride from Bakersfield was in San Luis Obispo County, a county as diverse as some countries.

While the AAA booklet breaks up the county into North Coast, North County, South County and San Luis Obispo; no mention is made of East County. "Nothing's there," is what I suppose people think.

One day, while my wife was at work, I decided to relive that early back roads experience so I stole her car for a drive in the country. Of course, I promised I would not take it over gravel roads, and I certainly wouldn't get it muddy.

I set the odometer for 0 at the Telegram-Tribune offices on Higuera and headed up the grade. I turned right on Highway 58 through Santa Margarita, past the Log Cabin office building and ranch style homes with hanging geraniums. The Santa Margarita auction barn stood as square as a crate next door to the Rainbow Hut which looked like two eyeballs; the one all face, the other all eyes.

Across the RR tracks I passed the city park and a home with lambs for sale. The road to Pozo was on the outskirts of town but I stayed on Highway 58

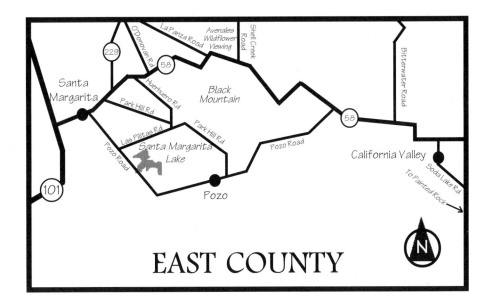

EAST COUNTY

going east. "Next services 82 miles" the sign said. I checked the fuel gauge.

The city was behind me and the road corkscrewed through the hills. In a short distance I gained long perspectives of valleys and distant ranges. A one-lane bridge for trucks and busses spanned the Salinas River. The buckwheat and deer bush still showed some life and the chamise and manzanita looked hardy following recent fires.

Roads to back country destinations flew by—Creston and Shandon on 229, Huer Huero Road, a Los Padres National Forest gravel road to the back side of the La Panza Range and primitive camp grounds like Navajo Creek, Black Mountain and Friis.

Gray pines, green and thin, grasped cones the size of bear claws. Poplars fluttered in the creek bottoms. Ground squirrels scampered across the road like it was blistering their feet.

Beyond O'Donovan Road (at odometer reading 25 miles from SLO) the road opens a bit, there are broader plains with more pines and blue oaks. The flower clusters of chamise were creamy-white to russet, otherwise it looked like a color photograph degraded to hues of blue—blue sky and the blue vegetation of oaks. The yellow and warm greens of the chamise with their showy flower heads made a subtle contrast. .

Thirty miles out (from SLO) La Panza Road went off to the left and Highway 58 turned easterly. I pulled off the road at Shell Creek Road and the Avenales Wildlife area, always a wonderful wildflower viewing area in springtime. The only thing blooming was jimson, or datura, a dark blue-green sprawling plant with big white bell-shaped flowers. It looked defiantly luxuriant in an otherwise parched environment.

An old windmill with an aero wind vane made in Chicago stood next to a water tank riddled with gunshot. This combination of windmill, water tank and overhanging tree is the trinity of the back country.

There's a world of dirt back roads to be explored from here; Los Padres National Forest roads spin through the hills to campgrounds in and around the Machesna Wilderness to the east of Highway 58. I decided to come back this way, crossing the summit and having a cold one at the Pozo saloon.

Forty miles out the terrain opens up. Blue Oaks continue to dot the hills, but soon I was in the treeless plains where cattle cluster under isolated trees. I got out to take some pictures in the heat of the day. The grasses were steeping in the hot dry air and there was a deliciously sweet aroma, like new mown hay. Summer felt good. Days under a foggy blanket along the coast leaves me homesick for hot summer days and sultry nights.

A Brahma bull watched me from the only available shade under a lone blue oak tree. The heat had drawn him out and his bullish sexuality made him look like a bronze-caste image. I got back in the car, shut the air conditioning off, rolled down the windows and went for it, doing 95 (degrees) without a sweat.

California junipers appeared on the hills, an isolated grouping along the grassy slopes. At the 50 mile point from San Luis Obispo the great plain of Carissa sprawled across the landscape to its eastern wall, the Temblor Range. I spotted the Arco Solar Energy plant, now defunct. The stanchions for the solar panels stood like light poles, stripped of their panels, wires dangling in the wind. The panels lie on the ground, soaking up the rays and not sending their energy anywhere.

Fifty-eight miles out of SLO on Highway 58 was Soda Lake Road and a wind-torn billboard sign to California Valley. "California Valley one mile." One mile to nowhere. "Soda Lake 13 miles."

I went beyond this junction to ride the roller coaster section of Highway 58 again. I picked up speed and met a Roadway semi coming over the hills, appearing, disappearing, reappearing, disappearing then suddenly reappearing as if he had crept up on me. He was grinning as we passed.

I turned toward California Valley, the forgotten community. Since I was here last the gas station has closed and the motel across the street looked deserted, although later in the day I saw a vehicle that I hadn't seen in the morning.

My hopes of finding food were dashed when I saw that the neighboring restaurant also was closed. I pulled out my emergency lunch, a bun slathered with peanut butter, an apple and a gallon of warm water.

The grasses of the plains were surprisingly long and a herd of cattle munched where people used to live. In 1960 this area was promoted as a potential community of 9,000 souls which were to include schools, a shopping center, swimming pools, a golf course and 25,000 acres of 2 1/2 acre plots. In hearings before the County Board of Supervisors, Fred Kimball wished developer Rick Walker success, "I hope you find oceans of water out there." They didn't. Now only a few homes are scattered on the grid of desolate streets that dead-end into the San Andreas Fault and the Temblor Range on the eastern side.

Seven Mile Road bisects the grids of California Valley, nipping the northern reaches of Soda Lake and heading back into Highway 58 eastward. I came to the sign of the Carrizo Plain Natural Area, managed by the Nature Conservancy, Bureau of Land Management and the California Department of Fish and Game. In a mile the shoreline of Soda Lake paralleled the road.

At mile 77.2 I turned right to the Soda Lake overlook. The road winds around the hill and mounts the back side of the hill. It's a short walk to the top and a marker and reference plate that identifies the natural figures, except that the raptors use this sign for a lookout point (also) and excreta flows across the diagram in confusing white streaks. Between the flows I could faintly read, "Soda Lake is the largest remaining natural alkaline wetland in California ...and the alkaline sink community which nurtures a narrow band of salt tolerant plants such as alkali heath and iodine bush. The Plain contains more rare and endangered species than any other place in California. Kit Fox, giant Kangaroo Rat, San Joaquin Pocket Mouse, Blunt Nosed Leopard Lizard and the San Joaquin Antelope Squirrel."

The sign gave the heights of visible mountains—Mt. Pinos, elevation 8831. Caliente Mountain, elevation of 5106. Midway Peak (just a minute I've got to scrape) elevation 3662...wait, (clean, clean), I think it's 3,664 feet.

Heat waves shimmered off the lake, still nearly full of water in mid July. The lake was edged in white, but in another month it will be a sparkling salt bed.

I looked to the west, trying to identify the dirt road leading to Painted Rock. A farm house with a cluster of buildings and three old combines was nearby. I remembered that the road ran by those three rusting combines.

Then a sign—Painted Rock Visitor Center. I pulled in. The road went toward the house and the old combines posing as rusting art. A new building had a sign "The Carrizo Plains Natural Area, Guy L. Goodwin Education and Visitor Center." I got out and into the heat. Grasshoppers scattered. "Closed for the season", a sign read. "But this is vacation time," I thought. A closed gate blocked the way to the rock.

There were other buildings nearby and a car that appeared to be from this century sat in the yard with four inflated tires. Maybe someone was here. A

CENTRAL

researcher answered the door. "The gate is closed because of mating peregrine falcons," he said. Phone calls later, we concluded that the gate was merely closed, not locked, and the falcons had fledged their young so it was safe to go out.

I went back to the car and rode through the undulating plains to the rock, crossing a small running stream with muck that sucked as I eased my wife's car into the creek. I slid in and bumped out leaving a chocolate mustache all 'round the tires. I thought about my promise to bring the car back clean. Maybe she would still be at her church meeting and I would be able to wash it before she saw it. I could hear her, "Where have you been with my car. It looks like you've been cuttin' cattle and forging streams again." By this time the car was a fine combination of prairie dust and stream bed muck so I continued, knowing I'd be in for a scolding later.

Sunbeams pierced the clouds and raced across the hills in a prairie light show. The road dipped and lost sight of the rock then rose again and came to a place out of view of the rock.

This was not Disneyland. There were no shuttle busses to the rock nor perky guides in uniforms pointing the way. Simply a trail marker. "Enter here, walk a quarter mile. Have a nice day."

I followed the marked trail, crested a ridge and saw the rock a quarter-mile away. There was hardly any grade and the aloneness of the moment immersed me in the atmosphere of this ancient Indian hunting grounds. Several California condors have been spotted near here, one of the few places in the world where these extremely rare and endangered animals can be seen. I scanned the sky. Maybe I would get lucky. There are only six in the world and one of them lives here; but the birds overhead were either kites or peregrine falcons.

The rock is a huge uplifted boulder in the center of a plain, with lesser rocks emerging from nearby slopes. The 20-foot portal leads to a circular amphitheater measuring 200 x 120 feet. The interior walls converge toward the top, giving the ground level walls protection from the elements. High back walls protect the enclosure from prevailing westerly winds.

The path cut through a garden of black sage humming with a million gathering honey bees. I sidestepped their favorite bushes and the cool ledges where they gathered. The images of the Chumash shamans are still there and discernible even after defacement from vandals who have chipped away sections and painted their own foolish imitations. These thoughtless and stupid acts are slowly degrading this priceless outdoor museum of Indian art.

The images were created by Chumash shamans and are considered to be religious and sacred. Having looked at sketches by Georgia Lee in Myron Angel's, *The Painted Rock*, published by Padre Productions, I recognized fragmentary forms of the mythological Coyote, thought to be one of the First People, and Lizard, and variations of the sun. I climbed the ledge and tried to figure out what was modern graffiti and what was ancient Indian rock art.

I left the opening and climbed the outside shoulders of the protected cavern and imagined the sounds of an ancient people who have resided here for 5,000 years trading with the Yokuts to the east and their fellow tribesman on the coast. They lived on this fruitful plain... "abounding in wild horses, elk, deer and antelope in countless numbers, and myriads of migratory birds of the arctic in their season, feeding upon its herbage." Myron Angel, *The Painted Rock.*

I decided to back track through Pozo on the ride home. Twenty-four miles from the rock, Pozo Road left Highway 58 and headed into the mountains.

The paved road began through oak woodlands. Valley oaks canopied the paved drive and blue oaks were silhouetted against brushed gold hills. It's as pretty as God makes it. For 8 miles it was clean and easy and very pleasant, then 12 miles of sporty driving over nice (?) gravel roads and perilous ledges to the summit of the La Panza Range. "Not recommended for campers and trailers," the sign said. "Or your wife's car," I might add.

I passed the last of the frontier homesteads and caught sight of an old stone barn and a collection of tiny cabins gathered in convention in a narrow meadow. Quail burst out of the thicket scampering along the road in their ditsy nervous state (DNS), chirping to each other, "Here comes a car, here comes a car, watch it, let's run, this way; no, this way; no, this way; no, this way...let's flyyyeeee." Near the top was the road to Queen Bee Camp, Pine Mountain Road and Machesna wilderness.

I finally came to the blacktop road near the center of the Eastern County Culture Center and cold drinks—Pozo. I pulled into the side lot of the Pozo Saloon, ready for a peaceful respite. But they were closed. I couldn't believe it. The thought of watering down here is what got me over the top.

I love this place. A couple years back my sons took me out on Father's Day and we sat in the back and listened to Louis Ortega. Other world famous acts come this way—a little of folk, 50s rock 'n roll and blue grass. Call them for times and details, 438-4225. The saloon is open Thursday through Sunday during the summer.

The macadam road winds through savanna woodlands to the little town with the flat front buildings and the Rainbow Hut which eyeballs travelers as they go by.

Who says there's nothing doing in the east county? I found it as scenic and more interesting than the first time I drove through it. Excuse me now. I've got to get this car washed before my wife gets home.

CENTRAL

SIDEBAR

* Round trip to San Luis Obispo is about 160 miles.

* The education center at Painted Rock is open from December to June.

* Tours from February to May include:
    1. Wildflower viewing
    2. Game and bird watching
    3. Geology of the San Andreas fault line at the base of the Temblor Range.
    4. Painted Rock.

For information call the Guy L. Goodwin Education and Visitor Center—(805) 475-2131 the Interpretive Center, or the Bureau of Land Management in Bakersfield—(805) 391-6000. Ask for the self-guided geology tour.

The gate to Painted Rock may be closed in December when the rains come. Roads become impossibly muddy when the rains begin, but that is also the time to see the sandhill cranes. Stay on the pavement.

There is no water or fuel in the plains. Bring your own. There are two campgrounds south of Painted Rock. Selby is two miles south off Soda Lake road and KCL is 10 miles south off Selby on Soda Lake Road.
Another way home from Painted Rock is by way of Soda Lake Road to Highway 166 near Cuyama. Soda Lake road is a well maintained dirt road that extends eastward for 30 miles before bisecting Highway 166. The pavement ends just south of Painted Rock.

Rainfall is usually 8-10 inches. It is usually dry by July.

There were about 2,000 sand hill cranes at last count.

THE RINCONADA TRAIL

(And the History of the Rinconada Mercury Mine)

My boys graduated from Cal Poly several years ago and moved on to the Bay area and to Portland to make a living, but San Luis Obispo remains home for these guys and I never get turned down when I invite them back for holidays and birthdays. I think SLO will always be their home, no matter where they live.

They love to hike, so when they come to town we invariably burn off the calories of a big family meal by hitting the trails. The Rinconada Trail was our selection so we drove out of Santa Margarita on Pozo Road and pulled into the trailhead parking lot, 2.7 miles beyond the road to Lake Santa Margarita.

It was the trail that we were interested in, but after pulling into the parking lot we began to wonder about the mine. At the far end of the parking lot is a sign and locked gate designating the Rinconada Mine.

It's not open to the public; but the fresh-air potty at the trailhead parking lot is open to the public and our group experienced the free-as-a-breeze, topless privy open to the hills. Never did nature call in a more natural setting. It's the only time we've rated an outhouse, "AAA".

The trail is on the left side of the parking lot with a sign, "Little Falls Trail 2 miles." We surmised that the Little Falls Trail was at the top of the ridge.

The winter sun was bright and pierced the cool air like laser beams as we swung into an easy gait on the lower trail. The ground wept from recent rains. Hiking boot prints, mountain bike impressions, horseshoe indentations and road apples told us this is an all-purpose trail.

The trail wanders upwards through grassy slopes and a copse of blue oaks. In some of the switchbacks we thought we identified cinnabar, the ore for mercury mining.

Toyon was showy with last year's berries and spring was in the lives of greening forbs. New chamise and manzanita sprigs burst from the charred crowns of recent fires. Ribes, or chaparral flowering currant, was blooming, its dusty rose buds and flowers soft and romantic.

The Santa Lucia Wilderness Mountains that we were hiking forms the western edge of the Santa Margarita and Pozo Valleys. Close to the top we looked northward to the telecommunication towers on Cuesta Ridge.

The Santa Margarita Valley looks like an unspoiled Eden from vista points on the trail. Texas owners want to develop it and locals fear it will become expensive ranchos with white picket fences.

Our group stayed on the trail and went through a gate at the top of the ridge where there was a road spur. It was not the Hi Mountain Road that we expected, but a short spur off of it. Hi Mountain Road was below us, out of sight.

We had lunch by a spoil area of black rock with mica. It was as if a monstrous earth mover had upset the crust of the earth.

Rinconada Trail spills down the slope on the southwestern side to Hi Mountain Road a half mile below, past islands of scrub oak and holly-leafed cherry. The trail bisects the road where there is a watering trough for horses and a large cement water tank. Five hundred yards beyond is the trail to Little Falls, which continues to the bottom of Lopez Canyon, a distance of 2.6 miles .

When we returned to our cars I turned to my wife. "Well, Toots, how do you rate this trail?" I know from experience that she gives poor marks to trails that make your pounding heart pop buttons off your shirt. She said, "It was fine." This I took as high praise. One person's "fine", is another person's "great." I think it's just right for a half-day land cruise with a lunch spot overlooking verdant valleys, unless you extend it to include the trails to Lopez Canyon. Then it will be a heartbreaker, unless you have a pickup at the other end.

While we were not able to see the Rinconada Mine, my curiosity was aroused and after a dozen contacts with reference librarians, local history books and folks at the Pozo Saloon, I got to talk with Mike Whiteford whose family owns the mine.

Many of the mines in our county were quicksilver mines. Cinnabar, a

The trail provides many views and vistas

vermilion colored rock found in hardrock formations, contains mercuric sulfide. When the rock was cooked in a retort, or oven, gases were driven off and condensed in distillation tubes.

The end-product was mercury, for which there were a variety of uses. Mercury was used for thermostat switches on furnaces; it was mixed with silver to form an amalgam for tooth fillings, and the silver bulb at the end of a thermometer is mercury.

During WW 2 mercury switches were used in places where sparks from "make-break" switches could be a hazard, such as in areas where there were flammable materials or explosives. The applications for mercury have decreased with time and the Rinconada Mine ceased operation in the 1960s. Presently there are no active mines in the county, although mercury is still considered a strategic mineral.

Most of the mines were in the mountains above Cambria; the biggest being Klau and Buena Vista Mines on Cypress Mountain Road; but county maps shows others as well. The southernmost mercury mine in the county was Rinconada, a minor player in comparison to the others, but its name is on a valley, a ranch, an earthquake fault, a store and now a trail. The original Spanish name for the mine was La Mina de los Amigos—The Mine of Friends.

The Rinconada Mine was in existence from the days of the Spaniards. Mike Whiteford's great-great grandparents, Rufino and Cecilia (Carmine) Pedraita, purchased the mine in 1897 from the Maho brothers. They came to Cayucos in 1882 as immigrants from Giubasco, Switzerland, and operated the mine until 1900 when they leased it.

Many different mining companies and partnerships operated the mine over the years. These groups expanded the operations of the mine and brought in extensive machinery.

When the mercury in the ore was recovered, the baked rock was hauled away and used by the county and the U.S. Army Corps of Engineers for roadbed throughout the Santa Margarita Valley. Much of the road to Pozo rides over red rock that came from the Rinconada Mine.

In 1941 the U.S. Army Corps of Engineers stored dynamite at the Rinconada Mine site while they constructed the Salinas River Dam which impounds Santa Margarita Lake, a project designed to supply water for Camp San Luis.

George Bell, grandson of the Pedraitas, capitalized on the development of Lake Margarita by building the Rinconada General Store at the juncture of Pozo Road and Santa Margarita Lake Roads, circa 1941. Behind the iron fence next to the store is a collection of buck boards, carved statues and frontier buildings lined up along an imaginary town's Main Street that were built by various lease operators of the store throughout the years.

CENTRAL

Currently the mine and surrounding property is owned by Carol Bell Blake and Juneln Bell Whiteford, great-granddaughters of the Pedraitas's. Mike Whiteford's two sons, Connor and Joseph, are the sixth generation to live in the Rinconada Valley.

Plans to develop the Rinconada Mine into a historical attraction went up in flames when a backfire was lit during the Las Pilitas fire (1985). The fire destroyed all the buildings and only the charred remains of machinery and equipment remain.

No, the Rinconada Mine is not open to the public, but you're welcome to stop at the Rinconada General Store and campground at the intersection of Santa Margarita Lake and Pozo Roads. Mike Whiteford is usually there and willing to share his knowledge of the history of the Rinconada area.

SIDEBAR

Distance from the Rinconada General Store on Santa Margarita Lake and Pozo Road to the Rinconada Trail by going east is 2.7 miles.
Distance from Rinconada Trailhead to High Mt. Rd. = 2 miles
Distance from Hi Mt. Road to Lopez Canyon via Little Falls Trail = 2.8 miles
Round trip distance from Rinconada Trailhead to Lopez Canyon via Little Falls Trail = 9.6 miles
Distance from Rinconada Trail to Hi Mt. Road—to Big Falls Trail—to Lopez Canyon Road—to Little Falls Trail—to Hi Mt. Road—to Rinconada Trail—to Pozo Road parking lot and the Rinconada trailhead = 16 miles.

Rinconada General Store and Campground are near the Rinconada Trail

CENTRAL

5

FINDING WILD TURKEYS ON TURKEY RIDGE TRAIL

(At Lopez Lake)

We knew there were wild turkeys at Lopez Lake but we were a little surprised when we started our walk up Blackberry Springs Trail at the end of Squirrel Canyon Camp. As we approached the trail head we saw the black silhouettes of two strutting males. Nearby a flock of disinterested hens pecked and scratched in the debris beneath the trees.

The Turkey Ridge Trail is one of their favorite places to roost and feed and they are in this area predictably each morning around 8 a.m. Rangers told us that in the fall when acorns drop from the valley and live oaks, the turkeys and deer literally graze the parking lots, eating the nuts that are smashed by the cars; but even in winter they feed from fallen acorns, and gather whatever vegetation can be had -- berries, fresh sprouts, seeds and occasionally insects.

We walked like native hunters, approaching our "prey" quietly, slowly, hiding behind trees, standing still, waiting, advancing slowly. It's surprising how much of the hunter is still in us. We were only shooting film but the technique for hunter or photographer is the same. The turkeys are trusting and accustomed to humans and we got very close. On another day I came by myself and spied on the lives of this flock of 20 birds. I was amazed how easily I could approach them. I crept from tree to tree, standing motionless for several minutes until the turkeys took me for a tree in the forest. Soon I was living among them. The hens gossiped in high chirping sounds as they scoured the ground while two mature males promenaded, vying for the title of "biggest and baddest."

At any time, one or several of the flock would raise their bright red heads like periscopes and with clear black eyes scan the horizon. If any movement was picked up, serious clucking began and the entire flock stopped feeding and 20 heads rose to assess the environment.

Turkeys have a terrible reputation, but it's the domesticated versions of the wild turkey that are dumb and foolish. Researchers have discovered that all the adaptive wild behaviors have been bred out of domestics, and with their white feathers, oversized breasts and chicks that don't respond to the distress signals of their mothers, they are no longer able to make it in the wild. But these birds at Lopez, and at other sites in our county, are wild and wary and able to survive cold and drought and marauding predators.

The males continued their rite-of-passage ritual. They pirouetted in front of each other, throwing their vivid blue heads back into an enormous chest of ruffled bronze. Bubbles and warts on their naked necks were puffed with ripeness and oozing with neon brightness. Their tails expanded into a black and

Two male turkeys exhibit strutting behavior

gold-banded fan. They were absolutely splendid and totally narcissistic.

The white and black-banded wing feathers dragged the dirt; the stiff center vanes dragging along the ground and making sounds like the rushing sound of a giant fan or propeller. It could be heard a 100 feet away. The center vein was worn flat from friction with the ground. Their frenetic dance crescendoed, their skin ripening perceptibly until they literally exploded into a climactic, "gobble- gobble."

I kept hidden behind a big oak tree, photographing them while this was going on. I learned their gobble-gobble call and soon was talking with them.

Meanwhile, the hens were running up the hillsides, clucking and feeding and doing sane and reasonable things, totally indifferent to the presence and calls of us males.

The heavy horizontal boughs of the oak trees come close to the ground along the side of the hill in Squirrel Canyon and with a rush the hens jumped into the trees, first one then another, then all the rest in rapid succession. The tree was like a giant ornamented tree at Christmas.

They walked, scratched and flew higher into the far reaches of the tree with the grace and commotion of flying umbrellas. Their long wing spans were too much for precision flying among limbs and branches, and their flights were comically clumsy and noisy. Sometimes they would take twenty-yard flights to the next tree, announcing their flights with histrionic calls and the breaking of limbs.

When one of them descended to the ground close to the two toms, the others followed, each one launching into space like a heavy bomber, steeply gliding and shrieking like excited kids, then leveling off as they approached the ground. Flaps down. Landing gear engaged. Touchdown. Legs a blur of rapid peddling. Screeching brakes kept them from running into each other. These flights were done time and again, without fault or accident.

I saw the turkey as the proper symbol of America - excessive, noisy, over-built and prone to accidents, but able to get the job done. To my great surprise I saw them take off from the ground where they had been feeding and fly back into the trees twenty feet above.

But back to our original purpose for coming to Lopez Lake...

Blackberry Springs Trail begins at the end of Squirrel Campground and winds up a canyon of live oak draped in Spanish moss. It's a marked and inter-pretive trail with numbered stations describing the features of the land and the plants in that vicinity. Blackberries line the trail in the cool canyons where ferns grow luxuriantly on a weeping wall, but on the upland slopes chaparral plants such as California sage, black sage, sticky monkey flower and pearly everlasting are the dominant forms.

The trail ascends a narrow canyon to the top of the hill where it joins the High Ridge Trail, a two-lane firebreak that runs along the ridges above the lake. Along this firebreak is the strata of the Santa Margarita formation, a seabed formation that existed here 26 million years ago before the land was uplifted. This was the period when camels, mastodons, rhinoceroses and sabre-toothed tigers inhabited the uplands around the edge of the inland sea. Some of the fossil specimens in this formation are as big as modern scallops and we found sand dollars and oysters.

We returned to the trail that skirts a hillside and eventually returns to the High Ridge Trail at a higher elevation, then crosses it and continues westerly along another sunbaked hillside of chaparral. We thought we had climbed to

CENTRAL

the top of the ridge, but the trail ascended another peak before we could rest assured we were downhill to the entrance station again.

Along the way are numerous wood rat nests, some of them five feet high and six feet across. Females live their furtive lives inside the den, caring for their broods while the males live an isolated life in nests of their own that are off the ground and in the brush.

An open field of grasses and spring flowers was passed before we were back in the forest of valley oaks and the habitat of the wild turkeys close to the entrance station.

This trail loop is only 1.8 miles, but if you get fascinated with wild turkeys it could take you all day.

SIDEBAR

Wild turkeys are as American as the buffalo and the grizzly bear. When the Spaniards first arrived in America they shot wild turkeys for game and learned to rely on the big birds for food. They were surprised and pleased to see that native Americans had domesticated turkeys.

Live turkeys were some of the first exports back to the old world and their domestication spread throughout Europe. Made in America exports were begun with native-born wild turkeys.

Turkeys haven't always been in California. Their natural range is on the eastern side of the continental divide, all the way to the Atlantic coast and south into the highlands of Mexico. They were carried across the divide and introduced into California as a game bird. They have adapted beautifully to the oak woodlands along the coast and in the Sierra Mountain foothills and now appear an integral part of the biota.

CENTRAL

6

I LOVE MONTAÑA DE ORO IN THE SPRINGTIME

I love Montaña de Oro in the springtime, I love Montaña de Oro in the fall, I even love it when fog enshrouds the cliffs and hides the peak of Valencia. I love it when the sun shines brightly and spangled breakers burst upon the shores.

I like it in the mist and dew when water beads on the meadow rue and water rushes in the creeks. I like it when it's quiet and foggy, and chilling to the bone. I like it in the campground when we're cooking out and a covey of quail scratch in the duff, and birds call from the thicket.

I like it least when winter storms strike it and waves gnaw at the edge of the land like a lion eating a deer; but even then, and particularly then, it seems like one of the last places on earth where creative forces live out their impulses unabated; wild, free, vicious, gorgeous, primitive.

But it's had its human inhabitants, its developers and its ranchers. Even the name, Montaña de Oro (mountain of gold), while fitting, was named by Irene McAlister in the 1950s. She saw "gold" in the shale hills and spent one fortune trying to make another fortune in oil. The ranch-(prospective) oil field went bankrupt in the sixties and the State of California purchased the lands which now extends from the mouth of Coon Creek all the way to Morro Bay. Eight thousand acres are within Montaña de Oro State Park.

As you approach the park along Pecho Road from the town of Los Osos on Los Osos Valley Road you may be smitten, as I was, not only with the magical views to the north of the sand spit and the big morro standing in the waves, but with the zoo of starved blue gum eucalyptus, growing in woeful deprivation like row crops of sugar cane. In their sterile environment nary an invasive weed or native plant takes hold.

But after a spring rain when you walk along the bluff trail and see a group of brown pelicans coming off Point Buchon, skimming the frothing surf, you know that this is a natural realm of the free and wild also. There are mountain lions, raccoons and wild hogs that still run free. There is the natural chaparral, the wild flowers, and of course the ancient rocks.

Ah, those ancient rocks! Faulted, twisted, and convulsed into distorted and painful forms, this land has been pushed from below and from all sides. At one time it was the sedimentary bottom of the ocean, but it was thrust upward as the Pacific Plate collided with the American Plate along the San Andreas fault. The evidence of these convulsive movements is seen graphically along the headlands of Montana de Oro.

Long chutes have developed as the sea wears away the softer fragments of the uplifted layers, and at the far end of the two-mile long bluff walks are doorways and arches cut into the rock by the sea.

We walked to the edge of the sea on a shelf of rock just beyond the high tide mark, mesmerized by the action of the sea as it surged in and out of the sea caves. The constant stirring and mixing of the water made it look like Perrier, and beneath the effervescence, was iridescent algae, swaying back and forth and flashing brilliant blue-green lights.

At the end of the bluff walk, which is two miles from the Spooner Ranch House and interpretive center, is the trail head to Coon Creek. At the mouth of the creek the native Chumash Indians had a village site.

We hiked Coon Creek Trail when the late afternoon fog filled the canyons, The trail along the creek is an entry into solitude of towering trees and luxuriantly growing shrubs. The grasses, weary from a day of nodding, hung over the path, dampening the toes of our shoes. The air was musty and quiet and a mourning dove called plaintively, while wrens chittered from the brush.

The riparian vegetation runs up to the base of the hills and ends like a thermocline. Beyond grows the dull gray chaparral.

In the black water of quiet ponds bay leaves lined up like schools of salamanders. Shiners darted through the water like silver arrows.

The trail opens up into a pleasant meadow. A fox or coyote finds this section of the trail his favorite dunging spot; and the added manure of trail horses made a fertile trail of animal leftovers. We didn't mind. They are silent, unobtrusive residents, and their contribution only enhances the naturalness of the area and enriches the plants nearby.

A beautiful live oak lies close to the trail, sprawling across the ground like a monster resting on its elbows. The ground beneath is clean , providing a resting place for lovers and travelers.

We met a young couple on the trail. She had a diamond in the corner of her nose and he had a red beard and lilac eyes. They seemed happy. They told us about a rotting log with turkey tail fungus up the trail.

The junction with Oats Peak Trail came up one hour from the Coon Creek trail head. If we went that way we would exit at the Spooner Ranch House in about 5 miles. At the head of Coon Creek is the site of Amasquito's cabin located in a grove of cedars, all of which date back to the 1900s. He farmed modestly and cleared enough land to raise a few farm animals and food for himself.

There are over fifty miles of trails throughout the park, including equestrian trails. Bicycling is possible on some of the park trails including the Islay Creek Trail, which runs alongside the creek to a waterfall and a historic barn.

Behind the old (1892) Spooner ranch house is a campground with fifty primitive campsites suitable for tents, trailers and motor homes up to 24 feet in length.

Day use facilities and picnic tables are at Spooner's Cove, Coon Creek and at the ranch house. Call park headquarters for information at 805/528-0513.

Views of Valencia Peak from the cliffside sculpture along the Cliffs Trail

CENTRAL

KAYAKING, IT'S REALLY EASY

It was before 8 am on Sunday morning. The atmosphere was still and misty. Nothing moved. It was the kind of day to sleep in, be quiet and read.

The phone rang. It was Dennis Sheridan. "It looks great, Ron. It's nice and quiet, high overcast but no fog. It's going to be really good. Are you ready?"

"Go back to bed and don't be so cheery, Dennis," was my first impression, but I faked it and grunted something agreeable. "Okay, Dennis, I'll see if I can wake Eva and get some breakfast on the table."

In 15 minutes Bill Deneen called. He had talked with Dennis, also, and was as bright as a chickadee. "It's a great morning, Ron. I'm loading the kayaks and I'll be over in 20 minutes."

"Hold it Bill," I cried, "Eva is still in the shower and we haven't had breakfast yet. Give us a little time to put ourselves together."

Sometimes the brightness of enthusiasm needs to have more respect for the darkness of melancholy.

Bill picked us up in his truck, kayaks hanging out the back. On the way to Morro Bay he explained that it was advisable to go out on the bay on a rising tide and come back when it is falling. We had it timed just about right; high tide was at 7 a.m. so we'd be going out as the estuary (where sea water meets a fresh water creek) filled. Nearly 70% of the estuary/bay is exposed at low tide. "If you go out on a falling tide," Bill said, "you could get to the sand spit or to Baywood and have yards of muck between you and the dock."

I remembered the last time I saw Bill on the bay, trying to rescue someone who got stuck in the mud at low tide. Bill ended up wearing the muck line at his crotch.

We helped Bill and Dennis unload their kayaks and studied these skinny boats. Dennis' touring kayak for two had more chine and beam than Bill's round-as-a-barrel kayaks, but it was sleek and racy. Eva got in with Dennis and they were quickly gliding like a great goose while Bill and I got ready. Bill threw a horse blanket in my kayak to cushion my tush, gave me a few rudimentary

Bill Deneen gliding like a swan

instructions and was gone. He had said earlier, "It's really easy, Ron. Every beginning kayaker who has never kayaked before, goes out in a kayak and in 30 minutes they've picked it up. One guy who had never kayaked before was racing after a little bit. I couldn't keep up with him." This was said obviously to make me look small.

I was left on shore to figure out how to get into this hollowed toothpick, stow my gear which included $550 worth of camera gear and the complete Eddie Bauer Seafaring Expedition Outfit (seemed like).

Once stowed and my fanny in place I had to figure out how to get in the water. The nose (bow) was in but in order to stay dry I didn't push it in very far, so I was sitting comfortably on shore...and avoiding the final step.

Push, shove, scoot, sweat, feel foolish. Inch by inch I crept into the water like an amphibian returning to its primordial haunt. I was finally floating...and wobbling. I couldn't believe how tippy this thing was. I felt like a lumberjack on a rolling log. The consolation was that I was in one-foot of water. If I tipped over I'd be able to stop my roll by putting my hand down (whereby my body would bring the opening of the kayak below the water line, wherein all my gear would be in salt water, thereby I would lose all my gear, my story and my pleasant Sunday disposition and my first kayaking outing would be *down the drain*, so to speak).

Good ol' Bill was in the same type of kayak but moved like a swan, effortlessly, without a ripple, his silver beard flowing in the breeze. Show-off.

I tried to get the hang of it, all the time thinking about the camera gear and food etc. at my feet. Bill said, "60% pull, 40 % push on the opposing paddle." I was still struggling with balance and he was giving me a mathematical paddling ratio to think about.

But things did come together, and soon I looked less like a *cerebral-deprived person* and more like a real-life kayaker. The others were close to a submerging mud flat and eel grass bed watching white pelicans and marbled godwits. The winter migration had begun and the estuary was filling with wildlife. Harbor seals were cruising nearby, unperturbed and apparently used to kayakers so close by. This is one of the marvelous things about kayaking. The wildlife seem to have an understanding that anybody in a kayak is a friend.

Elegant terns chittered overhead and Bill and Dennis got excited. The quiet of morning hung on like the aroma of a second cup of coffee. We sat on our paddles and watched. Wispy cirrus clouds filled the sky and made a dramatic backdrop for Hollister Peak and the chain of volcanic plugs called the Seven Sisters. There is no better vantage point for this string of mountains than in a canoe or kayak on Morro Bay.

We headed for the sand spit before the wind came up later in the morning. Dennis and Eva beached their kayak, then I came to shore, untangled my legs from the cubby which entombed them, tying to figure out how to get from the middle of the kayak to the shoreline without taking a dunking. There's no way to stay absolutely dry kayaking, and by this time I was damp and my gear generously sprinkled. Wet isn't bad. Everything dries and is washable.

We walked the dunes, identified plants, saw places where rabbits eat, defecate and urinate. When you're with naturalists, you get the whole unadulterated story.

Heading back, the noon winds picked up, making small ripples, nothing disturbing, but this shallow estuary can get sizable white caps after an afternoon of wind and it's advisable to do this sort of thing in the morning.

We stopped for lunch at the Bayside Cafe, a picturesquely-situated restaurant behind glass walls with pretty views of the waterfront and the comings and goings of kayakers. The State Park Marina rents canoes and kayaks and is a good place to begin. Most of their rentals are of the more reliably stable variety and they give brief instructions, provide life jackets, helmets, paddles and encouragement. They don't expect anyone is going to be doing Eskimo Rolls, so the usual admonition is, "If you fall in, stand up. If you can't stand up, stay cool. You're afloat, your kayak is afloat and someday you'll be together again."

Following this pleasant Sunday with Dennis and Bill, I heard from Jack Beigle. He heads the SLO Paddlers Canoe/Kayak Club and told me they were going onto Lake Santa Margarita the next weekend. Would I like to come along?

My one day of kayaking whetted my appetite. There are many shapes and styles of kayaks and I was eager to try another less-tippy-kind. He told me about Central Coast Kayakers in Shell Beach, close to both of us in the south county that rents and sells kayaks, so I went over and talked to Paul Schiro, owner. He and his sidekick, Rodney Way, gave me the skinny on types styles and uses. They sponsor sea cave tours using a broad-beamed *sit-on* (rather than sit-in) kayak, and they recommended I use the Cobra XL for touring Lake Santa Margarita, a kayak with hard chines, broad rails (works like outriggers) and sizeable keel for good tracking.

"How much if I wanted to buy this kayak?" I asked.

"Four hundred fifty dollars for the basic model, but if you want us to put in hatches and sell you a nice seat and stringers, paddles, helmet and life jacket, maybe eight hundred to a thousand," he said

On Saturday morning I picked up my kayak complete with helmet, PFD (personal flotation device), paddles, pack and water bottles, secured it in my pickup and headed for Lake Santa Margarita. It was a different experience than the Morro Bay kayak trip in Bill's tippy kayak. I got so fluid, so absolutely cool, someone said to me, "You can't convince me you haven't done this before."

"Last week was the first time, today is the second," I called back.

The group headed for their campsite on Lake Santa Margarita, then after lunch explored the coves of the lake.

Now if Bill or Dennis would call and say, "Let's go kayaking!" I would probably chirp back, "Terrific, I'd love to."

SIDEBAR

Here's how you can learn and where you can rent or buy. Rental rates vary but range from $6-$10/hour, $15-$30/half day, $25-$40/full day, depending on equipment.

Central Coast Kayaks
1879 Shell Beach Road, Shell Beach, CA 93449, ph. 773-3500, Paul Schiro, owner. Offer tours, and a good selection of touring and surf kayaks to rent or buy. Knowledgeable staff. Ask Rodney Way about his sea cave tours. Basic instruction for beginners.

Good Clean Fun Surf and Sport
136 Ocean Front, Cayucos, Ph. 995-1993, Steve Hennigh, owner Long established shop with new and rental kayaks. Specializes in ocean kayaking. Has lessons through Cuesta College, programs for kids, many clinics, experienced staff. Eco-tours along the Cayucos shoreline and in Morro Bay Estuary. Location is right on water.

Kayaks of Morro Bay
699 Embarcadero #9, Morro Bay, CA 93442, Ph. 772-1119, Lloyd Reeves, owner. Reeves is a world-class competitor. Rental location on floating pier at end of Pacific Avenue for clean and

CENTRAL

easy in and out. Knowledgeable owner and staff, extensive inventory, good assortment of rentals. Classes and tours. Show room in Marina Square, 601 Embarcadero, second floor.

Kayak Horizons
Morro Bay, 551 Embarcadero, Morro Bay, Ph. 772-6444, Frank Loving and Bob Reed, owners. Small shop, new owners, rentals and new boats. Docks on the water.

Morro Bay State Park Marina Kayak and Canoe Rental
10 State Park Road, Morro Bay, CA 93442, ph. 772-8796
Rentals of basic and touring kayaks, some instruction available.

Pacific Marine
331 Pacific, San Luis Obispo, Paul Coucaud, owner, Ph. 544- 4471 New and rental kayaks and canoes. Conducts tours on Morro Bay Estuary.

SLO Paddlers (Canoe and Kayak Club)
Arranges outings on Morro Bay, Lake Santa Margarita and Lopez Lake.
Phone Jack Beigle for information and a schedule of events, 773-2147.

CENTRAL

8

LOPEZ LAKE

(Mountains, Water and Scenic Trails)

Every time I drive into the Lopez Lake Recreation Area I am struck by the beauty of the place. It's the scenic combination of water and mountains that's magnificent, and if perchance you drive up in the morning when the mist is on the lake, every turn of the road makes the mind click like a camera. There's a modest day-use fee to get into Lopez Recreational Area, but it's what I call a bargain summer vacation.

At the end of Lopez Drive, beyond the campgrounds, the water slides and frenetic summer activity, is a sanctuary guarded by a locked gate...and the beginning of some very scenic trails.

Thanks to the scouts at French Camp, the Tuoutchi Trail creates a continuous trail system from the public camping and picnic areas of Lopez Recreation Area to the peninsula that separates the Wittenberg Arm from the Lopez Arm.

The Wittenberg road-trail begins at the locked gate which has a horse and pedestrian walk-through. Near the gate is a strata of Santa Margarita limestone rich in 26 million year-old fossils. If you have a geologist's pick, screw driver or hammer you'll be able to break apart the stratified stone and find perfect scallops and an occasional sand dollar.

To the left of the trail among the willow thickets in the Wittenberg Arm of the lake, empty milk crates tied in bunches look strangely out of place when the lake level is down...until you remember that these were the "thickets" for spawning bass in a lake bottom scoured clean in 1969 when the reservoir was filled.

As you walk the Wittenberg Trail beyond the locked gate you'll see a white tailed kite hunting in earnest along the creek, soaring, then hovering as it scans the territory with laser-beam eyes.

The road is ideal for mountain bikers and equestrians too, and in about a mile the Wittenberg Trail sidles next to Upper Lopez Canyon Road, a paved road that eventually leads to Little and Big Falls.

If biking is your interest, you can ride three tortuous miles from French Camp to Camp Good News Conference Grounds where the pavement ends. Then it really gets barmy. After 7 creek crossings over slippery algae-covered boulders, you'll come to Little Falls. Then if you're still alive you can do another half dozen crossings and 2.3 miles beyond Little Falls to Big Falls. Eventually you'll have to turn around and do the whole thing again.

Biking through the numerous creek crossings to get to the falls is like biking on marbles, but you could set some kind of record – for falls, for swollen ankles when you clank them on the rocks, for welts on your head, for...

But I'm thinking of walking – taking time to see the flowers and watch the birds. This is a great bird watcher's walk from the locked gate at the end of the road. Woodlands, open fields and water provide habitat for numerous wild creatures. Deer abound, wild turkeys are visible (although there are more of them in the populated areas than in the wilderness), and bear prints in the mud indicate they are not far away.

The Wittenberg road-trail turns into French Camp where it joins the Tuoutchi Trail. The scouts have created the trail and continuously maintain it by initiating their new recruits with picks and shovels.

By following the trail signs through the boy scout camp, you will be reminded that scouts are trustworthy, loyal, helpful, friendly, courteous, kind, cheerful. Says so on the road signs. Should the scouts be in session, however,

Lopez Lake is regularly stocked with trout

be mindful that boys in the woods do not have these virtues emblazoned in their hearts and they may be as predictable as bears in the woods.

At the edge of the clearing of the camp, near a shed that serves as the boat house when the lake is full, are signs (no doubt made by some loyal, helpful, friendly...scouts) pointing to the Tuouski trail.

The trail winds through the hollows and over the ridges, always selling the view of the lake. The walk is a wonderful study of the forms of oaks accentuated against fields of platinum grain and cobalt skies. Some grow like giant mushrooms, others are quirky and bizarre while still others are graceful and artistic. The trees grow in a random parkland as if someone tossed acorns to the wind, and wherever they landed trees grew.

Seasonal flowers give way to waves of grasses that fill every void. A red-shouldered hawk sails motionless in the sky and his cry pierces the quiet.

Straight across from the locked gate along the Wittenberg Arm is the beginning of the Two Waters Trail. The trail climbs to the ridge that separates Wittenberg from the Lopez Arm of Lake Lopez.

Golden star lilies bloom along the path sending a spray of yellow flowers up from its grasslike leaves. A bench along the way gives walkers time to catch their breath and be peaceful in the natural realm. Pearly everlasting, monkey flowers, toyon and black sage crowd the trail like small children eager to show themselves. I was alone and it was a popular summer weekend.

At the top of the ridge I had a choice of walking the ridge .5 mile westward on the Duna Vista Trail to a prominence with views of the dunes, or .6 miles down the other side to the Lopez Arm of Lake Lopez. I opted to do both, descending quickly on the Two Waters (designated the Lopez Trail at the top of the ridge) to the lake. This is not a popular hike and the trail is seldom used. The trail tumbles downward with nary a hint of the lake until you are on the water's edge.

And onto an old road bed – Lopez Canyon road – that canters out of the water for several hundred yards, then disappears again into the water. The last time this road was used was in the '60s before the lake was formed. It was a well established county road that served the folks in the back country, but it's a mere fragment of history now that brings back memories of ranch houses and strawberry fields. Boaters and skiers skim over the surface of produce fields where men and animals toiled for decades.

The road was built atop the Santa Margarita formation which yields an even older history – scallops and oysters that prove this area was formerly a tropical sea. Through uplifting, erosion, faulting and folding the pages are turned backwards and hikers and boaters who use the restroom here, can sample the past in fossils in the rocks along the road toward the shoreline. This is the same formation that shows itself by the locked gate at the beginning of the trail.

CENTRAL

Encinal camp is one of the very private, very primitive campgrounds in Lopez Recreation Area along this historic road. Boaters, canoers and kayakers make their way to the edge of the camp for evenings in the woods far removed from civilization.

Climbing back to the ridge that separates the Wittenberg Arm from the Lopez Arm, I walked the Duna Vista Trail to the end. This is by far the prettiest and least exhausting of the two trails that branch from the Two Waters Trail at the top of the ridge. The trail affords delicious perspectives of the man-made lake. At the end is a picnic table where you can dine in the clouds with views of the Nipomo dunes in the distance.

Here are some distances and brief descriptions:

Wittenberg Trail - to French Camp...1.0 miles. Easy and flat along the Wittenberg Creek.

Tuouski Trail from French Camp to the Two Waters Trail...1.25 miles. Moderate to easy. Great views of the lake.

Two Waters Trail...1.3 miles. Very scenic but steep and rough on the north side as it descends to the Lopez Arm. Climb is .7 miles to the top of the ridge, .6 miles down to Lopez Arm.

Duna Vista Trail...one-half mile. Easy once you get to the top on the Two Waters Trail. Very scenic. Great lookouts. See both arms of the lake as well as far away Nipomo Dunes. As good as Ben and Jerry's New York chocolate fudge chunk ice cream...well, almost.

Entrance to the Dunes near Pismo Beach State Park (Opposite story)

9

MOONSTRUCK IN THE DUNES AT MIDNIGHT

(Pismo Dunes)

It was a night of desert winds—warm, sultry, winds that caress the skin. Gone were the winds of the sea that were whipping cold, and which penetrated the bones. Once before we had spent a night in the dunes when the moon was full. We had huddled in the shelter of a dune crest while the cold dove deep to numb all things and make them sleep, and there was rest like death. But this was a night when bushes rustle and night birds call from the thicket.

We waited for the moon...

"Ascending
Up from the east the silvery round moon
Beautiful over the housetops, ghastly, phantom moon.
Immense and silent moon."
Walt Whitman.

From the crest of the dunes we entered the pubescent grasses of the foredunes. Wispy slender strands swayed in the mild desert wind, casting moonbeams in patterns; a theatrical moon that cast shadows of inky figures.

We glided like ghosts across ripples of sand, sculpted forms all the same, each one different. There was hard crusty sand, and soft pudding sand. Each step was a new land, a fresh beginning; then we glided down the back sides of the hills where the ocean is shut out and things live in a peaceful clime of damp, cool nights and quietness. We descended into the lush cover of the back dunes, the seed heads of goldenrod glowing softly in the warming rays of the moon.

Our bodies brushed dune heather, scratchy, and separated like braided hair. Pods of legumes rattled in the quiet night. I shook the branches again. A hundred seeds entombed in crusty ovaries lurched back and forth, calling for a life of their own.

What was that? Footsteps in the brush. Running toward us? We stopped, frozen in a moonlit scene. Hearts pounded. There it was again. Eyes strained, ears turned. It scurried across cereal-like ground, crunching and cracking. Foraging? Escaping? Attacking? Probably an opossum with its clumsy, shuffling through the understories.

Beyond was the big dune, looking like a new world, rising high to reach the sky. The melon moon rose from the east, just above the horizon.

We walked out of the cool hollow onto slopes gracefully glowing, every-thing flowing, like the contours of a woman's body in the moonlight – mounds and clefts and sweetly furrowed strands. The dunes were seductive, beguiling, rising endlessly until we breached the crest and looked across the village with all its twinkling lights, dimly shimmering. The village was quiet, like a child asleep.

Across the hills to the north, Pismo Heights sparkled on its hill. A neck-lace of twinkling jewels rimmed the shore from Shell Beach to Avila – and at the end, the brightest gem of them all, a ten karat diamond in a string of lesser jewels, the lighthouse beacon flashing, beaming brightly.

We laid down together, quiet together, my lover and I, beneath the moon and stars, alone and quiet...moonstruck.

Eva sang in a little girl's voice from her past " A foolish man built his house upon the sand...and the rains came tumbling down..."

Verse after verse, her hands gestured all the motions like a child ..."And the house on the sands went smack." "I learned that in daily vacation Bible school," she giggled, returning to her adult self-consciousness.

"Whatever made you think of that?" I said in surprised amusement.

"All this sand!" she exclaimed.

"You're funny. I love you."

Rising from our sandy lair we stumbled together back toward the ocean. The moon was at our back. Gone were the contours and the delicately shaded ripples, gone were the hills and rills and deftly flowing ravines.

Everything was flat like an ant's view of sandpaper. We stumbled up hills that we couldn't see, and cascaded down hills that gave no hint of their being. We were totally blinded, taking each step in darkness flooded by the light of the moon. Up and down and into sinister canyons of midnight forms and animals that rustle in the brush.

A lone tree overhung our path, its gnarly branches doubly grotesque, with shadowy fingers reaching across our path.

Finally we were on the edge of the sea, facing the surf that rolled in end-less silver scarves that reached the beach.

HOW TO SEE THE DUNES

1. Drive down Highway One to Pier Ave in Oceano, to the ocean. Walk the beach south, across the Arroyo Grande Creek. Enter the dunes and head inland to the highest overlook.
2. Take Highway One to downtown Oceano, west on 22nd street, toward the ocean, right on Silver Spur Place to the end. Walk the levee along the Arroyo Grande Creek, climb into dunes after you pass the rustic country house in the piney woods.

3. Drive onto the beach at Pier Ave in Oceano. Go south to the number 6 mile marker. Park your vehicle and walk the fence lines east into the dunes until you are at a high point overlooking the dune lakes. Do not trespass into Dunes Lakes Ltd, a private preserve.

4. Take Oso Flaco Road to the (end) parking lot. Walk into the dunes after you have walked the causeway between the lakes. Walk the boardwalk to the ocean. It's nine miles from here to Oceano following the boundary line between the State Park Vehicular Recreation area and the private dune lands further inland. Leave a car at Oceano near the airport.

5. Take Highway One through Guadalupe to Main Street, right, to the ocean, passing the guard house, (no four wheel drive vehicles) through the dunes to the ocean. Open during daylight hours.

CENTRAL

10

SAN LUIS LIGHTHOUSE

(There's Only One Other Like It)

It took 152 pages in the U.S. Lighthouse Service manual to explain the lighthouse keeper's chores. Every four hours the clockwork needed to be wound, there were wicks to trim, glass to clean, fuel to check, and myriad maintenance chores to perform.

Long nights and endless days of singing surf and whistling wind was the kind of isolation meant for people of immense strength and constitution. Food had to be raised, or stored in large quantities until the next ship arrived. In periods of storm, the lighthouse keeper's beacon brought floundering ships home, like moths attracted to light.

In 1888 the ocean steamer, Pacific, searched through the night for safe harbor after taking on water from an accidentally opened valve. She arrived in the morning, listing badly. Shortly after she tied up at the wharf, she slid below the water and was gone. This event and other sea tragedies made people think seriously about the need for a light at the mouth of San Luis Bay.

Two years later the Lighthouse Service appropriated $50,000 for a 30 acre parcel at the point along the Pecho Coast and began building a two-story Victorian home with the light tower in the northwest corner. It was completed in June of 1890, along with a duplex of similar design to house additional light-house keepers who manned the light.

In a blundering act, the US Coast Guard, who had taken over the respon-sibilities of running the lighthouse from the Lighthouse service, tore down the duplex in 1961 and bulldozed it into the sea. In its place are two graceless cement block buildings that served the lighthouse keepers until 1975 when the light was automated.

As more demolition and abandonment of old lighthouses took place, it awakened the public to the value of these remaining great national heritage landmarks.

The San Luis Light is one of the more charming lighthouse structures, situated on an idyllic point. You can't see it from the bay or the wharf, but you

CENTRAL

can see its blinking beacons from the coast along Pismo Beach and on the Nipomo Dunes.

Seven buildings like ours were prefabricated in Oakland and set out on the California coast around the turn-of-the-century, but only two remain, this one and East Brother Lighthouse on San Pablo Bay, near San Francisco. You can visit the East Brother Lighthouse because it is now operated as a bed and breakfast.

These buildings were not unimaginative structures made with common materials. They were finely crafted homes of solid redwood, exhibiting excellent workmanship and adornment befitting a home in town.

The fourth order Fresnel (pronounced Fray-nell) lamp weighing in at one-and-a half tons, is no longer in the tower, but you can see it in the San Luis Obispo County Museum on Monterey Street in SLO. The lights used five concentric wicks which had their light concentrated via the lenses in 800 candle power and shined 18 miles to sea. The wicks were fueled by whale oil, lard or kerosene, but in the 1930s most of the lights were converted to electricity. Presently airport beacons are used.

CENTRAL

The entire lens assembly rotated on a track at an interval specific to its site. Ships could interpret the period of eclipse pattern and refer to a light list which gave the characteristics of each lighthouse.

Before the Nature Conservancy became involved in the preservation of the lighthouse, PG&E granted permission to visitors. We set out on foot past the Fat Cat Cafe and approached the guard at the PG&E gate where we submitted a list of our names. One hundred yards beyond the gate is the road to the point. Presently there's a trail that winds through the coastal shrub chaparral and eventually reaches the road.

Our plan was to hike out to the lighthouse on the road, then walk back along the shore at low tide. We had done it before and it was no problem.

The two mile road winds in and out of the canyons and slopes, past a Chumash Indian burial ground, to the unbuffered western slopes. On the exposed western tip is the 1890 lighthouse and its company of homes and buildings.

We stood for a moment, imagining what the lighthouse keeper's life was like at the turn of the century, alone on a windswept point, rescuing the lost and helpless with the long arm of bright light.

We walked down the curving road until we were at the level of the lighthouse and saw dogs and kids and a huge 100-year-old eucalyptus tree with a swing in it. After lunch on the cement wall by the fog signal house, we walked around the old prairie Victorian with the tower in the northwest corner.

We headed back from the point along the shore because the tide was out and we could rock-hop back to the parking lot by the pier; except that our timing was off a little and the tide was coming back in, and a brewing storm was whipping the sea into large swells. While walking the shoreline at mean tide is lawful, it's frowned upon by the authorities. Neither the Nature Conservancy, PG&E , the Harbor District nor your mother espouse taking the shoreline walk back. In fact, after our adventure I can say that this is not the way to go. If you don't have the tides just right you could be swimming, or maybe worse.

At first there was a broad beach, 200 yards deep and 100 yards long. The going was easy and we had the wind to our backs. We stopped to look at the breakwater that extends from the beach to Whaler's Rock, an island used by turn-of-the-century whalers. The rock is now tied into the beach via a breakwater of boulders that came from the face of Morro Rock in Morro Bay.

Leaving the beach we entered a clinker field of jagged rocks, broken from the steep hillsides.

Martin and Paul, two of my favorite guys over 39 (way over 39), and a few of the others bogged down in the task of negotiating teetering rocks. In places the vertical wall pushed us to the edge of the sea and staying dry was a game of scrambling over the rocks before the next wave came crashing in.

Martin was hanging on to me tightly when we came around a corner. There wasn't time to leave the security of a good handhold and a sturdy rock when a huge wave rolled in, so we clung like crabs to the barnacled rock, letting the sea roll over us.

Martin muttered something about a perfectly good pair of Hush Puppies going to the dogs, a lousy pun at a perilous time, I thought, inasmuch as we had nearly met Davy Jones. We climbed higher, the surging foam chasing us. Finally we reached a point above the water line where we caught our breath and waited for an opportunity to continue.

Paul was behind us, assisted by Ted and Gene. It was a race of two game pensioners moving at the speed of a snail on a wet sidewalk.

We made it fine, and Paul won. After the seventh soaking he simply lost regard for dryness and went full bore, passing Martin in the final home stretch. The crowd cheered as the two elders jumped from the insecurity of the upended rocks onto the stability of the level parking lot.

Martin was still cursing the fate of his Hush Puppies, but then he'd look up and smile and say again-and-again, "That was fun."

I saw Paul in church Sunday. He slipped something into my hand and said, "Here's a little something for Martin, Ron. See that he gets this." It was a small black clinker he had picked up on the hike.

"Okay, Paul." I said. "I'll put it in his shoe."

If you're interested in seeing the lighthouse and knowing more about it call the Nature Conservancy at 343-2455. The Nature Conservancy and PG&E arrange docent-led hikes to the lighthouse.

Presently the Nature Conservancy offers two trips to the lighthouse. One trip goes to the lighthouse and back on the bluff trail, a round-trip distance of 3.5 miles. The bluff trail to the lighthouse affords the hiker magnificent panoramas of the bay and the distant Nipomo dunes.

The longer trail goes to the lighthouse and wanders the coastal benches of the Pecho coast, traversing vintage agricultural land to Rattlesnake Canyon, terminating in a grove of native oaks for a round-trip distance of 7.4 miles. The return trail reunites with the high bluff trail along the seaward side of the point and exits again at the PG&E gate.

All trips need to be arranged and reserved by calling the reservation number, 541-8735. Be prepared for a message that will describe this trail as though it were training for Outward Bound. A few clumsy walkers have probably not been able to negotiate the terrain which is rugged and steep at the beginning so PG&E makes it sound awful.

Trips leave from the PG&E gate located near the Harbor District office at the base of the Port San Luis Pier. Space is limited. Call for times—541-8735.

CENTRAL

THE ELFIN FOREST NATURAL RESERVE

At first look it didn't appear to be anything more than a typical chaparral community, a hillside community of hard-leafed shrubs that produce a mosaic of buffy-green mounds. As we got out of the car on 15th Street in Baywood Park and approached the trail to the Elfin Forest Natural Area, the plants appeared shorter than chaparral, less dense and with more open spaces. Over the tops of three-foot shrubs and herbs was Hollister Peak, north of where we were standing, and Morro Rock and the bay to the west.

The trail wandered among plants like black sage, sagebrush and mock heather. The aspect was a loose arrangement of plants interspersed with groves of taller shrubs.

Some of those taller shrubs were trees, pygmy oak trees, tiny trees of the same genus and species (Quercus agrifolia) as the towering live oaks that hold the hillsides; but they're dwarfed by the wind, salt air and sandy dune soil that percolates rainfall quickly away from their roots. Oftentimes there were many trees in one group creating a giant mushroom of gangly limbs in soft light beneath an interlaced canopy draped in Spanish moss (*lace lichens*).

The groves of pygmy oaks don't visually dominate the other plants in the Elfin Forest, but in their artistry they are the main attraction. Their stunted structures and thatched roofs harken to the days when we needed a tent site and a place out of the wind and they evoke feelings of homeyness and romance.

My three adult kids scrambled through the sinuous trunks and assembled themselves in gnarly limbs like a rock band posing for a record cover. It was quiet, and the parasol of leaves broke the misty light with a yellow glow. The soil was soft to the foot, and decaying leaves beneath their limbs emitted the sweet smell of ripening humus.

If left alone, the pygmy oaks will survive and reproduce and eventually own the land. They're on the march, but this is a dirge. They've been on the march for hundreds of years and they haven't conquered the hill yet. They've established a beachhead, sunk their roots, kept their heads down against the dry salt winds and struggled like pioneers. In the hundreds of years that dwarf oaks have lived on the side of these ice-age dunes, they have experienced grizzly bears, Chumash villages and developers. They have stood by and watched house after house move into their space, and in many places they have given up their lives to make space for living rooms and bedrooms.

Now, the kids from those homes hang in their limbs, play beneath their canopies, camp in their soft duff and don't come home for supper until Dad or Mom finds them.

And adults are struck with the magic of the Lilliputian forest. They arrange marriages and parties beneath the limbs. They have Mozart Festival Fringe Concerts under the pygmy oaks. In the grove called *Wood Rat Hole,* harps and cellos and viola de gamba are trundled down the hill, and players make music in a woodland setting ideal for early music concerts. Crowds squeeze in and drape their bodies over crooked limbs or sit on the soft forest floor while the music is played.

But the wood rats moved out. So did the mushrooms. They didn't understand Mozart or Haydn, and they certainly didn't understand why all those humans who have concert halls and homes came to the woods to play and hear music.

The cellist and harp player didn't mean any harm; cellists and harp players don't operate out of greed or malice. And the kids who make forts in trees and play cowboys and Indians didn't willfully destroy anything.

And folks with dogs the size of sheep who walk the trails don't mean to intrude. There's an idyllic harmony of man, dog and wilderness trail. Man's best friend is never happier than when it's running along a dirt trail, nose to the ground, excited by smells that must be (to a dog) as intoxicating as the bouquet of dirty laundry. In their exercise and excitement, **Caninus defecatus** leaves his *signature*, which the next dog reads, and it adds its *signature,* and soon hedgerows of canine markers dominate the view. Walkers turn their heads to find a view where nature is less spoiled.

Soon, the wildness we love loses its natural charm. Invasive plants, like veldt grass, planted intentionally years ago to stabilize dunes near railroad tracks, become as threatening as developers. Slender-leafed ice plant with its lemon-yellow star burst flower finds enough open space to grow and flourish. This is one flower and plant we should pick. How do we preserve wilderness? And do I, by the act of telling you, hasten despoilment?

Yolanda Waddell moved into Baywood Park years ago, fell in love with the nearby elfin forest and conducted walks through it with the Museum of Natural History docent services. When additional homes were being considered for this 90 acre tract of land, she and Carol Larsen Cochran got citizens together to form a wilderness protection society, SWAP (Small Wilderness Area

CENTRAL

Preservation). Eventually Rosemary Bowker added her organizational skills to the job, Money was raised, donations and sponsors recruited. Finally, the means were found to purchase the land. Ordinary citizens had monthly withdrawals taken from their paychecks designated for the Elfin Forest, companies and corporations chipped in, land lovers gave generously, and now it belongs to all of us. The county owns 39 acres, the state 60 acres, and SWAP has assumed the job of caretaker for the next ten years. Dennis Sheridan, Dr. David Keil and other specialists catalogued the life and a teacher's guide was developed.

Boardwalks are being considered to lessen the human foot print on the land. No more will we feel the soft duff of the forest floor beneath our feet, but how many pounding (artistic or otherwise) hooves can cross this land before it's irreparably hurt? Already the sanctuary/privacy of many groves of pygmy oaks has been violated. Access for seniors, the handicapped and for school groups will make it a sanitized version of a walk in creation. It's the price we pay in a period of increasing population and diminishing wilderness. The natural world cries for asylum. We form committees and do what we can.

The Elfin Forest Natural Area is not the garden of Eden. As Yolanda pointed out, "Over the many years the intrusion of people and dogs and cats, trucks, and ATCs degraded the land. It's natural but it's not pristine." But it's a priceless natural treasure despite its woes.

Here are directions for getting there and places to begin your walk. The Elfin Forest Natural Area is off South Bay Boulevard between Morro Bay and Baywood Park. Santa Ysabel Avenue runs westward from South Bay Boulevard past numbered streets starting with 17th. The principle starting point is on 15th Street, but don't park in front of anyone's mailbox or driveway. Trails also begin on streets between 17th and 11th. Cul-de-sacs are being considered at the end of some or all of these streets in the "development" plan.

An even better approach is from South Bay Blvd. This way you don't intrude on the neighborhood and your footprints will be less noticeable. Park off Turri Road where it connects with South Bay Blvd. Walk across the bridge alongside the highway, south, until you see the sign to the Elfin Forest Natural Area. Cross the cement drainage ditch and enter the Don Klopfer pygmy forest. This is one of the oldest groves in the 90 acre area.

By staying to the right, parallel to the highway, you'll descend a slope where the pygmy oak forest becomes green with moss and lace lichens drape the trees. The humidity is high, fresh water springs keep the soil moist and Jack O' Lantern mushrooms and blewitt (blue hatted) mushrooms thrive in the loamy soil. A grove of wax myrtles grows at the edge of the fresh water fringe and the trail ends in a profusion of thimbleberry and impenetrable thicket where Townsend's warblers and marsh wrens flit through the dimly lit understory.

Backtrack and return to the place where you entered the forest. Go straight through it, aiming for the open ridge above. You'll see a lone pine tree, then the trail winds through chamise and coffeeberry and other chaparral plants that are tall and dense, with hard leaves and stout stems.

We heard a group of people talking when we were on this segment of trail, but we couldn't see them because of the density and height of the chaparral on the north slope. The trail corkscrews to the top, the vegetation thins until you are near the smaller plant communities typical of the coastal sage scrub community near the 15th street trail head.

Oak groves and manzanita are scattered and the landscape has the feel of patchwork groups. Manzanita is a fellow-traveler with the pygmy oaks and together they form a biological complex. This manzanita (<u>Arctostaphylous morroensis</u>) has evolved in a special way in a special place. Its range is the south end of Montaña de Oro to the north end of the Elfin Forest Natural Area. Some of the manzanita are small, and some are giant reaching to 20 feet. Old dead forms leave grotesque sculptures in a landscape of round, green plants.

Celestial Valley is near the top of the ridge, an open meadow with a slight rise on all sides that insulates it from city lights and noise. On a dark night at new moon you can be alone in a world of inky black and twinkling stars.

The absence of trees and the darkness of the soil in Celestial Valley suggests that this was a Chumash camp site. Nearby, kitchen middens hold the discards of numerous Indian meals—shells, bones and pottery fragments.

Walking to the edge of the bay on the bluff you will see the Morro Bay estuary, and if the tide is falling and the bay is draining, the mud flats will be streaked with receding rivulets where thousands of waterfowl feed from the emerging land. For a moment you can sense the timeless surge of life that has gone on here since last ice age 10,000 years ago, when oaks and manzanita were beginning their long march across the dunes to the place which is called the Elfin Forest Natural Area.

Leave behind your dog and your viola de gamba, and tread lightly lest we see your footsteps, or your signature.

THE NEW ROAD TO POZO

HEADLINES:

Commerce Between Arroyo Grande and Pozo Increases
(from the Arroyo Grande Herald, July 18, 1896)

"The new road to Pozo, cutting off twenty miles, has been formally thrown open to the public. In the nature of things, it cannot be a first-class road until one winter's rains have packed it and the necessary repairs, such as putting in culverts, repairing washouts, etc. have been made. Then it will begin to assume importance as a through-fare connecting two of the fairest and most productive valleys in the states. Arroyo Grande and Pozo will reap the benefits from the building of this road for all time to come..."

Over one hundred years ago, they officially celebrated the opening with a brass band and speakers predicting a new day of burgeoning commerce between Arroyo Grande and Pozo. The ladies served cake and lemonade and everyone had a grand time.

I didn't see any evidence of celebration, revelry, or excitement on the 100th birthday of the road to Pozo, AKA Hi Mountain Road, in 1996 so I had my own commemoration. I saddled Ol' Blue (my blue Toyota pickup, an inappropriate substitute for a real trail mule) and rode through the valley of Arroyo Grande to pick up the trail and see how things have improved.

The old road has had a hundred years of packing down. There has been a little grading after winter rains, and a few culverts have been put in place; but it's a rough and ridiculous way to get to Pozo from Arroyo Grande and in the absence of the expected culverts are a myriad running creeks (in the wet season).

In the 1890s, the weekly mail route went from San Luis Obispo to Arroyo Grande and on to Pozo. In 1883 a road was built between Pozo and La Panza to the east where there was another mail stop. That tied the coastal town of Arroyo Grande with La Panza and the Carrizo Plains, and the Carrizo Plains was a short ride over the Temblor Range to the San Joaquin Valley. When Valley residents came to the coast on summer vacations, many came this primitive route. It was thought that a widening of the road and regular maintenance would create a busy avenue of commerce and travel.

The road to Pozo, now called Hi Mountain Road, begins near the entrance to Lopez Lake Recreation Area. A sign indicates the distance to Pozo as 16 miles.

Hi Mountain Road continues straight ahead into a lush valley that was home to L.T. Musick, where there was a post office, and the Steele Brothers who ran cattle on the arable portion of their 4,500 acre Arroyo Grande Grant, known as the Ranchita.

It is now a nearly suburban complex of ranchettes called Ranchita Estates. Only a rustic ranch house painted red remains, glaringly disrespectful of the designer homes with pastel colors. Good-bye, herds of Herefords lowing on open ranges. Hello, quarter horses living like pets behind white fences.

Six miles from Lopez Lake Road is a semicircular parking area on the left side of the road, big enough for equestrians' trucks and trailers and bikers' cars. San Luis Obispo County Parks has cut a new trail in the hills of Ranchita Estates. It wanders along a creek and through oak forests, eventually exiting again on Hi Mountain Road at a higher elevation.

I stopped a half-mile along the trail to listen to the high strings of summer insects and to watch water striders skating on a pond. I caught the sounds of someone coming up the trail and saw Diane Woodward on horseback, a second horse on a tether coming behind, and her three happy dogs licking up the dust. The dogs ran right past me and dashed into the water, belly to the pond, slurping loudly. The horses, also, without hesitation splashed into the water and drank like fire hoses. Diane sat high and dry as we exchanged information about the trail.

The trail is used frequently by equestrians for endurance riding and she was giving her steeds some training. The dogs were accessories to the event, but they were the first ones back on the trail, urging her to get going again.

It's a two hour leisurely walk up the trail to where it crosses Hi Mountain Road again. A one hour walk on the road back to Ol' Blue made a total round trip time of about 3 hours.

Hi Mountain Road gets gnarly beyond Ranchita Estates, going up and around canyons, crossing Salt Creek too many times to count, passing the Kessler onyx mine hidden in the hills, climbing uphill grades that are so washboardy they made Ol' Blue chatter as he tried gripping the rolling stones and loose gravel. We were down to 5 m.p.h. an hour.

CENTRAL

After a few ascents over ridges and descents through dry creeks, I crossed into Los Padres National Forest land and a junction in the road that pointed left to Hi Mountain Campground 1 mile, Hi Mountain Lookout 3 miles, and straight ahead to Pozo, 4 miles. I went left, past the primitive campground to the top.

The lookout is to the left on a short spur. The little house on stilts was still manned until the '80s. When it was officially closed, vandals moved in and broke all the windows. The Osborne Fire Finder used to sit in the middle of the room, but it's gone, as is the bed, table and cook stove. The garden still shows sign of order, irises struggle against the drought and a small walkway lined with cobble stones leads to the outhouse down the slope.

Dale De Blau was there on the grated walkway with his sons observing the Highway 58 fire. I mounted the long staircase and observed the world 'round. Below us to the west lay Lopez Lake, shimmering blue. Beyond the lake was the Nipomo Dunes, our eyes trailed southward all the way to Mussel Rock. Turning around we looked down the slope to the cowboy mecca of Pozo, a speck in green pastures, a bustling 19th century frontier town now reduced to the Pozo saloon and part of the Pozo Hotel.

By the time I finished talking to Dale and his boys, I was ready to renew commerce with Pozo. A Pozo martini (beer in a pint jar with an olive) and an ortega burger was very much on my mind. One last creek crossing on the 4 mile descent, which had an unbelievable amount of water running through it late in the summer, was a cleansing before entering the fertile valley.

Rhonda was tending store at the 1858 Pozo Saloon when I swaggered up to the bar in my Reeboks and stretch denim jeans to order the house special. She set me up and I sat outside with the cat where the warm wind whispers in the trees and acorn woodpeckers ratchet overhead.

If you're a genuine wimp, take Highway 101 from San Luis Obispo to Santa Margarita and ride the black top road to Pozo.

The "Made in Pozo Christmas Fair" is scheduled for Thanksgiving weekend, there's a New Year's Eve dinner dance, Highland Scottish Games happen in April, and other events are scheduled throughout the year. Call their Special Events Chairperson, (same person that runs the bar) at 438-4225.

Or you could simply take a ride in the country and settle for a Pozo martini and an ortega burger.

SIDEBAR

Coming up to Hi Mountain Lookout at night is a kick. I came up one night, stumbling over the washboard, boulder strewn, creek-crossing-road to the lookout and observed constellations of blinking lights, above, and the twinkling lights of villages below. It's an extraterrestrial experience, but do it from the Pozo side, which is a mere 4 miles.

CENTRAL

The abandoned Hi Mountain Fire Lookout on Hi Mountain Road

CENTRAL

THE SAGA OF MIGRATING BUTTERFLIES

It was the week before Christmas. People were seated on the benches in the midst of eucalyptus forest, quiet, simply sitting and watching like a congregation at worship. There was an expectant quality to their vigil as if something miraculous was about to happen...like the birth of a king at Christmas.

Turns out it was a miracle. They were watching the spectacle of the Monarch butterflies who follow their guiding star to the eucalyptus groves at Pismo Beach State Park each winter. One to five million butterflies sail from their homes in Canada, and as far east as Zion National Park in Utah, to winter in the towering trees of Pismo Beach and other locations along the California coast.

The butterflies cling to each other in long drapes on the pendulous limbs. Thousands, maybe tens of thousands, can be seen in one tree making draperies of orange and black wings. In some places the trunks of the trees are totally covered, each butterfly grasping the other for warmth and protection during the night and the cool days.

At temperatures below 40 degrees the mass is totally immobile, but as the temperature rises above 55 degrees the warming rays of the sun heats the outer layers of insects until they are able to move. When the monarch's body temperature reaches 81 degrees F, it can fly controllably, but anything less than that makes them wobbly and erratic.

To get warm the monarchs expose themselves to the sun, using their wings like thermal conductors. As the day warms they peel off like airplanes from home base until they are all in the air, flickering silhouettes across the sky.

If their body temperature goes above the normal range of 82-105 degrees they fold their wings dorsally, reduce the amount of sunlight hitting the wings and allow the thorax to radiate away excess heat.

On the soft ground a male and female found time for love. With deep and repeated "kisses" the male clasped the female and injected her with packets of sperm from the end of his abdomen.

Exhausted they wobbled up to their congregate nest on the branches of the eucalyptus and pine trees. They will wait for the feeling of spring in March before embarking to places like Sacramento and Arizona.

Most females mate many times on their winter holiday on the coast. There's no doubt she'll be pregnant with all the suitors she has. The protein rich infusions of sperm from the many males act not only to fertilize her eggs but also serve to feed her through the winter as she absorbs the extra spermatophores into her body. Only the last is best, and it is those sperm that will fertilize her eggs when she flies off in spring.

Thousands of butterflies are tagged each year to discover more about where they go, and how long they live. On November 7, 1987 a monarch butterfly was tagged in Santa Barbara County and ended up in Portal, Arizona on April 9, 1988, a straight line of 660 miles.

Because butterflies fly erratically and achieve long glides on fickle wind currents, it's likely the distance the butterfly flew to Arizona was considerably farther than 660 miles. The previous long distance record was in 1957 when a monarch flew 565 miles from San Francisco to the Grand Canyon.

On good days with tail winds the Monarchs can fly at 10-15 m.p.h., and when they are being pursued by voracious predators, they can achieve speeds up to 30 m.p.h.

In their summer ranges the females find food for their eggs. How this gauzy creature knows what to feed her babies is a mystery; after all she is a drinker of nectar. All winter long she has drunk the sap of eucalyptus flowers and other forbs, yet she seeks out the milkweed plant and lays her eggs on the underside of the leaves.

In a short while the eggs hatch into ravenous larvae that devour the plant and grow to 2,700 times their original size. The larvae ingest all the noxious toxins of the plant, and in their eating become themselves distasteful to the birds who prey on them.

But not all. There are a few clever birds and beasts around that have found that not all of the body is distasteful or toxic. Chickadees, phoebes, mocking birds, shrews, mice, wasps and ants have been seen eating monarchs, and several species of wasps and flies lay eggs on the body of the growing larvae (caterpillars).

The birds are able to pick out the best part of the monarch to eat, like the muscles of the butterfly thorax that power the wings, and some animals will eat the nectar-engorged stomach of the butterflies.

In the miracle of metamorphosis the caterpillar changes into a chrysalis of emerald green. It takes anywhere from 28 to 35 days for the transformation.

During the summer there may be three to five generations of monarchs that grow from egg to larva to pupa to adult. 'Round and round the cycle goes throughout the weeks and months of summer, but as the daylight hours wane

CENTRAL

the last generation of summer monarchs eat more than previous generations. Their metabolism slows and the result is a butterfly that is as fat as a blimp.

Struggling into the air the heavyweights beat their way to places warmer, for surely the harsh winters of the mountains and inland fields will kill them. They have no tolerance for continually cold and freezing temperatures. Pismo Beach becomes the target for many of these timid creatures because the temperate coastal environment is high in moisture and there is an adequate source of food. Pine trees, eucalyptus, sycamore, and cypress are useful as roost sites.

It's not the food of these plants that's important, because the butterflies have a large store for the winter; but the limbs of the trees act as hangars for the huge clusters. The eucalyptus is especially significant because its flowers bloom during the winter months providing the butterflies both rest, food and moisture.

The eucalyptus are in bloom around Christmas, displaying showy white flowers. As the flowers grow inside their green acorn- looking shells, they pop-off the top and a myriad of creamy white stamens unfold themselves, dangling deliciously over and around a corpulent pistil, the ovary of the flower.

They're pretty, fragrant and a hopeful sign of the rejuvenation of nature following the winter rains. They are also a source of food for the butterflies and other nectar feeders who need a rich sugary diet at this coldest time of the year.

There are 100 permanent wintering colonies along the California coast, with nearby colonies in Nipomo, Montaña de Oro State Park and San Simeon, but Pismo Beach is one of the largest with upward of 80,000 animals...where people sit on benches like a congregation at worship—quiet, simply sitting and watching.

SIDEBAR

White paper tags are placed on the right forewing of thousands of butterflies each season. The tag has a number on it and instructions to return the insect in a letter envelope to the Natural History Museum at 900 Exposition Blvd., Los Angeles, CA 90007.

If you see a live butterfly with a tag take down the number and record the time and location. Send this information to the museum in Los Angeles, but do not otherwise disturb the insect.

TOURING CENTRAL COAST PIERS

They're like tinkertoy highways in the ocean—a slab of boards on sticks, a way of treading water without getting wet.

Of course they have their uses. Ships tie to them, people walk on them, fishermen fish from them and lovers stroll hand-in- hand on them.

Surfers love them too. The pier pilings create resistance with incoming swells, so the surfers are out in the cold briny getting high on waves and creating a visual spectacle for the rest of us.

And fish like them. The pilings provide a place for barnacles and sea weed and a hiding place for small fishes. The pier becomes a reef for marine creatures, safe in their Venetian blind compartments of streaked light, where crumbs and crackerjacks fall from above, and leftover bait at the end of the day is cast into the water and descends like manna from heaven.

Stormy winters, like the pier-wrecking storms of 1983, turn piers into flotsam, driftwood for the beachcombers and firewood for the campers. They're wobbly on their spindly legs, always threatening to fall down, but the appeal of standing two or three stories above the foaming breakers is so strong they will always be.

THE PISMO BEACH PIER

It cost 1.9 million dollars to restore the Pismo pier after the 1983 storms, but it has emerged straight and strong and is considered the latest in pier design. New 75 foot steel tube pilings go down through 25 feet of sand into clay and bedrock.

Three diamond shaped platforms, buttressed with batter pilings, set at angles to the bents (a group of pilings), are designed to help the 1,184 foot pier endure the crush of the open ocean and to allow fishermen to cast underneath the pier where all those little critters hide.

The Pismo pier is the most exposed pier along the coast, protruding into

Pismo Beach Pier

open water with no breakwaters, shoals or terraces to soften the force of the sea.

Halfway out on the Pismo pier is a bait and tackle shop where you can rent fishing poles and buy bait (no license required in California when fishing from public piers), purchase food and beverages and ogle a variety of shell jewelry, figurines, trinkets and a tasteless arrangement of a plastic Jesus in an abalone shell.

They're catching perch, flounder, tuna, jack smelt, red snapper and sharks from the pier, and while we were there a fisherman created a spectacle when he pulled up a three foot shark and bloodied the beast in an effort to kill him. Tourists grimaced and wondered aloud if that is what Californians do for fun.

"Steelhead," somebody called out. Then up and over the railing came a two pound fish, flopping around until the fishermen picked it up and held it with both hands in front of his face, like a father admiring a young child. A very happy man eyeballed a very sad fish.

We wandered back into Pismo Beach along Pomeroy, the epicenter of beach culture. Long-haired kids on skate boards and surfers in customized pick-ups cruised the streets and music from Harry's Bar spilled onto the sidewalk.

AVILA BEACH PIER

We turned off Avila Beach Road onto San Miguel Street which runs right into the Port San Luis Harbor buildings. The Avila pier is a straight narrow pier, 20 feet wide in the middle (stem) and 60 feet wide at its terminus. In its 1984-85 remodel it was lengthened to 1,680 feet and raised at its terminus to 22 feet above the water at mean low tide.

It's a good fishing pier and in the fall is a great observation point for an unusual phenomenon. The anchovies run along the shore and not far behind are the albacore (tuna). In a complex play of characters the small bait fish get chased up to the surface by larger predatory fish below. Wiggling masses of silvery anchovies near the surface set the gulls, pelicans and hordes of shearwaters on a feeding frenzy. The birds circle in a counter- clockwise vortex close to the water, then plunge into the mass of little fish, gorging themselves. The splashes of plunging birds and the patter of a million little feet of the shearwaters running across the surface makes the ocean glisten with activity.

A few pelicans broke from the pack and were fishing on their own. From 30 feet above the water they spotted their prey, then with needle point accuracy plunged into the water. The metamorphosis of pelicans from improbable flying machine to streamlined diver is remarkable. No sooner did they surface with a gular sac full of fish than bothersome gulls tried to steal the food, right out of the pelican's baggy chin.

As mysteriously as this feeding phenomenon began it would end; the birds would scatter and the sea would be quiet. The sun would set and we'd go home, wondering where all those birds were going to spend the night.

CENTRAL

PORT SAN LUIS

The Port San Luis pier could be called a wharf. It's the only pier open to motor vehicles, but access is restricted to vehicles loading and unloading only. Stop in at the harbor office located near the pier for permission to drive to the end.

The wharf hasn't changed much since the times the Pacific Coast Railway ran over it beginning in 1872, when it was called Port Harford. From the gate to bent 91 (a transverse support to bolster the upright pilings) the pier has nearly the same foot print. The pier used to extend back to where the Fat Cat Cafe is situated, but in 1965-67 that was all filled. Today the pier is 1,456 feet long with an 18 foot wide drive and an 8 foot walkway.

Near the end is the Avila Bay Seafood Company, a fresh fish market and restaurant serving fish and chips, clam chowder and hamburgers from a window near outdoor dining tables.

Across the way is Olde Port Inn with its fresh fish market, bar and second floor restaurant overlooking the bay and fishing boats tied up alongside. The downstairs bar and restaurant has glass bottom tables that peer through holes in the pier. Mirrors set at angles give the viewer a look at the creatures of the sea swimming beneath them. Seating is both in their indoor patio and outside on the pier. Phone 595-2515 for information and reservations.

Port San Luis Pier, also called Pier 3, is a busy commercial pier, with the hustle of boats unloading, particularly in the mornings or early afternoons. Five albacore boats from San Diego, Los Angeles and Monterey were tied up together at the far end of the pier when we were there, going about their business of unloading and tidying up for their next trip.

At Port San Luis, Paradise Sportfishing has boats going out daily. They can provide you with a day license and all the necessary gear for a day of deep sea fishing. They have half-day trips and full- day trips and twenty-four hour Albacore tuna trips where they go 70 miles to sea, leaving the port at 11 P.M.

They also have halibut and salmon trips, and whale sight-seeing trips during the winter months.

Call them for rates and schedules because the trip depends on good weather and a substantial number of customers. Avila Sportfishing , 805/595-7200.

MORRO BAY

The Embarcadero is a mile long series of gang planks and docks on the bay side of the town's businesses. On the south end of the Embarcadero are a number of public access piers for viewing the boats tied up at the floating docks— at the end of Marina Street near the Morro Bay Aquarium; on Pacific Street by the huge American flag and by the Exxon dock pumps; north of Zeke's Wharf, at Front Street by the public restrooms, and at Harbor Street.

But the authentic fishing village face of Morro Bay is down by the PG&E stacks and Giovanni's Fish Market. Here are the choice spots for viewing the fishing fleet and walking out onto the T-shaped

CENTRAL

piers. The atmosphere is rife with the smells and sights of fish and fishing.

The skyline is a confusion of booms, masts, stacks and hoists, and the two huge piers have ships tied up on all five sides. There are lubberly trawlers looking like the mothers of the fleet, drag boats with huge spools of fishnet, and local boats with homey touches and names like Bonnie Marietta, M'Lady and Shan-gri-la.

The municipal T-pier comes first, just south of the PG&E stacks near the Great American Fish Company. North is the floating dock of Tiger's Folly, a simulated paddle boat that gives tours of the harbor and features a Sunday brunch and evening dinners. Outside the Harbor Hut a banjo trio dispels the foggy gloom with old-time American tunes.

Next door is Virg's and Bob's Sportfishing, and north of that is the T-shaped Coast Guard pier with its high-speed cutters and a variety of commercial and pleasure craft docked along the outside edge.

A little boy with a fishing pole sits there on the edge of the pier, smiling and pulling out aquarium size fish like an image from a Norman Rockwell painting. I think the chamber of commerce hires him because he's always there.

For information and rates for sportfishing call Virg's Sea Fishing at 772-1222, and Bob's Sportfishing at 772-3340.

Morro Bay T-Pier

CAYUCOS PIER

The Cayucos pier is one of the oldest surviving piers in the county, built in 1875. This county-operated pier is a 1,000 foot straight walkway with the 250 foot terminus rising 5 feet above the stem. There are no bait or souvenir shops, no frills or fancy stuff, just plain pier.

At the base of the pier is the Memorial Building where all local events take place—an antique show on Labor Day, a gem and mineral show in June, and parties and dances the rest of the year.

Along the waterfront, shops rent wet suits, surf boards and other gear. Up from the pier on Ocean Avenue, the main drag through town, is the 1876 Way Station Restaurant and a variety of shops selling nostalgia and Americana to palpitating hearts.

A block up is the weathered Victorian home of Captain Cass, the early pioneer merchant who put Cayucos on the map, more or less.

In early days sailing schooners found it easier to slide up to the Cayucos and Port Harford piers than negotiate the narrow channels of Morro Bay, so Cayucos had its share of shipments of dairy products, beef and hides from coastal farms; in fact at one time there was a 700 foot hitching post outside the warehouse next to the wharf where as many as 125 teams of horses were hitched to wagons on "butter days." Today Cayucos seems half asleep and not at all missing the bustle of yesteryear.

SAN SIMEON

San Simeon was a place of Playano Indians; the original holding of the Mission San Miguel; a seaside rancho in 1810; a whaling town and presently the W.R. Hearst State Park.

On San Simeon Bay there were a number of piers that predate the present pier. From 1864-1894 there was a whaling operation on the tip of San Simeon Bay, and 50 feet below the small settlement of homes was a flensing wharf where gray whales were cut into sections before being rendered into oil in vats.

In 1869 Senator George Hearst, father of William Randolph Hearst, built a pier out on the point where the masted schooners could catch the wind, but a number of mishaps led the schooners to stay at sea and float their cargo into the beach, and soon the pier was no longer used or profitable. A few years later storms destroyed it.

George Hearst built another pier at the center of the bay in 1878, and in later years constructed a beautiful Spanish style warehouse with residences along the beach for his favorite employees. This was the pier used by William Randolph Hearst during the castle building years of 1919-1940. The pier broke up during the '40s and was never rebuilt.

The present pier was built by the county in 1957. It's a 1,000 foot long, white railed pier high above the swells of San Simeon Bay. The setting is exceptionally beautiful, with a white crescent beach sweeping around to San Simeon Point.

This point was naturally barren, but George Hearst had rows of Monterey cypress, pine and eucalyptus planted prior to his death in 1891, and now the mature trees give San Simeon beach and harbor a beautiful windbreak.

Fishing is good out of San Simeon. Long boats leave at 7 am and come back with 15 pound cow cods, and 45 pound ling cod (honest, a fisherman told me) after a day in waters around Pacific Valley. Short day boats fish in 300 foot water for rock cod, and olive and yellow bass.

In winter southwest swells cause trouble for moored ships in the bay so the boats pull out to the safety of Morro Bay.

Leaving the pier, I walked the beach northward, fascinated by George Hearst's Spanish style buildings. At the base of the warehouse just above the beach, is a vestige pier piling from the 1878 pier that began to break up in the 1940s.

North of the Spanish warehouse is a storage building William Randolph Hearst erected to store his many earthly treasures before they ended up in his "little something" on the hill.

The trail at the end of the beach goes along the eucalyptus grove George Hearst planted in 1890. He was hoping they would grow into new pier pilings, but this is one time George didn't get his way. The easily splittable eucalyptus never proved to be reliable construction material. The trail wanders out to San Simeon Point over private property, to the former site of the Sebastian store and whaling village, circa 1852-1878.

George, Phoebe and William Hearst succeeded in time to buy everyone out on San Simeon—except the Sebastian store—and eventually all the origi-

nal adobes homes and fences of early establishments disappeared. For years it was only the Hearsts', but in 1951, following the death of William Randolph Hearst, a Memorial Park was given by the Hearst estate, and now the opportunity is there for everyone to enjoy this pristine cove and beach.

Stop by Sebastian's 1852 general store to look at its collection of whaling implements, books and curios. This building was moved to its present location on horse-drawn skids from Whaling Point in 1878 when the whaling operation declined.

Driving distance back to San Luis Obispo is 42 miles.

CENTRAL

NINETEEN "SECRET" BEACHES AND COVES

(From Pismo Beach To Avila Beach)

Okay, the beaches are wonderful. But the sun and the sand and all those beautiful bodies leave me wondering if there isn't more. It's the tremendous herding of people that gets me; it may be why everybody goes out there, but there is another approach that I think is better. It's finding the hidden beaches, the mysterious sea caves, and the staircases that lead to obscure coves.

If everybody knew about these places they wouldn't be hidden and obscure, so put a lid on this information and keep it just for yourself. We'll begin at the Pomeroy Street staircase in Pismo Beach and work north to the pier and beach at Avila.

1) Pismo Beach's main street is Pomeroy, and at the end is a short pedestrian spillway to the beach, north of the pier. This is where everybody goes, so you won't want to go there.

2) The Wadsworth Street staircase, just north of the Sea Gypsy Motel, is a short, uninteresting way to the beach, but if you're going to play volleyball you're close to the stanchions. It's the same beach with all the painted dolls and the sculpted hunks...and the wind...and the sand. Boring.

3) Behind Bank of America on Dolliver Street is the Kon Tiki Inn. This private (for guests only) staircase is where the beach thins and the headlands rise.

4) The city staircase at the end of Wilmar Street, north of Trader Nick's, is a hundred feet high, and from the top you get a grand panoramic view of the beach and dunes. There is parking for 25 cars at the top. To the right of the staircase is the beginning of the rocky ledges and tidepools.

5) North of the Wilmar Street stairs is the private Tides Motel staircase. When you park in their driveway, you're competing for parking space with their clientele. Be courteous and don't leave your car for the day.

6) Deep in the rocky headlands, at the end of the beach, is the Sea Crest Motel behind the Marie Callender Restaurant off Shell Beach Road. Walk through the building by the reception area to the ocean front gardens and walkways. The staircase is at the end of the walkway. There is a bench at the top of the stairs

CENTRAL

and magnificent views up and down the coast. This is the last staircase that reaches the beach.

7) The Cottage Inn by the Sea staircase, north of the Sea Crest, zigzags down a white cliff of tuff, ending at ocean level by a cave. The water rises and falls, swirling and washing around in the grottoes and caves at high tide.

8) North, at the Shore Cliff Lodge, is a safe and sturdy public access to the Elmer Ross Beach. The circular stairs are alongside the restaurant (north side) and lead onto a concrete breakwater. The beach is hidden and very private.

9) The public access walkway along the cliffs on the sea side of Shelter Cove Lodge on Price Street (Shell Beach Road) is along the fenced reserve of the nesting peregrine falcons. At the north end (at Don Dyke's fishing point) is a natural auditorium where the booming waves send shivers through the ground. From the highest vantage point, the scene southward is like a graveyard of grotesque headstones with the surf surging around them.

There is another sliver of beach that can be reached from the trail at the north end of Shelter Cove. The trail takes off from the oceanfront footpath, then descends under the gazebo walkway to a secluded beach. Be careful. The last half is rough and stony, but there is a railing and guide rope going down the slope. At the beach level you can see a big sea cave that has broken through; the sea now surges in and out, producing thunderous roars. This coastal area is undergoing extensive erosion as the sea divides the land by wave action and drags the crumbly rock to the bottom.

10) From Shell Beach Road, take Cliff Avenue to Dinosaur Caves, a fenced-in sea cave where the ocean has invaded the cliff's softer elements. It's a fascinating hole in the ground where adventurous climbers scale the fence and lower themselves to the seaside at low tide by way of a nylon rope. You didn't hear me recommend it.

11) Nearby, at the end of Cliff Street, is Margo Dodd Park, an excellent place to see seals on the smooth outcroppings offshore. In stormy weather this point provides breathtaking views. At Pier Street, a hundred yards north of Margo Dodd Park, a staircase leads to a stony beach, picturesquely sequestered behind freestanding monoliths. There are the same beautiful bodies, sun and wind as on the big beaches of downtown Pismo, but the scenery is much more spectacular and usually there are not many people here; unless you've been telling.

12) Ocean Boulevard continues north of Placentia Street, running past luxury sea shanties. Ocean Park, by Palomar and Montecito Streets, is a pleasant grassy knoll with benches where Shell Beach residents gather at sunset with raised glasses to toast the end of another day. Nearby are two staircases to the tidepools and small beach, the farthest north being at the very end of Ocean Boulevard, near Vista Del Mar Avenue.

13) North on Shell Beach Road, Coburn Street joins Baker Street, which runs

CENTRAL

Margo Dodd Park - Shell Beach

down to Sea Cliff Street. Left on Sea Cliff at the turnaround is a public access walkway next to a house numbered 177. The access parallels the driveway, then turns right on a sidewalk to a platform on the edge of the sea.

14) Drive down Spyglass Drive, past the restaurant, until you come to Spyglass Park. There are picnic tables, a playground and benches facing the ocean. Take the road-trail down the canyon at the south end, to the upended rocky shelf and mini beaches. The surfers love this area, riding the waves as the sea rolls over the shallow shelf.

15) The Cliffs Hotel off Highway 101, a half-mile north of Spyglass, spent $35,000 to give the public access to their descending staircase at the north end

of the hotel. You can now reach Turtle Beach, a crescent-shaped beach that has been the exclusive domain of surfers who love the big waves on the north point. At low tide there are miles of ocean ledges to explore.

16) In Sunset Palisades at the end of Topaz Street is an easy walk to the water's edge by the house with the beautiful geraniums. At low tide you can walk north to the sea urchin beds. All along this section, homes perch precariously above the surf like divers ready to hit the water.

17) Indio Street leads to a gated community along the coast, but a designated public walkway allows us to park at the entrance and walk a cultured path northward towards Pirates Cove, which can also be reached from Avila Beach Drive and Cave Landing Road.

18) Another approach to Pirate's Cove is via Avila Beach Drive, opposite the San Luis Bay Golf Course. Take Cave Landing Road up the steep grade to the top. The promontory of rocks at the top of the road is exceptionally beautiful, with many scrambling rocks and scenic views of eccentric rock formations and foaming sea. Several paths lead down to the nude beach. Wave to me if you go. I'll be the one in the swimming trunks.

19) If you follow Avila Road around westward, you'll come in to Avila Beach and all the small staircases leading down this nearly always sunny beach. Protected from northerly winds, Avila Beach continues to be popular with the locals; of course you're back to the maddening scene of throngs of gorgeous brown bodies ripening in the sun...and the wind and the sand. It's your choice.

CENTRAL

16

HIDDEN TREASURES OF SAN LUIS OBISPO COUNTY

Sometimes I can't win. If I write about the obvious places of interest in our county some critics will say, "C'mon. We know about that. Find us some place we've never seen before."

So I bust my keester and find some obscure place nobody ever heard of...except a cell of people who have garnered this place for themselves. Then I'm a bum for telling everybody about THEIR place. And if I should, perchance, reveal the place of Indian pictographs or petroglyphs, I'm in deep...trouble. Never mind that Painted Rock is now publicly administered with a visitor's center, campground, parking lot and directional arrows along the road.

It's heartening to know that as a result of reading this column a pestilence of humans will descend on a place. Oftentimes I'm not even sure anybody reads this stuff.

So, with an attitude of reverence and respect for all unspoiled places, and a confidence that responsible people like you are the ones most likely to pack a picnic lunch and go out and experience the back roads and explore the hidden treasures of San Luis Obispo County, I go on.

Many of the places I write about are public lands, and they in fact do belong to all of us, but let us go with the burden of stewardship, to love and cherish, and to pick up after ourselves and tread lightly.

HUASNA ROAD AND THE STONY CREEK AREA.

At the end of Huasna Road, forty miles into the back country from Arroyo Grande is this puzzling scene—a large slab of concrete with a beautiful stone fireplace sits in the middle of Stony Creek Campground. What's going on here, you ask?

I say this is the former home of a CCC camp which was full of unemployed guys of the 1930 depression who did anything for a buck, like build roads and trails in the back country. They intended to build a road from Stony

Creek Campground, to High Mountain Road behind Lopez Lake, but never finished the job.

The slab and fireplace are what's left of a huge recreation hall that was burned to the ground after the camp was abandoned. Old timers say the hall was so big you could drive a team of horses through the front door and circle around in the interior. Tent cabins were placed around the camp, and there was a shower house up the hill.

The fine stone work the CCC did on the bridges that crisscross the creek is impressive. This road, beyond the campground on the opposite side of the creek, is getting overgrown but there are some Indian grinding rocks along the way and I would imagine some caves with Indian pictographs.

About .8 mile back down the dirt road that leads to Stony Creek Campground, is a truck trail to the right, (west). There may be some iron stakes in the ground near this junction. Follow the road across the creek (park your car and walk if you don't have 4 WD) and continue a quarter mile to the Indian caves and grinding rocks.

Follow a foot trail into the boulder field and when you come to a flat rock with grinding holes in it, turn around and walk back 25 feet and go right. In this area are a number of Chumash pictographs in the caves and overhanging rocks.

Look, but don't touch. These invaluable relics are rare and a precious record of the people who preceded us in this land.

On the edge of this high plateau is another grinding rock where Indians prepared their meals and where you can prepare yours.

To get there: Pick up Huasna Road off Lopez Lake Road a few miles out of Arroyo Grande and drive through the oak groves of the Huasna Valley, crossing a wooden bridge over the Huasna River.

From there the road becomes gravel and you'll pass the 51,000 acre Huasna Ranch, a part of the original Huasna Land Grant given to Isaac Sparks in 1843.

Keep going through cut hay fields, open range and creek bottoms to the junction to the Joughin Ranch. Stay left and drive 23 miles to the Los Padres National Forest sign. You'll pass Aqua Escondido campground on the right side, and the Avenales Vista Point on the left (worth a stop). Three miles beyond is Stony Creek campground and the end of the road.

PERMASSE ADOBE

Twenty years ago the road between Cuyama and Santa Maria rode high in the hills, parallel to the existing highway. It cut into and out of more than 60 canyons on its way to Maricopa and Taft, and travelers would stop halfway at a gas station where they could get fuel and a bottle of coke. Rumor has it that they could get more than Coke during the Prohibition years, and that moonshine was made in a little adobe down the hill from the wayside station. The gas station on the old highway is gone but the little adobe still exists, and now it is on the highway, the new Route 166 built in the '60s and '70s.

The adobe is 22 miles from Santa Maria, on Highway 166, just beyond one of the many bridges that spans the Cuyama River. A parking area of the Los Padres National Forest for access to the Adobe Trail comes first, then around the bend is the adobe.

The adobe can be seen from the trail and from the roadside. I visited it one hot summer day when the wind sang in the pepper tree and everything was quiet and oppressed. The interior was cool and an animal had moved inside.

The last time a human lived here was in 1937 when cowboys John Skinner and Frank Reed were herding cattle for the Gifford Cattle Company which ran cattle on the Permasse Ranch.

Bernard Permasse came from France in 1888 and homesteaded 200 acres with his partner, Pete Labord. Permasse built the adobe in 1890 and lived in it for a number of years, but when the partnership dissolved Labord took possession of the 100 acre tract that included the adobe and Permasse moved up the canyon (west) several miles where he built the permanent Permasse home on the old (prior to 1960)) highway.

BIG ROCK MOUNTAIN

Four miles beyond the Permasse Adobe and the Adobe trail head is the Big Rock Ranch and Branch Creek Road. Turn left, (north) for a pleasant outing among the peanut-brittle formations of Big Rock Mountain.

On the far north end of the mountain, a trail wanders between these unique formations. Climbing to the top you can see for miles.

The adobe trail, near the Permasse Adobe, has a branch which ends at Branch Creek Road in the vicinity of Big Rock Mountain.

PAINTED ROCK OF SANTA BARBARA COUNTY

I'm cheating a little bit by mentioning a Santa Barbara County point of interest, but it's so close to Big Rock Ranch and the Permasse Adobe that it's easy to group it with these San Luis Obispo County features.

The coastal Chumash Indians often traded with tribes to the east, the Yokuts, and along the way stayed at camps where there was food, shelter and water.

In the Sierra Madre Mountains, not far from the Big Rock Ranch, is an idyllic area of springs and high mountain meadows which served as an Indian camp. There are also rock outcroppings and caves where Indian shaman performed their art and symbolic paintings.

The inaccessibility to this area makes it a rare and special find. One way is to take Sierra Madre Road, which comes off Highway 166 near Big Rock Ranch and Branch Creek Road, 26 miles from Santa Maria. This is a well maintained gravel road that travels up to McPherson Peak. The Johnson corrals block the way so it's on foot from there for the five mile walk along the ridge road (fire road) until you arrive at Painted Rock.

This is a pleasant walk with little change in grade, but it will make a 10 mile round trip. If you have a mountain bike, drive your car or truck to this point and throw the bikes onto the trail.

Another way to get to Painted Rock is to drive to the town of New Cuyama, take the road into the village all the way to the end, passing through the oil fields, to Lower Lion Springs. From the parking area walk up 26W01 (Perkins Road) to 27W04 Lions Canyon or Rocky Ridge Trail. This is a gorgeous but strenuous five mile hike with healthy (as in heart pounding) increases in elevation. Painted Rock is on the ridge road, west of the junction of the trail with Sierra Madre Road.

Note: There is a PAINTED ROCK IN THE CARISSA PLAINS, which is not to be confused with the Painted Rock of Santa Barbara County.

To visit the PAINTED ROCK IN THE CARISSA PLAINS, follow Highway 58 out of Santa Margarita to the towns of Simmler and California Valley. Turn right on Soda Lake Road and follow the signs. Twelve miles from the gas station you'll see the road and parking lot to Painted Rock. Painted Rock of the Carissa Plains is now under the jurisdiction of BLM, the California Department of Fish and Game and the Nature Conservancy who administer the newly formed Carizzo Plain Natural Area.

Drive your car to the end and walk the quarter mile distance to the cave paintings under the horseshoe-shaped rock. The wall murals have been badly vandalized over the years, supporting the point of view that to disclose the place of valuable ancient relics is to put them in harm's way. Pictures from the turn of the century show most of the painting intact, but today the walls are badly fragmented and chipped.

EL RINCON ADOBE

When Francisco Ziba Branch came to the Arroyo Grande Valley in 1837 he brought a wife and his infant son, Ramon, from Santa Barbara. It was a lonesome life in the Arroyo Grande Valley in 1837 and the only other human inhabitants were the Indians living in Corallitas Canyon where they raised crops for the mission in San Luis Obispo.

For the first years the small family lived in a lean-to on the 17,000 acre

Santa Manuela ranch, but later Branch built a large two-story adobe on Branch Mill Road.

When Ramon grew up he built a two-story adobe on 4,000 acres of his father's ranch after marrying Maria Isabella Robbins of Santa Barbara. She was of the distinguished Carillo family of Santa Barbara.

Ramon and Maria Isabella raised 12 children in this house. There were four bedrooms upstairs and a kitchen, dining room, parlor, storeroom and two bedrooms on the main floor. The walls were very thick and large sills were sufficiently big for the children to sit in them. A porch extended around all sides of the house. The driveway to the house was lined with olive trees and the house was surrounded by fruit trees. Much of the family's food was raised on the premises. Wheat, barley, corn and beans were raised in the fields around the adobe. Hay barns and dairy buildings were also constructed. Two Chinese cooks were employed to help Maria serve her large family.

The family and descendants of Ramon and Maria lived in the adobe until 1892, and recently the adobe was brought out of oblivion by Talley Vineyards. They refurbished the old structure and proudly retell the history of this early Arroyo Grande family in a photo album in their tasting room.

To see the El Rincon Adobe, drive out on Lopez Lake Road, a half mile east of Corbett Canyon Drive. The Talley Vineyard Tasting room is open 12 noon until 5 p.m. daily throughout the summer. The winery is on the left side of the road at 3031 Lopez Lake Drive, near the reservoir.

El Rincon Adobe

MACHESNA MOUNTAIN WILDERNESS AREA

There's a new wilderness in our neighborhood and there's an easy way to see it.

Take Pozo Road out of Santa Margarita to the "town" of Pozo and continue out of town, passing the Parkhill Road on your left and the Avenales Ranch Road on your right. The road is broken macadam, but not too bad.

At the Pozo summit (elevation 2,635) park your car near the trail head (16E01). The trail ascends a thousand feet in four miles to the top of Pine Mountain with Machesna Mountain looming off in the distance at an elevation of 4054 feet.

At two miles there are some choices. The left trail goes to Machesna Mountain and Queen Bee campground. The right trail goes to Pine Mountain at an elevation of 3,777 feet and a beautiful stand of Coulter Pines.

The trail to Pine Mountain can also be reached from Queen Bee Campground and is a better maintained trail. Take the road over the Pozo summit 4 miles to La Panza campground, then one mile beyond to Queen Bee Camp.

SANTA RITA OLD CREEK ROAD

Now this is a road less traveled, a bit of wilderness close by and a pleasant interlude from city life.

Santa Rita Creek Road is a remnant from the past and runs from Templeton to Cayucos. Pick it up at Vineyard Road near Templeton and travel through the wooded slopes and country estates before getting the feeling that you've lost your way.

The road becomes dirt and is usually a bit rough and dusty. It skirts precipitous canyons and follows the curves of the rugged mountains, passing over the highest point where views of the ocean and Whale Rock Reservoir come to view.

This section of the county is our hardwood forest and the scenery is quite different than what you see on the eastern side of Highway 101. In ten miles you'll approach Whale Rock Reservoir and from there to Cayucos is all downhill.

SANTA ROSA CREEK ROAD

If you travel from Highway 101 near Paso Robles and drive west on Highway 46, you'll come to Santa Rosa Creek Road, which is the old highway in use since 1860. During the winter months it was frequently washed out as the creek overflowed its banks, so the present highway was built.

Take Santa Rosa Creek Road from Highway 46 into Cambria following the creek for 18 miles, catching numerous windows open to the ocean. Orchards and berry fields thrive in the alluvia of the creek. Four miles from Cambria is Linn's Fruit Bin, a favorite roadside bakery and berry-picking farm. They sell olallie berries and boysenberries and make them up into scrumptious pies.

TEMPLETON

Somehow this little town fascinates me. For one thing, there isn't another town around with a five story grain elevator in the middle of town. This monstrosity dominates the scene like a skyscraper. Trucks come and go and farmers hang around and jaw and the place feels like a pure farm town.

Secondly, there isn't a town in the county that has a livestock sale barn right on the edge of town. I love to go there and experience the smells and sounds of cattle. This is a wonderful place for an outing with kids.

On Fridays around noon, ranchers fill the parking lot with cattle trucks. Terrified cattle are ushered into the sale barn and bidders sit on bleachers scrutinizing potential purchases while responding to the auctioneers incantations.

As quickly, the cattle are driven out and penned according to the number of the buyer. Be sure to go in the back and watch the penning of the animals by the horseback riders.

On Saturday morning they auction pigs, sheep and goats, so if you've been thinking about a special gift for someone, it might be on the hoof right there in Templeton on Saturday morning.

Thirdly, nobody has more first class cowboy saloons (I think that's what you call a respectable western eating establishment that's good and rowdy) than Templeton. There's A. J. Spur's and McPhee's, both excellent red meat emporia (they're actually much more than that) featuring the finest animals sold down the street at the sale barn. So if you want to see your dinner live, go to the sale barn first and eat later.

Fourthly, the Country House Inn Bed and Breakfast, originally the Chauncey Phillips residence built in 1886, is a six room Victorian home that dignifies the image of downtown Templeton. Staying there overnight is a good way to get out of town and out of sight. The bawling cattle and train whistles in the night will transport you far away.

Country House Inn Bed & Breakfast - originally the Chauncy Phillips residence

YORK MOUNTAIN WINERY and PESENTI WINERY

In the early days of Templeton the hills west of town were deeply wooded. The first settlers cleared the woods to plant vineyards, prunes and apples. East-west valleys allowed the coastal fog to temper the heat and made dry land farming possible. Thirty-five inches of rain falls each year at York Mountain Winery and 20 inches at Pesenti, with lesser amounts eastward.

About 2.5 miles from Templeton on Vineyard Drive is Pesenti, founded in 1923 by Frank Pesenti and Al Nerelli. They began their operation when Prohibition was in force and sold a lot of grape juice. When the ban was lifted in 1932, they were ready to go into full wine production.

No drip irrigation or overhead sprinkling is used on this 69 year- old vineyard, and some of the vines are originals. The 20 inches of rainfall is sufficient to keep the deep-rooted vines going all year. They explain that while yield is reduced with dry farming, the varietal character of the grapes is enhanced.

Admittedly, Pesenti Winery is not a HIDDEN treasure, inasmuch as it has been a part of our county history for years, but it's worth a ride in the country to visit their wine tasting room and sample over 30 different generic and varietal wines.

York Mountain Winery is 3.5 miles west of Pesenti Winery on Highway 46. York Mountain Winery dates back to 1886, about the beginning date for the town of Templeton.

York Mountain gets 30 inches of rainfall each year and is at an elevation of 1,658 feet. The winery makes a good dry sherry, as well as chardonnay, pinot noir and their inimitable Mountain Appellation. The tasting room at York Mountain is vintage California and the grounds are a favorite spot for benefit parties and celebrations. York Mountain IS hidden from view from Highway 46, so as you head west look for York Mountain Road and turn right (north).

ADELAIDA AND CHIMNEY ROCK ROADS

When I think of retirement, one of the places I envision is a cottage along Adelaida Road, where stone fences mark boundaries and the woods are big, and people talk about the last sighting of the mountain lion that comes down to the spring. I think of Mac Gillivray's place and quiet lanes under boughs of towering oaks, and hen turkeys scratching in the duff under the walnut trees.

There's a gentlemanly quality to these parts and the people who live here possess the land and their homes like a priceless inheritance.

Adelaida Road comes off Nacimiento Lake Drive, north of Paso Robles and saunters into the countryside, weaving over wooded slopes and brush lands and past manicured walnut groves. This was the old mail route between Paso Robles and Cayucos and Cambria, going over the top of the Santa Lucia coastal range where it junctioned with old highway 46, now called Santa Rosa Creek Road.

Adelaida Road circles north and ties into Chimney Rock Road, where the points of interest are the Adelaida cemetery, the 1917 Adelaida schoolhouse and the old road bed across San Marcos Creek which is believed to be the wagon road from the 1880s The mission cart trail, referred to in early descriptions of the area, may be this early road. It is supposed that the trail went from San Miguel Mission to Cambria and the wooded slopes of the Santa Lucia Mountains where the beams for the mission were cut. Near G14 is chimney rock, a not too prominent landmark on the south side of the road.

An interesting approach to Adelaida and Chimney Rock Road is from Vineyard Drive from Templeton, then northwest into this valley of charm and serenity.

JOLON (an Indian word meaning valley of oaks)

El Camino Real ran to the San Antonio Mission and through the bustling town of Jolon in the 1880s. Jolon was the commercial and social center of the San Antonio Valley where 700 people made a living prior to 1900.

Antonio Ramirez came to Jolon in 1848 and built an adobe structure in Jolon that later became known as the Sutton Hotel. In 1876 Captain Tidball, a veteran of the Civil War, came to Jolon and joined with George Sutton in the operation of the hotel. The Sutton Hotel reached its zenith in 1880 when the town supported two hotels, 3 general stores, a saloon, a blacksmith shop and 8 residences.

Tidball and Sutton separated as partners and the Tidball store came into existence (1878) and operated as a hotel, general store, post office, and residence until 1948. During WW 2 Ramona Sutfin operated the Tidball store as a beer garden and lunch counter for the troops stationed at Hunter Liggett and Camp Roberts. In 1948 she moved the business over to Mission Road and renamed it the Ruby Mine Saloon. It was the last move out of the historic town of Jolon, leaving the town deserted.

The Sutton Hotel was used by the military in the 1940s for a variety of purposes and was on the national register of historic places, but it has fallen on hard times and is open to the sky. A few walls hardly have sufficient strength to hold the windows.

Several events doomed Jolon. The first and most crucial was the coming of the Southern Pacific Railroad in 1886 through King City, not through Jolon as was anticipated. The highway (present Highway 101) was routed away from

Jolon in 1896 and Jolon became a backwater town. Mining activity kept Jolon alive until 1900, but by this time Hearst was prowling around, gobbling up what he could for his cattle empire. Jolon, depressed and forgotten, was easy prey.

Hearst owned the entire Jolon Valley and set up his ranching operation in the old Milpitas Ranch house, a country vernacular adobe-frame home which burned to the ground in 1929.

Mr. Hearst built the present ranch headquarters in 1931, It is a gilded, domed building with a ranch manager's home at the far end, a number of beautifully appointed guest rooms, a "bull room" where the cowboys entertained, a dining room and kitchen facilities and bunk rooms for cowboys and ranch hands.

He did this in the grand style of his castle on the hill overlooking San Simeon, hiring Julia Morgan to design it. I imagine Hearst said "Let the building be placed on a knoll, which I shall create. Bring in truck loads of dirt and let the building face the setting sun, with mature plantings brought in so that it looks like it hasn't just been built, because I don't have time to wait for things to grow up and look properly. And let the name be Milpitas Rancho."

"And let the earth bring forth living creatures according to their kind, cattle and creeping things and beasts of the earth according to their kind."

And Hearst saw that it was good...and so did everyone else.

When the second world war loomed, the government bought 149,000 acres of William Hearst's ranch, including the town of Jolon and the ranch headquarters. The ranch house is now military headquarters for Hunter Liggett and you can stay there. The military was ordered to be more self-sufficient so they have turned it into a guest lodge and restaurant called The Hacienda. Call them for reservations. Staying out there is a blast. 408/386-2511.

At the end of the valley is the 1771 San Antonio Mission, considerably more modest than Hearst's villa on the hill. The mission was the third of 21 built from 1769-1823. Much of it had fallen into desperate conditions...and so it was that the Lord laid heavily on the heart of this rich man, the task of reconstructing it.

And his heart was softened and his purse stings loosened, and he gave of his wealth and the mission was restored. And the people saw that it was good and praised him for his worthy deeds.

The chapel is the only building of the San Antonio Mission that did not collapse, and is the highlight of the mission.

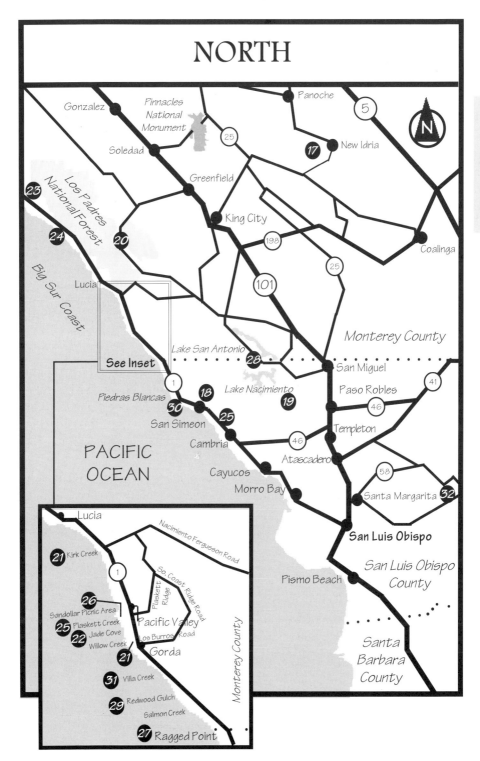

Gonzalez

Pinnacles National Monument

Panoche

5

25

Soledad

17

New Idria

Greenfield

23

Los Padres National Forest

24

Big Sur Coast

20

King City

198

Coalinga

101

25

Lucia

Monterey County

Lake San Antonio

28

San Miguel

See Inset

41

1

Piedras Blancas

18

Lake Nacimiento

Paso Robles

46

30

25

19

46

Templeton

San Simeon

Cambria

46

Atascadero

PACIFIC
OCEAN

Cayucos

58

Morro Bay

Santa Margarita

32

San Luis Obispo

San Luis Obispo
County

Pismo Beach

Santa
Barbara
County

Lucia

21 Kirk Creek

Nacimiento Fergusson Road

1

So. Coast Ridge Road

26

Plaskett Ridge

Sandollar Picnic Area

25 Plaskett Creek

Pacific Valley

22 Jade Cove

Los Burros Road

Willow Creek

21

Gorda

31 Villa Creek

Monterey County

29 Redwood Gulch

Salmon Creek

27 Ragged Point

A BACK COUNTRY ROAD TO NEW IDRIA

(An Old Quicksilver Mine)

Highway 25 between Priest Valley to the south and Hollister to the north is probably one of California's most scenic back roads. Car and driver magazines like to send people here to try out the latest road monsters, but Buick owners and easy riders, not to mention motorcyclists and bicyclists, like it too.

In the spring the hills are guilded with mustard and the San Benito River runs through flower-covered hills; but in the fall the poplars are golden and the chamois hills look buttered in the long rays of autumn sun.

We started at San Miguel where we picked up Indian Valley Road, then onto Peach Tree Road and Highway 25 north through burgs like Bitterwater and San Benito, identifiable by the intersection of two roads and three or more buildings within a quarter mile...and finally on to Hollister.

From San Miguel, Indian Valley Road follows Big Sandy Creek, sometimes high above it, sometimes running through it. In the springtime this road is often flooded, but in the sunshiny days of spring following the threat of floods, this is a prime wild flower viewing area.

There is a quiet peace to this inland country, and many bicyclists, our only companions on our ride northeast, have discovered the sweetness,

The terrain becomes heavily wooded as the road ascends the Cholame hills before it intersects with Peach Tree Road, a picturesque road of dipping curves, rolling road and ancient barns tucked into wooded slopes.

Highway 25 is more of the lovely Bavarian-like hillside interspersed with clearings and woods.

For every romantic with dreams of life on a farm, this route stirs fanciful images of life in a cottage with kids and cats and bleating sheep in the fold, and a big-eyed dairy cow named Nellie...or Dolly...or Marilyn.

We drove to Pinnacles National Monument (Highway 146), where we stayed a spell and explored the surrounding countryside.

We took off from Pinnacles National Monument one afternoon, to explore the roads to New Idria. Following Highway 25 south from Pinnacles we

Hiker stands amid the boulders at Pinnacles National Monument

turned east on San Benito Lateral (not on the map) to Old Hernandez Road, going east - southeast along the San Benito River.

Old Hernandez Road rides high on a ridge overlooking the expansive San Benito River valley. Magnificent bulls, hung with testosterone, snorted and pawed after fertile heifers lounging in a natural wonderland.

The road dropped down to the water's edge and we plowed through stream beds unfit for trailers, motor homes and automobiles—then up again, and down again, across one lane bridges and cattle guards.

We intersected with Coalinga Road and then with Clear Creek Road where we stopped to read a BLM sign. Two rugged guys leaning on a pickup watched us. I pulled up.

"Pardon me, guys, is this the road to New Idria? (I pronounced it New Id'ree'ah). They looked at me... "You mean Eyedra?"

"Well, it says New "Id'ree'ah" on my map."

"We call it Eye'dra."

"You guys local?"

"Yeah."

"Swell, well you should know. So, how long will it take us to get to Eye'dra from here?"

They sauntered over, unsure they wanted to tell us; but finally the instructions came—"You just wind all the way up the mountain then you wind all the way down the mountain. When you wind down you stop, and there'll be a sign—Idria (pronounced Eye'dra, remember?) eleven miles. Take a left there and it takes you right into Eye'dra; and when you come out you'll just shoot right out on New Idria Road to Paicines or Hollister."

So we stuck it in gear and headed up Clear Creek where we saw an information sign giving us directions to the Clear Creek Management Area and the San Benito Mountain Natural Area—all BLM managed land. Eva read off the road signs the numerous mines of the hills - Clear Creek Mine, Arroyo Mine, Wonder Mine, 4th of July Mine and Picacho Mine.

We passed numerous camp grounds where dirt bikers gathered in clusters

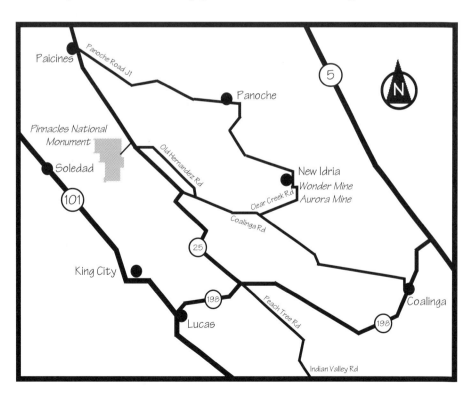

Ore crushing plant at New Idria

with their bikes, trailers and motor homes. We were surprised at the size of some of the motorhomes, because this road is rutted, dusty and very steep.

But pretty. The chromatic hills are beautiful...and ghastly, striking in their rainbow pastels but unhealed from years of mining.

Staging area 2 came up in several miles. More bikers were coming back from a day's ride. A road sign read: "Soil, dust and water in this area contain asbestos which could be hazardous to your health". Most of the bikers wore masks under their helmets. We shut the windows and ran the air conditioner, trying to minimize our risks.

We made many creek crossings, and went up and down and over and around, passing Sawmill Creek Road and Wildass Road, until we crested the final hill and caught views of the San Joaquin Valley and the town of New Idria. (The original Idria Mine is in Austria).

This was a live town in the last century, beginning around 1850, when more than 300 men worked the cinnabar (mercuric sulfide) mines and the mill at New Idria; but times and need change, and the industry, fumes and dust of the mining days are history.

We rolled into town, past deserted homes, the town hall, fire station and post office. It was like high noon in Tombstone. No cars, no people; no sign of life. No movement save for the dust devil that danced down Main street. On the edge of town a huge stamping mill with chutes and scaffolding and machinery creaked and shuddered in the wind.

At the end of the empty main street a woman sat at a table beside the only habitable building in town, working on papers and listening to the voice of the outside world on a radio that blared for all to hear.

She and a company of others are part of Futures Foundation which now owns the town stamping mill, the town and 880 acres of the surrounding land.

Futures Foundation provides drug and alcohol therapy to persons who need to be away from the temptations of their old environments; but if the booze and drugs doesn't get 'em, the loneliness and isolation might, because New Idria is nowhere, with no life of its own, save for the few souls who are being quarantined and purified.

We took J1, New Idria Road, out of town toward Hollister, running on the good macadam road through treeless ranches and desolation reminiscent of the Carissa Plains.

An authentic adobe sat along the edge of the road like a country cottage in England. A venerable cottonwood towered above it and Eva, only 5 foot tall, looked tall as she squinted through its windows and narrow door.

At the town of Panoche we looked at the Panoche Inn and tried to imagine who might seek out such obscurity for sanctuary. Then miles of monotony and grayness in the last rays of day's light to Paicines and Highway 25, a total of 50 miles from New Idria on J1, and a total distance of 112 miles round trip back to Pinnacles National Monument.

NORTH

A HISTORY WALK TO SAN SIMEON POINT

NORTH

First there were the Indians who lived at San Simeon, fishing, picnicking and enjoying magnificent sunsets.

Then in 1542 Juan Rodriguez floated by and noted the harbor. Next came Sebastian Vizcaíno, in 1602, a Spaniard who was looking for safe harbors for a fleet of Spanish galleons. He decided to lend his name to a small grocery store that would exist on the point in 1852.

In 1797 Padre Fermin Francisco de Lasuen named San Simeon and claimed 66,000 acres of coastal grazing land for San Miguel Arcangel, the 16th California mission located near Paso Robles.

By 1836 the missions had become secularized and San Simeon became the rancho of Jose Ramon Estrada; but in 1865 George Hearst of San Francisco acquired it and it has been Hearst's ever since.

Actually, the Point remained independent from the Hearsts until 1894, and from 1852 to 1880 a whaling village operated there.

There were 22 families who made a livelihood chasing whales and dragging them into the beach where they rendered the blubber in huge trypots. There are stories of the women of the point having great donut bakes when the pots were hot with oil.

Sebastian's store was there and so was a blacksmith shop, a barber shop and a saloon. Forty-five buildings perched on the treeless point, but by 1878 the operation fizzled and the Sebastian store, the lone survivor, was placed on skids and dragged to its present location at the head of the beach.

George Hearst planted rows of eucalyptus, pine and cedar on the point in the 1890s, and today San Simeon Point is densely wooded, and hardly a trace of the whaling village can be found.

The scene is strikingly beautiful, with the white crescent beach accented by deep blue water and white fishing vessels riding at their moorings. The point arches aesthetically to the south, a forested peninsula standing high above the beach and bluffs.

NORTH

We began our walk near the 1878 warehouse, across from Sebastian's General Store and walked to the end of the beach where a trail goes up to the bluffs, parallel to the Hearst's Ranch fence.

Through the trees we saw a flock of white egrets nesting in the limbs of the big pines overhanging the edge of the bay.

It's a short walk to the point on grassy carpets among pines of grotesque shapes, their limbs bent and gnarled like figures in a mystical forest.

Offshore we caught the image of a white dunging rock, decorated by the pelicans and cormorants who at that very moment were painting the rock, as they have for years.

One hundred year old cedars hug the western and northern edges of the point, their limbs draping gracefully to the terraced slopes in horizontal sprays.

The trail wanders across fields of ice plant and chaparral, open to the sea and the wind. Occasionally the windrow of cedars encroach on the trail and hikers have to slip through tunnels of darkened limbs where little children mount their daddy's back and hug real tight so the branches wouldn't snag them.

And then to the city dump of 1852, where villagers discarded their old bottles and broken dishes, and the bones of the animals they ate.

In a half mile from the point along the terrace trail, we came to a beach of black sand on the leeward side of a more northerly point. Four miles away

Sebastian's Store is the oldest store on the Central Coast

San Simeon Bay and Point

Piedras Blancas Lighthouse winked at us.

Finally we left the wall of cedars and ventured out into the open fields, crossing a finger of dunes that worked its way inward. We turned right, and headed back toward Hearst's black forest.

In a quarter mile we were back in woods of eucalyptus, planted neatly in rows. Their scaling bark and resinous leaves have created a sterile forest where nothing but their kind grow.

In ten minutes we approached the edge of the bay again where we caught the descending trail to the beach, and passed in front of the 1920 Spanish style warehouse.

Access to San Simeon Point is also available from the north along Highway One at the first lookout point beyond San Simeon State Beach. A staircase over the fence allows walkers to follow the trail to the obscure point.

19

ADELAIDA, ADELAIDA

I had a yen to go exploring so I pleaded with my wife for the use of her car, but she's getting wiser and more skeptical with time because I invariably end up on dirt roads and through muddy creeks, and when I bring the car home she's standing there with her arms folded and a scolding look in her eyes.

So I took the '75 Audi which helped raise a family of teenage drivers who broke it in good and sent it around the horn several times and made it beyond caring for. I call it *Schmielopp* a Dutch word my father used for anyone or anything totally contemptible. The Audi still runs but when I turn too sharply the wheels lay over and the car comes to a halt like a cow going down on her front legs.

But this little road trip is good for old hacks and Mercaaedeez Benz and everything in between. Honest. When the wife and kids are nagging you to take them somewhere, jump in the family chariot and head for the hills of Adelaida.

It was high noon by the time I started my northwest passage, picking up G14 beyond Spring Street in Paso Robles and heading north out of town. I followed the signs to Lake Nacimiento and Lake San Antonio reservoirs, passing almond orchards and arriving at Adelaida Road in just a few miles. I turned left.

"No services ahead", the sign read. Resthaven Park on the north side of Adelaida Road is still cooling passing travelers as it has for years when it comforted the horse-and-buggy sojourners coming out of Adelaida and the quicksilver mines. All the horses are under the hoods now and the covered wagons and buckboards are slab-sided aluminum types with awnings and roof air conditioners.

Adelaida Road winds through thickly wooded groves, but much of the land has been civilized, and orchards of walnuts and almonds grow where nature had its way. Regiments of dark green walnut trees march across the hills with the orderliness of crosses at Shiloh.

There's an idyllic quality to these hills, and folks fleeing big cities, crowds

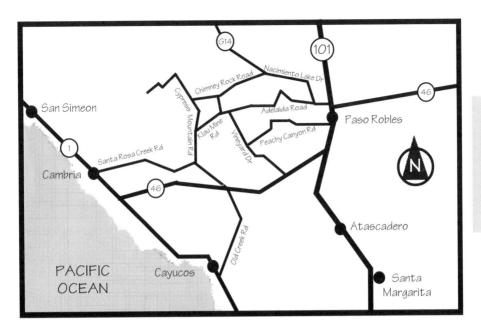

and smog, tuck extravagant cabins into the hills and live the romantic life among orchards and curving country roads. Ranching and wineries appears to be the leisure-time activities of industrialists who come to Adelaida to mix business with art and recreation. The bridled order of vines, trees and crops must be the rancher's psalm.

> *Oh beautiful, for spacious skies*
> *for groves of fruitful trees*
> *for streams and woods and winding roads*
> *that lead from slope to sea.*
>
> *Oh Adelaide, Oh Adelaide*
> *God shed His grace on thee*
> *and crowned thy good*
> *with wineries...*

Lichens hang from the trees. Some of the hills are so steep that mass wasting has divided the hill in two as if someone cleaved it. The earthy tentacles of hillside oaks dangle grotesquely like veins and arteries from an illustration in *Gray's Anatomy*.

Adelaida Road reaches beyond the shallow valleys of almond orchards and looks across broad expanses, longing to make a lunge for the top where it

NORTH

can catch vistas across stone outcroppings of waving grass that sweep to the edge of the sea. Upwards toward the summit the hills are brushed gold with grasses interspersed with islands of oak.

Don and Elizabeth Van Steenwyk, industrialists and gentle farmers of Hidden Mountain Ranch, nurture a 1600 acre home of 2,000 walnut trees lined up picturesquely. The (Diamond) nuts that we get at the grocery store may come from one of the many co-op nut ranchers in the hills east of Paso Robles.

I stopped at Adelaida Winery and sipped their cabernet sauvignon, an educated Stallone with huge muscles and a raspy voice. Or was it a musky, heavy red with the sweetness of horse flesh and saddle leather. I couldn't make up my mind. Then I read the press release of this same wine from Wine and Spirits Magazine—"...a strong sense of terroir (soil) while pleasing with a full range of aromas, including floral and herbal notes." We think alike, don't we? (Describing wines should be a national sport).

Susan Rescola, of Adelaida Winery, told me about Adelaida's cult of Epicureans called *The Tribe of Esau...* "where the simple lentil is revered over kingdom, wealth, metaphysics and other such non-comestibles." The Biblical character, Esau, is portrayed as an outdoorsman, hunter, chef and lover of good times. His treacherous brother, Jacob (Israel), cheated Esau to win (unfairly) their father, Isaac's, blessing. Isaac blessed Jacob, thinking he was Esau:

"Ah, the smell of my son is like the smell of open country
blessed be the Lord.
God give you dew from heaven
and the richness of the earth,
corn and new wine in plenty." Genesis 27: 27-28

In several miles I spotted a white frame cottage with latticed balconies overlooking the creek. This was Marie Brown's place. The last time I was through here we chatted and she told me of deer, coons, badgers and a mountain lion that drank from the creek. The thick woods have no sign of man or viticulture. Oaks canopy the road and thickets of blackberry fill the understory.

Across an open field I caught sight of a water tank and small cottages, the realm of Fraser Mac Gillivray, then views of his old English style house dating back to 1885 (at 8910 Adelaida Road). It was midday and there wasn't a breath of air. Spanish moss hung lifelessly from the trees. Acorn woodpeckers ratcheted and mourning doves cooed from the distance. The Mac Gillivray place has the feeling of originality, a homestead that depended on the productivity of the land.

Just ahead was Vineyard Drive. If the Adelaida Winery is your destination (only), a good alternative drive is to take Vineyard Drive off Highway 101 near Templeton, then turn left on Adelaida Road. But if you can stand to get your Mercaaedeez Benz dusted and jostled, keep coming along to the center of Adelaida where wild turkeys scratch in the duff and time rolls back.

Beyond Tablas Creek Vineyard I spotted the stone wall of Mac Gillivray's west border. A good mason placed that wall with great care, some of it crumbling now but sections of it is splendid in its joiner work. The thistles have turned into platinum buttons and strike picturesque poses around stone walls and old buildings.

There is a little tiny house next to the Ramage place where you can stop for cold drinks, snacks and something to read if your afternoon is completely blank. Help yourself, leave your money behind for the things you buy. No one is home and no one is looking. In the adjacent garden tomatoes ripen, beans are coming on and the basil is ready to be picked.

A short ways beyond is the heart of Adelaida in 1877, at 2825 Adelaida Road, 200 yards south of the junction with Chimney Rock Road. Of the original buildings, only some of the outbuildings of the 1880s Dubost sawmill remain. A little store, service station, post office and dance hall comprised this back country Camelot. It began to disappear in 1936 when they closed the post office...which is where the story of Adelaida begins. It's a mystery never solved.

Realm of Fraser Mac Gillivray - circa 1885

Respite along the road

Was Adelaida the 15 year-old daughter of Jose the blacksmith and Susana Corelle who lived next door to the post office in 1877 when Milton Sunderland was postmaster? Did Milton abandon his wife, Adra, for the affections of this young woman and rename the post office after her? Or was the town named after Adelaida Carlon, a member of an influential family? Or the wife of Captain John. M. Price of Pismo Beach; or Adelaida Brizzolari, wife of Bartolo Brizzolari who had financial interests in the nearby mines?.

What we do know is that in 1877 Las Tablas, later renamed Adelaida, was on the mail route to Cayucos and Cambria. There were no road connections to Paso Robles miles and hills to the east. The life line to this tiny community was over the mountains to the coastal communities of Cayucos and Cambria. Las Tablas, or Adelaida, was a suburb of Cambria. All of Adelaida's cattle and produce followed the same road your Mercaaedeez Benz is traveling today.

I turned left on Klau Mine Road. Staying straight on Adelaida Road takes you to Chimney Rock Road and back to G17, another beautiful ride on a warm summer night. The road is paved for a spell and seems to be going downhill.

After a few miles it became dirt. I hung a left on Cypress Mountain Road. The roadside gutters turned alkaline white from the runoff from the mines and soon I observed a scene which looks like land disembowelment.

In 1871 cinnabar (mercuric sulfide) was discovered and mined. When price supports for strategic metals ended in the 1960s, mining stopped. Today the corrugated sheet metal buildings creak and pop in the noonday sun and the underground ovens that heated the ore, are cold. The Buena Vista Mine is on the left of Cypress Mountain Road as you climb the hill. Klau Mine is further along on the right.

Several one-lane bridges cross the creek. A deer bounded from the bush and I nearly hit her. The habitat changed to sycamore, bay trees, and big tooth maples. I drove past the 7X Ranch campground, donated by Dee and Minnabel Fitzhugh for the youth of north SLO Country. Large gray tree squirrels ran up the trees and watched me from their perches.

The road got rougher. I passed Ranchos Dos Arroyos in *My Indecente Carro*. (Give your ranch a dandy Spanish name, will you? I will not be out-done).

I wouldn't want to be come home on a rainy night in this part of the county, but it's wild and pretty. Turkeys scratched along the side of the road. They're an eastern species, brought over the continental divide as a game bird by U.S. Fish and Wildlife Service. They have adapted very well to the oak woodlands and are a pleasant sight. In the evenings they roost in the trees, coming down in the morning to scratch a little, talk a little, eat a little. They run like horses but are excellent fliers for short distances.

Madrones with mulatto-skinned trunks line the road. The road claws its way to the top, cascades over the crest, and winds and twists in tight spirals through windswept grassy slopes to the beginning of Santa Rosa Creek far below. The road parallels the creek, sometimes intimately, sometimes remotely, eventually becoming a paved road again

I came to a junction with Santa Rosa Creek Road at the bottom. To the right was Cambria, 12 miles away to the west. Left on Santa Rosa Creek Road brings you to Highway 46, five miles away. Beyond Highway 46, it is called Old Creek Road, running past Whale Rock Reservoir and entering Cayucos.

If you begin your trip from Cayucos, you can pick up Old Creek Road south of town and get to this point and look up and say, "I'll bet its pretty up there, but I'm not going to get my Mercedez Benz dusty. I'm going to just keep on going and have some pie at Linn's."

The spring storms have undermined the roadbed and great dips make the going uncertain along Santa Rosa Creek Road toward Cambria. Dayriders stop to dabble in the creek. This is the creek that sometimes babbles and sometimes screams, as it did in a recent year when it ran through Cambria and brought water levels to the window sills.

Four miles from Cambria I stopped at Linn's Fruit Bin, a great place for afternoon carbs—a small raspberry-rhubarb pie and a cup of coffee; and a big pie to take home.

They were having a different season in Cambria than they had in Adelaida. The temperature gauge came down on *My Indecente Carro* and I had to roll the windows up to stay warm.

Turn right on Business Highway One if you want to go into town. If you really did take your Mercaaedeez Benz over those dirt roads, stop in town and get it washed. In no time it'll forget it's been back in time and over a century of mule trails.

NORTH

20

ARROYO SECO ROAD

(And The San Antonio River Gorge)

NORTH

The paved road runs through a park of blue and valley oaks, rolling over hills and through creeks. Fort Hunter Liggett now has control of these lands west of the San Antonio Mission in the valley of Jolon and it's a crazy mix of tank trails and peaceful woodland settings.

We drove the 75 miles from San Luis Obispo along Highway 101 through Paso Robles to Jolon Road, then to Lockwood and onto Mission Road on the military reservation.

Beyond Nacimiento Road, and coming up to the gold-domed military head-quarters, formerly Hearst Ranch headquarters designed by Julia Morgan, and now an overnight inn called The Hacienda, we turned left on Del Venturi Road. A sign indicates that Santa Lucia Memorial Park is off in the distance.

The creek crossings were paved and the recent rain hadn't sent any water running, so we continued pulling our fifth wheel into the foothills of the Ventana Wilderness. We passed a gate which is sometimes closed for military maneuvers.

Six miles from Mission Road we arrived at rock outcroppings that appeared suddenly and dramatically. The whole mountainside is composed of tilted rock—slabs, layers and boulders. The russet colored buckwheat was striking and the poison oak fiery.

We entered Los Padres National Forest and came to the Indians Ranger Station. Nobody was home. There is camping across the road in what we assume is Santa Lucia Memorial Park. Most of the campsites are around the perimeter of a large circular clearing. There were no signs; no campers either. We dropped the fifth wheel at a campsite and continued past the pipe gate onto Arroyo Seco Road, also called Indians Road on some maps.

This road is closed in winter and treacherous even for four wheel vehicles during the rainy season. The sign warns off motorhomes, trailers and vehicles over 25 feet. We wondered if we could pull our fifth wheel trailer up to the Escondido campground, three miles north.

NORTH

Arroyo Seco Road is steep and narrow, with numerous places where two vehicles meeting each other would have to back up to let the other through. I can imagine that two vehicles with trailers might be in a standoff for days, because backing down a mountain road with a trailer on a road that has no shoulders and few pullouts, is very tricky.

Escondido Campground is secluded and high in the hills in a grove of oaks. We chose a campsite and then went back down to pick up the trailer. Lucky for us we didn't meet anyone on the road.

In the center of Escondido Campground is a horse corral, and alongside the corral is a well used trail that leads to the Gorge. It's a long, very steep descent on slippery rocks and crumbling dirt, full of genuine hazards. After 20 minutes we arrived at the gorge in the last light of day.

Water lay in inky pools against the white rock. Stickleback and native squawfish swam below the still surface, and water striders walked on water is if it was glass.

On the opposite side of the gorge the rocks were crusty with moss and

Leanne Parkes overlooks the San Antonio River Gorge

ferns but crispy dry after a long and exhausting summer. In the spring these rocks are in dripping elegance as water seeps from the rock to enter the gorge.

In the morning our friends from Arroyo Grande came out to visit and to have breakfast with us on the table in the sun. We explored another trail at the end of the campground which also descends to the gorge, then runs up the western side of the mountain and disappears over the hill to Fish Camp, Lost Valley, Marble Peak, and eventually ends up in Big Sur. This is the place to set off on backpacking expeditions into the wilderness.

At noon Frank and Liane left us and Eva and I jumped in the truck to discover the rest of the wilderness north along Arroyo Seco Road.

The road becomes bumpier and dustier, but is still suitable for all vehicles including family sedans. This is no place for a camper or a car-trailer combination, however. In some places we were down to 7 m.p.h. on very narrow roads with deep drop-offs and vertical walls of fractured rock.

It's a treeless wilderness of chaparral, steep mountains and wooded gorges. Few things seem alive in late summer, save the poison oak that gets prettier as the dry season worsens, and the rabbitbrush that thrives when others faint. Standing four to five feet high its willowy branches, bare at the bottom, are bright green at the tips with clusters of tiny yellow flowers that give it a yellow broom look.

For ten miles we plied the dusty road, stopping frequently for long views. From on top we could see the descending switchbacks to Arroyo Seco Camp and picnic area, and beyond that to Sycamore Flats and the city of Greenfield.

We returned to the south end of Arroyo Seco Road, near the Indians Ranger Station to discover more of the gorge of the north fork of the San Antonio River. In the first half-mile of Arroyo Seco Road, north of the Indians Ranger Station, is a place for a several cars. From there we walked a trail to the gorge, an extensive area of sculpted sandstone formations.

We climbed from one sandstone ledge to another, visiting the deep grottoes and caves caused by the erosion of the river. There are endless surprises and enchanting water holes. Sycamores and alders overhang reflective pools and kingfishers watch from limbs overhead. Turtles basking on the rocks in the sunlight literally ran for the water as we rounded another corner.

In places the sandstone has been rendered into tiny beaches. Summer brings a lot of folks looking for an old-fashioned swimming hole, complete with ropes strung to the limbs of overhanging trees.

We walked for more than an hour in this natural riviere, scrambling from rock to rock, until we came to a place where a trail led back to Arroyo Seco Road.

The gorge is the main reason to come to this area; its beauty and recreational value is outstanding. A close second is the scenic roadway into Indians from Hunter Liggett. The stone parks beg to be explored and there are many hiking trails to intriguing places like Junípero Serra Peak which is on my list of things to do when I return.

Near the Indians Ranger Station are also back country trails to Cone Peak (9 miles), Cooks Camp (6 miles) and Madrone Camp (3 miles).

Some of the Salinan Indians who were disenfranchised and homeless following the closing of Mission San Antonio in 1835, went to live in the oak woodland and open range near the headwaters of the San Antonio River where deer and game were abundant.

An enterprising Salinan Indian family, Eusebio Encinales and his wife Perfecta, purchased 100 acres in the northwest corner of the Milpitas Land Grant along the north fork of the San Antonio River and put some of the homeless Indians to work as cowboys. They knitted a community that survived until the turn of the century. The area of their habitation is called the Indians.

They buried their dead on a knoll overlooking the adobe where they raised 13 children. The home, later modified by a private gun club, and still later by the Los Padres National forest, is on a dirt road near Lucia Memorial Park. The road and house are not open to the public but can be viewed from the outside.

There was a period of hope when Franciscans from Monterey came down to minister to the Indians who hadn't fled the area. The Franciscans and a handful of Indians lived a minimal existence until 1845 when the mission lands and cattle were turned over to influential people. In 1851 Father Ambris came to take up the ministry and recreate a parish; even though the mission and its lands were no longer held by the church, but when his ministry ended in 1882, the mission entered its final period of decay and destruction.

The Mission was rescued from oblivion when the Milpitas Land Grant was bought by William Randolph Hearst. Hearst poured his wealth into its restoration, and now it is one of the key places to visit in the Valley of Jolon.

Presently Father Leo Sprietsma has gathered together a collection of historic memorabilia of life at the mission and the people who worked and lived there, including photographs of Eusebio Encinales and Perfecta who can be seen standing with their family and friends in front of the mission in 1904. The mission is open to the public.

21

FOLLOWING HISTORIC ROUTES ABOVE CAMBRIA

(Willow Creek Road & Kirk Creek Campground)

NORTH

The gold rush of California in 1849 was centered in the foothills of the Sierra, but San Luis and Monterey counties also had their rush, although it paled in comparison and few were made rich by it. Still, there were gold rush towns like Mansfield (originally called Manchester) that counted over 200 souls searching for gold in the Santa Lucia Mountains. At its height, Mansfield had many miner's shacks, a hotel and the necessary number of saloons where miners could invest their wealth.

W.D. Cruikshank discovered gold in 1887 south of the towns of Gorda and Pacific Valley. His mine was about 10 miles inland from the coast in an extremely remote area, and the town sprang up around him. The town's principle supply route was a long day's ride on a rutted wagon road over the mountains to the small town of Jolon, near the San Antonio Mission.

As the ore became more expensive to extract, the town dwindled. In 1909 the town burned and no buildings were replaced. Mansfield left nary a scar or a foundation to contemplate, and now the land looks like it did before the invasion—hills and rills with pines and firs, and manzanita and madrone filling the understory. In the creek lands, redwoods grow, and the land looks wild and natural.

In search of the Mansfield of yesteryear, I took the 69 mile ride from San Luis Obispo to Los Burros Road, aka Willow Creek Road or Los Padres National Forest Road 23S01, a mile north of Gorda, about ten miles inside Monterey County.

It's a wonderful road to travel when you have a day to dawdle because there is so much to see. But the pace is serpentine, forced by the steep terrain and the numerous lookouts and side trips that delay your passage. At times the road is so steep the only view out the windshield is the sky.

Redwoods begin to appear in the wet draws as the road wends its way across streams that feed Willow Creek. At a thousand feet, I drove through a grove of oaks on the north facing slope with tanbark trees and gooseberries

NORTH

nestled in the clearings. Pines and firs appear at the 2,000 foot elevation, and large toothed maples grew in the swales. The madrones in winter are strikingly beautiful with their smooth mulatto skin and small orange berries borne at the end of their branches.

After 6 miles of travel from Highway One, I was near the top, but still climbing. Pipe and construction materials at road spurs suggested miners were here. Many of the claims are still jealously protected, so wandering off the road in search of open mines and buckets of gold nuggets generates commotion.

A house on the road nearby sucks up metallic junk like a magnet and has a scolding sign alongside the road... "Go Slow, No Dust." A kid's plastic tricycle sits in the road, the only level place for a kid to ride a bike, and evidence a family is in residence. On my return trip I got proof of residency when the "lady" of the house bawled "SLOW DOWN." So I did as she said, and went real slow and ducked lest Daisy Mae let fly with a 30 aught six and remove the top half of my pickup. You meet the nicest people up here.

Shortly beyond the road house with the junk (that loathes dust), is a sign to Alder Creek Camp, the approximate location of W.D. Cruikshank's Last Chance Mine and the town of Mansfield. This is a good place to stop for the day, have lunch and go back; or go on as I did, until the road becomes narrow and the roadside vegetation leans into the vehicle like bristles at the car wash.

If you continue on Willow Creek Road, you'll eventually reach the South Coast Ridge Road (32S02), a high-in-the-sky road that begins near the Plaskett Creek Campground, just south of Pacific Valley. The South Coast Ridge Road runs the spine of the mountains northward, through park lands of coulter pine and oaks, eventually bisecting Nacimiento Road at its summit. Turning east takes you to Jolon, duplicating the original supply route.

The distance from Highway One to the South Coast Ridge Road on Willow Creek Road is about 14 miles, a travel time of several hours if you take time to look and wonder. At the summit of Willow Creek Road are the junctions to Three Peaks (7 miles), Lions Camp (5 miles) and Miguel Camp (6 miles).

There was another curious historic feature that we had come to investigate along this section of Highway One just inside the Monterey County line. When Highway One was being built in the early thirties, convict labor was used. Convicts from Alcatraz had the choice of working with picks and shovels in the great outdoors of Big Sur, or live the life of dreadful sameness in the prison on the rock.

Their camps were situated on level terraces along the highway, and one of these convict camps was at Kirk Creek. It is now a Los Padres National Forest campground on a terraced slope with panoramic views of the ocean and the Big Sur coastline, north of Pacific Valley.

The clues to its past lie in the vegetation. A row of blue gum eucalyptus line the road, and Bermuda grass carpets the grounds, wonderful features for a campground, but hardly what you would expect along the coast.

And then there was the pampas grass, eight-foot high platinum plumes waving gently, scattering the light, being stunning and providing hedgerows of privacy to the campsites.

Not that pampas grass should be considered all good. Its foothold on the coast's slippery slopes is both reason for awe and concern, for its eradication is impossible and its adventurous desire for all the real estate up and down the coast seriously threatens native plants.

All this exotic vegetation suggests that some time ago (1930) someone decided to landscape the camp with quick growing wind breaks, hardy lawns and an inexpensive decorative, low maintenance hedge. Looking through the photographs of Rosalind Sharpe Wall's book *A Wild Coast and Lonely, Big Sur Pioneers* , we saw a picture of the Kirk Creek Convict Camp with its rows of tents behind a line of young eucalyptus. The drive into camp came from the north then, and the trees followed this descent into camp. Checking out our suspicions, we walked to the entrance, which no longer enters from the north, and found the original grade overgrown with vegetation, but with military ranks of eucalyptus flanking it.

The present site is a modern campground with utilities and easy access to the wild features of the coast. A trail runs alongside the fence, south, to Kirk Creek, and then through a poison oak garlanded trail to small beaches, steeply faulted magmatic rock and pockets of rolling stones where I retrieved a number of fascinating green rocks which I took to be jade.

It's a wild and beautiful walk along the shore at low tide and there are several crescent beaches that can be reached. But beware, lest you get caught as the tide comes in for you could spend many hours waiting for the tide to turn. These beaches become isolated at high tide and the vertical cliff walls provide no avenues for escape. A doorway in one of the volcanic rocks, now isolated from land, offers smashing views of galloping white breakers that hiss and roar and vie with each other for passage. With great commotion and confusion, they snort and tear at each other in a one act play of ruthless characters and violent conflicts.

Monuments and headstones make this section of the coast look like a graveyard as the sea works to divide and conquer, endlessly gnawing and pounding the land until it is broken and buried in the surf.

The trail from the campground north through the pampas grass is the tame way to the sea. The beach is broad and uncluttered and is the reason why many folks come here. The trail is free of poison oak and easy going. Every morning, campers tote their lunches and chairs to the beach and spend the day in the sun

NORTH

and surf.

This campground has become one of our favorites in fair weather, because it offers even grassy slopes and panoramic views of the sea and the coastline. This is a National Forest Service Camp and sites are offered on a first-come, first-served basis.

Nearby Sand Dollar Beach (to the south) is an ideal day-use area for picnicking and walking the prettiest beach on the coast. Excellent camping is also at Plaskett Creek Forest Service Campground a few miles south.

A couple of miles north is Limekiln Beach and Campground, a private facility with deep woodland campsites, as well as sunny beach sites.

Across the road from Kirk Creek are the trails to Vincente Flat Camp, 5 miles; Stoneridge Trail, 5 miles; and Cone Peak Road, 8 miles.

Kirk Creek Camp is at the junction of Highway One and Nacimiento Road, about 75 miles from San Luis Obispo.

Campers descend for a day at the beach near Kirk Creek Campground

NORTH

22

JADE ON THE BEACH AT YOUR FEET

Bill Begley sent us over to Willow Creek, but we didn't see it at first. All the pebbles looked alike, all beautifully rounded from the ocean's tumbling action.

Then someone picked up a few rocks and found hiding beneath them a sliver of stone as green as a 7-Up bottle, and nearly as transparent. It felt hard and dense, and slick to the touch. A knife blade didn't scratch it. Then we knew we had found some.

Everyone went back to searching, knowing better what to look for. Another green stone was found, and another. After 30 minutes we had a plastic cup full of...JADE.

We ventured closer to the sea, following the waves like shore birds chasing the bubbly edge. Then CRAAASH! In one giant clap the sea slammed into us, soaking us to our waists. Now there was no more need for caution. If we had snorkels and masks, I think we would have been on our bellies in the water picking up rocks. Finally, after another cold dousing, the passion for jade subsided and we decided we had enough.

We met Dixie Montgomery and Ray Haux at Jade Cove. They had come up for the day to hunt and collect. Dixie, a veteran jade collector, wore the most outrageous rainbow-striped socks with star-spangled tennis shoes for standing in the surf. She said the "jading" is best when the ocean is stormy and the turnover is the greatest.

We learned to discriminate jade from serpentine and soapstone by visiting the Big Sur Jade Company, a genuine grit and grime gem workshop above the general store in Gorda, on Highway One, 70 miles north of San Luis Obispo.

This is not a jewelry store with trinkets and earrings hanging from driftwood. This shop smells like kerosene and looks like a machine shop, a place where field stones are collected in milk crates and cuts of boulder-size jade are bisected for scrutiny.

Wild Bill Begley was the man in charge, a guy who blends a backwoods style with an articulate understanding of the world of jade. For 50 cents a square inch the shop will cut your hunk, or they'll help you with the evaluation, and if they think you've got a winner they'll cut it for you and keep half, giving you first choice.

For three months the shop's big six-foot diamond-embedded drag saw gnawed day and night through a slab of jade the shape of a redwood burl. Into that slice you can look down through layers of swirled green colors, dark bands contrasted with milkier greens.

In the back of the shop, a 30-inch saw with a kerosene-oil bath and pump was working its way imperceptibly through a promising jade boulder—14 1/2 inches in 14 1/2 hours.

With a hardness of 6-7, on a scale of 10, diamond being 10, the network of interlocking fine needles of jade resists being messed with; but once it yields itself, the mystical secrets spill out. I can understand why the Chinese considered it more precious than diamonds. Artisans of the first dynasty in 1400 BC carved it and buried it with their dead as the richest token of this world to the next.

Jade from New Zealand is nephrite, while jade from Burma and Japan is jadeite, the designation also given to California jade. Botryoidal jade is a California exclusive, a bubbly or grape cluster mass of exceptional hardness and translucency found only in the southern part of Monterey County within 10 miles of Gorda.

Jade has been "cooking" in the earth's interior for millions of years. Often associated with serpentine and easily confused with soapstone (soft enough for a knife to score), jade is usually smothered by accretions of other materials.

The tumbling action of waves and other stones makes identification of beach jade easier than identifying specimens in the hills where it is mined. Some of the best pieces have been discovered under water by Scuba divers; beachcombers repeatedly bring in high quality gems from Jade Cove, Willow Creek and Sand Dollar Beach.

One mile north of Gorda, on Highway 1, a bridge spans Willow Creek. To the left, south of the bridge, a road goes down to a small parking area by the creek. When the tide is out (call Port San Luis Harbor Control, 772 6254/6256, or the U.S. Coast Guard weather hotline, 772- 4620) get your sand bucket and little shovel and begin working over the rolling stones at the edge of the sea. Combers in this area constantly turn up good jade. The distance from San Luis Obispo to Gorda is 70 miles.

About 3.2 miles north of Gorda on Highway One is Jade Cove. When you see the sign, park opposite it and walk the staircase over the fence past the California Sea Otter Refuge sign. At the edge of the terrace is a rough trail down to the cove. Because of its remoteness, few people venture to the cove and the pickings are good. You're not allowed to take anything above the high tide mark but scrounging beach stones is no problem.

A half mile north of Jade Cove is Plaskett Creek Campground, a grassy-

Jade seekers explore the beach

NORTH

green camping area where we camped and met a young couple from Aachen, Germany. After a camp supper we walked the short distance along Highway One, north to the Sand Dollar picnic and beach day use area. Beyond the parking spaces, two stiles go over the fence onto the terrace. A sign on the north end marks a trail through a set of posts to the beach below.

This huge beach is another favorite jade collecting area. The south end has large deposits of boulders and rocks that yield good specimens, but some of the best are right underfoot beneath the sand.

By the time we had returned to the highway near Plaskett Creek a sliver of moon was casting a faint glow across a sky of milky clouds. We met our German friends again and stood in the middle of the deserted highway exchanging notes about each other's country.

The night was cool and quiet, but out of the stillness came the distant sound of a motorcycle. There was nothing to see as the sound came around a curve in the road, but the roar of the engine told me that in a second he would be upon us. We dashed for the side of the road, and out of the waning light came the dim image of a motorcyclist with long flowing hair. In an instant the lightless rider roared by us and down the road. "Was that Wild Bill Begley?" I wondered.

The next day we returned down Highway One, stopping at The House Of Jade in the San Simeon Plaza. They have a fine collection of finished works as well as prime examples of botryoidal jade. No, we never did find out who the midnight rider was.

SIDEBAR

Big Sur Jade Company is no longer at Gorda but they have a shop in the hills and are open for special orders. Their message number is (805) 927-5574.

THE OLD NORTH COAST ROAD

We rolled up Highway One past towns and settlements with names from the past—San Simeon, Lucia, Partington, Pfeiffer (old timers pronounce it Piefur), Deetjen's, Castro Canyon, Ventana and Andrew Molera.

For many years this part of the Santa Lucia Mountains was inaccessible, and Spanish padres didn't attempt to establish missions along the coast. Instead, they planted their seeds in the fertile valleys to the east of the coastal range—San Miguel, San Antonio, Soledad and Carmel.

The Esselen Indians had an early history on the coast, however, and datings from human remains, artifacts and fire pits on the Post homestead near Ventana Country Inn Resort, place them on the coast for over 3,000 years.

They were also using the natural hot baths from mountain springs at what is now the Esalen Institute. After their incorporation into the other Indian tribes at the missions, and because of their inability to withstand the smallpox and cholera diseases transmitted by the Spaniards, they were decimated.

In 1853 the land to the south (of Monterey) became available through the Homestead Act and settlers began to dribble in from the north.

But there were no roads, and the gorges at Bixby Creek and the Little Sur River were impossible to cross. Travelers were forced inland, following animal trails and primitive roads picked out of the granite and limestone by home-steaders. Beginning at Carmel Highlands and meandering inland and along the coast to Bixby Creek, the roads wandered through the hills until descending to the coast near John Cooper's Rancho El Sur, now Andrew Molera State Park. (Andrew Molera was a great grandson of John Cooper).

Michael Pfeiffer and his French wife Barbara came across these trails in 1869, along with their four kids, chickens, a cow, seeds and supplies, and settled at the mouth of Sycamore Canyon. Others were soon to follow. John Bautista Cooper, the claimant on the 8,946 acre Rancho El Sur at the mouth of the Big Sur, was a seaman, and he began to establish seaside supply points for the early pioneers. Ships would anchor offshore while settlers rowed out to the ship to

Bixby Bridge, built in the 1930's, was one of the longest single span bridges of its time

barter and buy.

After a few years the Pfeiffers were joined by William Brainard Post and David Castro, and for a time that's all there was at Big Sur.

Eventually, roads were picked and graded from Castro Canyon on the south where Deetjen's Big Sur Inn is situated (you can see the old coast road if you pull into the restaurant and inn and walk the horseshoe shaped canyon to the other side), then it went alongside the Post Homestead (the red cottage at the entrance to Ventana) to the mouth of Sycamore Canyon in the vicinity of Pfeiffer Big Sur State Park, and parallel to the Big Sur River, crossing it 13 times until it approached the Cooper Rancho El Sur (Andrew Molera State Park).

We walked some of that original road by pulling into Andrew Molera State Park, where the original Cooper ranch home has been preserved, turning left toward the livery stables before we entered the parking lot. Giant sycamores line the 120 year-old road which winds through the riparian woodland.

Across from the entrance to Andrew Molera State Park, the historic trail leaves the river's side and goes straight up the hill on the east side of Highway One.

We picked up the (north) Old Coast Road one fall afternoon and examined the footprints of those pioneers who spent a dozen hours in a light spring wagon with two horses to make it into town (Monterey).

The road was so washboard I thought the truck would come unraveled as we climbed steeply into the treeless hills away from the broad valley of the Big Sur River. Soon we were seeing for miles, catching a glimpse of the glistening traffic on Highway One far below us and deep chocolate valleys of alders and redwoods lying between buff suede ridges of short grass.

It's a roller coaster ride, sky high, then descending into verdant green creek bottoms of tall trees, a strange juxtaposition of dry upland slopes and wet redwood gorges. The road got more even as we rode and I no longer feared the truck would come undone. This is not a truck or jeep trail and any vehicle will handle it easily. In wet weather, however, you'd have a different kind of experience.

As we crested a hill a buck pranced across the open field, graceful and self-assured, suggesting he felt safe and was probably surprised to see us.

We observed that the trees in the numerous redwood gorges along the way grow in circles, and in the middle of their ring is the stump of a giant. We surmised that these are not old growth forests, but rather regrowth following logging of the virgin timber. Later discussions with park rangers corroborated our suspicions.

One of the reasons these roads were built was to access the redwood forests, but they chose the best trees to harvest and left the less desirable ones standing, which are today's giants. But even the 100+ year old trees are impressive and we stopped frequently to look and walk, for this indeed is beautiful country and the land has healed following intensive 19th century lumbering and mining activities.

About the time I was thinking that this 11 mile circuit from Andrew Molera State Park to the Bixby Bridge would be a great mountain bike circuit, I heard bikers round the bend in the road where we had stopped. I ran back to the truck, blew the horn and waited for the guys to turn the corner because we had stopped dead in the middle of the road to take pictures. We just about had those guys over the tailgate. I sensed their impatience with us.

How dare we stop on a one lane road with little regard for other motorists. Hey, we thought we had the country all to ourselves. They were the first and only ones we saw.

Four miles into our 11 mile ride on the old coast road we came into another redwood forest of giant trees. These were the biggest we had seen. Our map indicated we were probably on the south fork of the Little Sur River.

We spotted an old moss covered bridge that spans the river and wondered where it led. We learned later that we were at the site of the historic Idlewild Resort, and this was the bridge used by the horse and buggies to reach the resort which lies in the woods a short way from the river. Some say that the two-story hotel is still standing in the woods on the privately owned Rancho El Sur.

The four-horse stage left Monterey at 8:31 a.m., stopped for lunch at Smith's stage station at the mouth of Palo Colorado and reached Idlewild for dinner. The fare was $1.50/ day for family table, everything included, including a limit on trout from the stream.

The temptation to walk the main supports of the green velvet bridge was too strong for Eva and soon she was out over the water walking the balance beam like Nadia Comaneche.

Downstream I spotted a giant redwood lying across the stream and went to investigate. The water of the river wore saddle shapes in the trunk as it spilled over in the spring and these depressions were made to order for human derrieres. It was a natural lunch spot. Our feet dangled above the water and we munched while the crayfish had their lunch on the bottom of the stream and water striders walked on water casting shadows like Mickey Mouse faces.

Eva stretched out over the giant tree with her face to the water watching the crayfish; at least a dozen ugly guys were sparring with open claws and scrounging for the crumbs that falls from nature's table.

The large-toothed maples were beginning to turn color and I thought of how colorful this drive would be in late September or October as the nights turn cooler.

It was up and down into redwood forests and treeless plains and over one-lane bridges before we made the final ascent toward the road to Bixby Bridge.

These roads were built by ranchers, loggers and mining interests of the

NORTH

late 1800s. Lime was quarried from nearby Pico Blanco at the top of the divide at an elevation of 3,709 feet, and a swarm of Japanese and Italian workmen toiled and stoked the kilns to treat the ore during the years of 1906-1910, sending the finished lime in barrels along a high cable tram to the landing at Bixby Creek.

And finally there it was, after several hours of travel and 11 miles of scenic back roads, this monument to human engineering, the Bixby Bridge, 714 feet long and 285 feet above the surf, one of the most photogenic bridges on the west coast and the largest single span bridge of its time.

Then back on Highway One with the fast crowd for the 10 minute drive back to our beginning at Andrew Molera State Park and a look at the Cooper ranch house.

Big Sur is about 100 miles from San Luis Obispo.

Coastal redwoods growing in gorges along the coast

PARTINGTON COVE AND TANBARK TRAIL

(To Redwood Groves And The Historic Tin House)

There are only a few redwood canyons in the Big Sur Country that can be explored along established trails. All the others are a bramble of impenetrable thickets, waterfalls, vertical canyon walls and fallen trees.

After a harrowing experience along Villa Creek several months ago, Ben and I decided to explore Partington Creek in Julia Pfeiffer Burns State Park. Our map indicated that a trail ran up Partington Creek, then traversed the slopes southerly until it came into McWay Creek, near the park entrance and parking lot.

We set out on a sunny morning and found the turnout for the Partington Creek trail 2 miles north of Julia Pfeiffer Burns State Park, and 100 miles north of San Luis Obispo.

One trail heads down the slopes from the highway to the ocean. The broad trail is beyond the iron fence and descends into the stream habitat where a grove of redwoods grows happily along the running creek. Picnic tables and benches make this an inviting lunch spot.

If you continue on the quarter mile trail toward the ocean you come to a rugged little beach where the fresh water creek meets the tide; or turning left you cross a wooden foot bridge over the creek and face a hole in the wall that leads to Partington Cove.

In the 1880s John Partington and his partner Bert Stephens cut 50 feet through the sheer rock cliff to make a 6 foot high by 8 foot wide beam supported tunnel to the picturesque cove on the other side. A hundred years of weather and storms haven't seriously weakened the passageway, so you can safely pass through and sit on the memorial bench alongside the azure blue cove where the seaweed sways in and out with the tides. The boom that hoisted goods onto ships in the 1880s is still intact.

Partington shipped out tanbark, redwood and lime. Tanbark was the source for tannic acid which was used for tanning hides, dyeing and as an astringent.

The period in Big Sur history from 1880 to the turn of the century was a time of intensive exploitation of all the resources of the woods and hills. More that 40 million board feet of redwood lumber and 50,000 cords of tanbark were sent down to waiting ships at Partington Cove and other landings. Lime was smelted in Limekiln and Bixby Canyons, and all the slash from lumbering operations were gleaned to stoke the fires of the kilns. The canyons were stripped of all their natural beauty and the rivers ran dark with eroded silt.

The land has had time to heal, and a new ethic has evolved that treasures the redwood forests for more than picket fences and redwood tables. The riparian woodlands are beginning to resemble the paradise it must have been before this period of destructive commerce.

Partington Cove is also the entrance to the 1680 acre underwater sanctuary of the state park. Certified scuba divers can plunge down the steep sea wall to grottoes, caverns and natural bridges. Permission to dive is required, so don't just pull off your shoes and have a go of it.

Above Highway One, where we parked our car, we started up the Tanbark trail, along the south side of Partington Creek. The gurgling of the stream and the density of the redwood forest soon shut out the noise of the ocean and roadway. The soft forest floor is carpeted with sorrel, and redwoods spread their limbs across the sky, creating thin, sharp rays of light.

Old hollow stumps tell of the cuttings a hundred years ago, but along their rim many small saplings have sprung, forming rings of maturing trees. The path follows the creek for a half mile, meandering through the Babcock family of redwoods, then ascends along a sheer cliff where a wooden foot bridge supports the trail across a hanging canyon. A million lady bugs were clustered on the fallen tree limbs.

In a half hour of leisurely walking up the canyon we came to the Mclaughlin grove of redwoods. Beyond this the trail begins to switchback out of the creek bottom as it winds toward the upper ridge of 3,000 feet. For hikers looking for heart thumping exercise it's upward and onward. For the less physical this could be a good end point.

Tanbark trees fill these upland slopes, the young trees being lush and green, and as symmetrical as fir trees when growing in open spots. The mature trees, competing with the laurels and redwoods, tower with spindly limbs 60 feet into the upper canopy.

This is the time of year for tanbarks to drop their acorns, and they ricocheted through the limbs like pinballs through the chutes. The ground was crunchy with a million nuts determined to fill every inch of soil with tanbark seedlings.

Tanbarks have acorns very like an oak, but their prominent parallel venated leaves and deep green color make them look like a chestnut.

After two hours on the trail we came to a beautifully constructed stone wall near another family of redwoods at an elevation of 2,000 feet where we stopped for lunch. The redwoods continue to grow along this north slope even though they are far from the creek. Two of the giants have grown together here, the limb of one penetrating the other and now the two have become inseparable.

A half-mile beyond, the trail divides. We opted for the left branch which took us near the top of Partington Ridge by a small house with a green Buddha in the crotch of a tree. Backtracking we came to this same fork and went right, (straight) until we came to the fire road trail.

The fire road trail leads to a large green house called the Tin House, built during World War 2 by Lathrop and Helen Brown who donated much of their land to the park in the 1960s. Helen complained about the constant fog they experienced at their Saddle Rock home near McWay Creek, so they built this sun house high above the clouds (elevation 2,000 feet) on the steep slopes facing the ocean. Materials during World War 2 were scarce so they scrounged materials from old metal gas stations and erected their tin house. The blinds hang crazily across the windows and plaster sags in sheets from the ceiling, but the old place is still in pretty good shape.

Ewoldsen Trail to McWay Creek begins at the Tin House, but it may be closed due to fire and storm damage. The way to return can be by way of the fire road, or return on the Tanbark Trail.

The fire road descends down the slopes toward the ocean in a sharp spiral, and in an hour we were back on Highway One. From the fire road at Highway One it's a half-hour walk back to the cars at Partington Creek.

Total hiking time up Tanbark Trail to the Tin House and back along the fire trail road is about 4-5 hours.

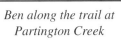

Ben along the trail at Partington Creek

PEAK EXPERIENCES ALONG THE COAST

(San Simeon Creek Road And Plaskett Ridge Road)

We took a drive up the north coast one sunny autumn day looking for fall color and new places to discover. We concluded that California's fall color is green except for the yellow of big-leafed maple and the scarlet red of poison oak. Everything else seems to subtly transform the tired foliage of summer for developing buds of early winter and spring.

I've often wondered what's up San Simeon Creek Road so we turned right off Highway One just north of San Simeon. The road runs by San Simeon State Park and meanders alongside San Simeon creek where pumpkins, cherry tomatoes and gourds grow in the luxuriant flood plain alluvia of the creek.

The road climbs the hills where sycamores arch the road and coveys of quail burst from the thicket. As the road climbs higher the riparian habitat becomes rich in alder and bay trees.

At 5.7 miles from Highway One the paved road winds tight, rising quickly through red mountains. The active stream gurgles and dribbles over the rocks, wandering close to the road so that it is almost always in view.

At 7.5 miles we seemed close to the top. We spotted a sunny terrace where we pulled off and caught lovely vistas toward the sea. Nearby is Red Mountain at 2,085 feet and farther in the distance, at the top of the ridge, is Rocky Butte at 3,438 feet.

In a half hour, 8.5 miles from the highway, we came to a closed gate and the end of the public use road. If this road continued straight through it would tie in with Chimney Rock Road on the eastern side.

What makes this road worthy of an afternoon jaunt are the numerous spots along the creek for picnicking, and the wonderful roadside pullouts. Total time to ride up and down is about an hour. If you plug in time for lunching, sitting by the creek and a little afternoon delight it could take you...all day.

We drove beyond San Simeon to where the rugged Big Sur coast begins. It was time for lunch so we stopped at Ragged Point. We bought sandwiches at the takeout restaurant and headed across the lawn to the descending cliff trail.

A short way down is a bench that faces northward along the coast. We dug fruit and juice from our basket and settled in for a moment of peace in a beautiful place. We finished our meal with imported French wafers filled with raspberries, a gift that required a moment like this.

We drove farther up the coast to Gorda, a watering hole, gas station and restaurant. Three and a half miles north is Plaskett Creek Campground State Park.

On the southern edge of the campground is an obscure dirt road that runs into the Santa Lucia Mountains, traversing the ridges until it meets Nacimiento Ferguson road 12 miles north. On some maps it's called Plaskett Ridge Road, on others it's named South Coast Ridge Road, or Forest Service Road 23S02. The road runs along the south edge of the campground, then climbs quickly into the hills along the ridges, providing phenomenal views of the coast. It's another one of those roads that can take an hour to drive or a day, depending on your curiosity and inclinations.

In a half mile the county road ends and the forest service road begins. No matter. This is one of the best graded and accessible roads in the national forest. I wish the foot trails were so well maintained.

Your family sedan will do just fine here, but don't come when it's wet and muddy. There are no shoulders and the drops into steep canyons could make this road treacherous in wet weather.

In two miles we entered a ferny redwood canyon where water trickled and the moist earth supported ferns, sorrel and giant trees. A short climb beyond brought us to a hilltop terrace where a doe and her fawns grazed peacefully in a meadow parkland of pines and oaks.

Three miles out and still climbing the road runs along a ridge with full views of the ocean and tiny Highway One below. Wispy clouds lay over the sea at elevations below us.

We finally reached the top of the ridge road where we met a spur that goes south on the ridge road (Coast Ridge Trail) to places like Lion's Den Camp, Three Peaks and Los Burros Road (county road 4406), but we continued north toward Nacimiento-Ferguson road.

We stopped at a clearing and sat beneath the embracing limbs of an ancient oak that overlooked the redwood canyons and the Big Sur coast. The sharp, cold winds of autumn were chilling, but the warm rays of the afternoon sun comforted us.

In this mixed evergreen forest, oaks mingle with Coulter and Ponderosa pines. The giant foot-long cones of the Coulter pine lie about. Camping beneath these trees can be hazardous because they smack the ground with tremendous force and have been known to seriously injure people.

Each cone cradles the next generation of pine trees disguised as winged

Eva Stob overlooks the grand terrain from Plaskett Ridge Road

nuts. You can see them parachute to the ground, spinning on a single wing to new soil away from the nurturing tree. The splendor of the ancient oaks along these ridges is an arborist's dream. There was a huge, gnarly black oak with shelves on its trunk like folds of adipose on a fat person.

"It's like the bark of the trunk has settled down and the skin wrinkled," Eva said. "Like an English bull dog."

Nearby were other giant trees, each with its own personality. Some were military straight, with muscular trunks and orderly branches, others were bent and as disheveled as a poet.

The road continued through a burn area. Many of the trees are dead but some of the large oaks have survived. Tanbark trees sprouted vigorously in the clearings.

There's a world of side roads on these heavenly ridges high above the ocean, and innumerable places to picnic and camp. On a side road to Alms Ridge we stopped to view Sand Dollar Beach, Plaskett Rock, and the campground where we began our ride.

Eight miles out we approached Chalk Peak, a mountain of white metamorphosed limestone. Along the way we spotted many mature madrone trees with their smooth, mulatto-skinned limbs.

After 12 miles we reached Nacimiento-Ferguson Road at its zenith. The ridge road goes across Nacimiento-Ferguson to the Cone Peak Trail, some 6 miles distant. There it ends.

Nacimiento-Ferguson Road winds down toward the sea for 7 miles in a series of scenic spirals. From there it's a 75 mile drive back to San Luis Obispo.

SIDEBAR

Check with the locals before making the loop on Plaskett Ridge Road. The road is sometimes blocked off.

NORTH

PLASKETT CREEK CAMPGROUND

(A Hummy Sort Of Place)

The coastline from Gorda to Pacific Valley is being conquered by the erosive work of the sea. Numerous caves and doorways have been developed in the basement strata where the sea washes and makes a great commotion.

The headlands and steep cliffs are a paradox of beauty and brutality; frightening in its raw energy and outrageous in its colors and formations. Sometimes I see it as grotesque, at other times sublime.

Waves rush the black rock and smash in foaming breakers then fall in formless streams of dissipated energy.

Spiny-backed rocks, like huge Stegosaurus dinosaurs, are undermined with caves where the waves swish and boom.

Sand Dollar Beach is a paradisic crescent of sand that lies between these black rocky headlands. The hand of the Creator is masterful here.

Surfers were in the water, and families who were staying in the nearby campground trundled blankets and toys and baskets of edibles for a day on the sand. The combination of excellent camping with close access to coastal splendor and recreation, makes this area one of the most coveted recreational areas on the coast, yet not many people take the 72 mile drive from San Luis Obispo to ever see it.

There are two staircases over the fence surrounding the parking lot of the Sand Dollar Picnic Area and Beach. The one in the center is a bluff trail, and the one at the right leads directly to the beach. The trails are interconnected, and by aimless wandering you'll see it all.

A handsome wood staircase winds off the bluff to the beach where beautiful bodies and ebullient dogs liven the otherwise desolate beach.

As we walked the beach we felt the presence of a million little creatures squirming in the water. With each new wave a new army of Pacific Mole Crabs swarmed to the surface, and all in unison, myriads of them, in all sizes and generations, scrambled toward the ocean, digging back into the sand before the water receded.

Their actions were as quick as a wink, and after the wave receded, the beach surface was flat and quiet like there wasn't anything going on...until the next wave came and the sand wiggled again with a million little creatures swimming and (simultaneously) filtering detritus from the sea water. These little fellas are part of the hoards of creatures who clean the sea and make it so pleasant for us big kids.

Plaskett Creek Campground is only a 100 yards south of Sand Dollar Beach, a parklike campground of grassy expanses and rows of giant Monterey pines and cypress. We set up our fifth-wheel trailer and made lunch, catching a nap on the blanket under the warm spring sun on the lawn around our campsite. A purple finch warbled in the tree overhead and time stopped in an idyllic moment of peace and harmony.

In the afternoon it was more walks for me, while Eva rested and read.

There is a series of trails that run across the terraces, from Sand Dollar Beach all the way to the remains of Pacific Valley Center (which burned to the ground a number of years back), a distance of about a mile. These are excellent biking and walking trails, with spurs that run to the bluffs, and more gorgeous views of jagged headlands and white foaming surf.

Going north from the charred remains of Pacific Valley on Highway One is a staircase over the fence at Pacific Valley Station (the Los Padres National Forest fire station and office which issues permits to back country overnight backpackers). This trail ends at the bluffs where there is a cliff/beach, high above the surf. It's a perfect picnic spot with expansive views of the entire coastline.

Another crescent shaped beach, north of the path from Pacific Valley Station, was enjoyed by one couple who had the beach to themselves, until I arrived. The rim trail descends a gully to the beach where I inadvertently destroyed the Shangri-La quality of this couple's romantic solitude.

In the springtime these terraces are covered with wild flowers, and even in June the fields are green, and yellow with splotches of mustard. The terraces and hills are part of Los Padres National Forest, and as such are part of our legacy of accessible public lands. Wherever you see a staircase over a fence along this stretch of highway consider it your invitation to explore the coast and all its coves.

Plaskett Rock stands off shore from Sand Dollar Beach, the largest, whitest, most guano-covered rock, named after an early family that lived in these parts in the late 1800s. William and Sarah Plaskett raised 11 kids on the ranch land in these parts. Their son Byron, and his son Ed ran the mail over the mountains from Jolon and King City (where the Southern Pacific had a depot) to the coastal communities of Gorda and Pacific Valley. Their mule train hauled mail, freight and groceries over the McKern trail, which is now called Plaskett Ridge

Road or South Coast Road 23S02. This road runs along the south boundary of Plaskett Creek Campground.

Within walking distance (south) of Plaskett Creek Campground is Jade Cove. The spot is well marked with a sign. The staircase over the fence puts you on a short trail to the edge of the bluff and down a rickety hand rail to the rocky cove, strewn with gems.

Some of the stones are jade, to be sure, and some are inconsequential jewels worn smooth by tumbling in the surf. Each has its own signature and personal beauty. When we go down to the cove we end up with a cup of beauties, being unable to discern the "precious" stones from the ordinarily beautiful. The law reads that it is illegal to take gems or materials from the beaches that are above the mean high tide mark.

That night at the campground we punished our neighbors with the smoke of fresh catfish in wine sauce simmering over hot coals. It was a hummy sort of day, as Winnie the Pooh would call it. The purple finches were still warbling from the trees and everyone seemed to be at the right spot in their lives.

Note: Plaskett Creek Campground is a Los Padres National Forest Campground. There are no hookups or running water at the sites. Water spigots and flush toilets are placed throughout the grounds. The 44 sites are available to campers on a first-come, first-served basis. Tenters and medium-sized motor home travelers can be accommodated in the camp. There are no pull-through sites but rigs with trailers will find the sites clear of debris and easily accessible.

A remote section of the park is designated for group camping. Group sites for up to 50 persons requires reservations. Call (408) 385 5434

Trail leads down to Sand Dollar Beach

RAGGED POINT INN

(And a Fascinating Trail Through Seacliff Botanic Gardens)

The hills around San Simeon were so colorful one spring, they looked like floral carpets. It was awesome (as distinguished from teenage "awesome"). As far as you could see there were yellow tidy tips, goldfields, indigo lupine, poppies and seaside daisies.

Near the motels of San Simeon Acres, Hearst's zebras and cattle grazed in a field of lupine, creating a surrealistic picture of striped animals against a cerulean background. Newborn foals, which are brown and white, lay knee-deep in flowers. The range of the Santa Lucia Mountains and Hearst's Castle in the background completed a picture reminiscent of scenes from The Sound Of Music.

Flower shows happen every April and May along this part of the coast, with some years being better than others. You may get so mesmerized and stricken with the beauty that you just stop here, take a bunch of pictures and go back home, maybe you were on your way up north, but you forgot where you were going.

But if you get out of the grasp of San Simeon in springtime, venture north along Highway One where the marine terraces end and the highway follows the torturous contours of the steeply faulting slopes of Big Sur.

South of the Piedras Blancas Lighthouse are the elephant seal beaches. Here's another place that sucks you in and doesn't let go. The hoards of elephant seals have become a county phenomenon. Our beaches are going to get awards for the biggest seal colonies on the west coast. The numbers of seals are greatest in May, but the most outstanding spectacle is the calving and mating season in December and January.

But let's say you tear yourself loose and drive further north. In another four more miles (total of fifteen miles from Hearst Castle) is Ragged Point Inn (look for the Union 76 sign). If you get there at the close of the day, be prepared for a sunset of peach chiffon clouds and a fiery orange ball piercing the clouds like on a Pentecostal Sunday.

Ragged Point Inn isn't the splendor of Post Ranch or Ventana Inn, and it's not the funk of Deetjen's Big Sur Inn, but its position on the edge of the ocean is what makes it delicious, and its rooms are an echo of the redwood forests along the Big Sur watershed—simple, natural and elegant, and without the smothering Laura Ashley decor you find in other places that try too hard to wrap you in loveliness. Their moderate prices, unparalleled views and gracious

The Ragged Point trail crosses a roaring creek on the way to a black sand beach

accommodations, make them one of the best buys in lodging accommodations along the Big Sur Coast.

When we went there for our special date, we stepped into our room and looked through the glass wall to the Pacific Ocean. This is where we would sway to the song of the surf. We pulled in the bags and decided that there was still enough daylight for a stroll to the point. A gravel path led out and joined other gravel paths to the gardens and the cliffside trail to the point. From the top of the ridge we looked north, the ancient cedars making a picture frame for the foaming surf that crashed against the black sand beach. Motorists were still scurrying along the Big Sur Highway, eager to find their place of rest.

When the sun goes down, highway travel stops and Highway One becomes a walking path. Not that I would advise that. The first time we took a walk on the highway under moonlight near Plaskett Creek Campground, a local biker decided that this was the kind of night he'd like to ride his chopped Harley at full throttle, with no lights, in the glow of the moon. If we hadn't heard him coming, I'd be writing from another place.

Ragged Point has a new restaurant and chef. We used to eat from their takeout restaurant next to the gas station, and that was okay, but it was the usual fare of burgers and fries. We began with Stuffed Mushrooms with Herb Cheese, graduated to Spicy Rosemary Pasta with Grilled Chicken Breast, peaked with the New Zealand Rack of Lamb and climaxed on Banana Raisin Bread Pudding with Whiskey sauce and the Creme Brulee. Life is good.

The little masked faces didn't show through the glass doors on the night we were there, but the raccoons of Ragged Point are sometimes as ubiquitous as cottage cats, begging to be fed and entering your room if you get too friendly with them. Just as well they weren't there; Eva wasn't eager to have raccoon paw prints on her pillow.

In the morning we ambled over to the main office where the lounge was set up for breakfast. It was more than the usual continental breakfast and included fruit, juice, oatmeal, cereal and milk, Danish and coffee. Owner Wiley Ramey stopped by to talk us into going horseback riding. The inn has a wrangler and a stable of steady steeds for plodding the 1500 foot peaks above the point; but we deferred that for another time and opted instead to walk down the inn's cliffside trail before seeing the elephant seals on the beaches near the Piedras Blancas Lighthouse.

The path to the cliff walk is beyond the restaurant and toward the point. An overhead sign designates the trail which winds down a three-hundred foot precipice of black granite, switchbacking like a goat trail, wandering past seeping walls and ambling over a cascading creek on a wooden bridge. Dudleya and saxifrage dig themselves into cozy corners of the cliff and into the fissures of large rocks, and other flowering plants cling to the precipice to compose a rock

NORTH

Eva Stob views the Ragged Point Trail

garden of unbridled beauty. Cutting sea-breezes sweep up the face of the slope and shear the vegetation into rakish forms no higher than five feet tall.

The beach is a disquieting scene of black sand, rolling stones and white foaming breakers. The unpredictable size of the waves makes walking the beach perilous because you never know when large waves with the power to drag you to sea, will come ashore.

The trudge upward from the beach made Eva groan, and me wince with the sweet satisfaction of making a body work. Benches along the way gave us time to perch and observe the coast from a falcon's point of view. Many timid souls find this splendor a bit too raw, a mite too strenuous, so this hike is left for the rest of us who rather like it.

But the path is well maintained and the poison oak is trimmed back like an English hedge. If you're not in high heels or absolutely gawky, you'll make it easy.

Every time my wife and I go to Ragged Point, we think it can't be as good as the last time, but it gets better. I think it's the seclusion of the inn and its edge-of-the-sea position. Now with a fine restaurant, it's even better.

For reservations and information write or call the Ragged Point Inn, PO Box 110, San Simeon CA 93452. Phone 805/927-4502

28

SOME LIKE IT HOT

(Lakes San Antonio and Nacimiento)

It was late in the afternoon by time we got to our campsite at Lake San Antonio; time to be purified in the kiln-dry air of late day. We leveled the motor home, pulled out the lawn chairs, poured a cool one and sat like dried flowers in the sun.

The acorn woodpeckers and magpies kept up their chatter, and the deer came out in such large numbers the camp resembled a farm yard. People fed them corn on the cob and lichens from the trees despite the admonition not to feed wild animals.

The light of day dimmed until only a hundred little campfires glowed and smoky fires sent a smorgasbord of aromas through the blue oaks. By ten o'clock there wasn't a hint that anyone was going to bed. Kids ran and screamed and adults sat around fires talking and playing games.

It was a peek at our tribal heritage when the extended family celebrated the return of the hunters, and the women and men were reunited and kids jabbered and played and the tribe affirmed their unity.

Not until the chill of evening bathed the skin did the hunters and the food gatherers begin to think of retreating beneath the thatched roofs and hide skins of their Winnebagos and Coleman tents.

And that is the magic of the north county—hot and dry during the day, and cool and dry every night. By the time we were ready to snooze, there was a chill in the air, and by early morning when people first stir, many of us were digging under the covers for another hour of sleep.

In the morning I walked down near the lake where rental cottages afford a house for folks who don't want to camp. They prepare their own meals in a real kitchen, and spend hours boating or sitting on the decks of their cottages overlooking the lake.

Western Grebes were screeching from the water. The little ones, now the size of their parents, sat on the water begging. The parents dove and snared small silver fishes and brought them to the surface. The hapless fish flashed and thrashed in the sunlight until the fight was out of them, whereupon they were repositioned until they faced their tormentor and got ready for the ride down that long sinuous neck and into the acid inferno of the grebe's stomach.

Adult males and females, immune to the interminable whining of the babies, twisted romantically toward each other, each mirroring the elaborate neck stretching movements of the other. For the moment, not even fish was on their minds.

The beach is a half-mile away from the campgrounds on the Lake View Drive. I was the only one walking. Vans loaded with flotation devices, kids, dogs and food drove by and waved. I trudged on.

Heart break trail went up the side of the hill, part of 26 miles of hiking and mountain bike trails at Lake San Antonio. These trails become part of the May Wild Flower Festival and Triathlon that attracts thousands of athletes each year.

I passed a small cove where several families occupied a tiny beach, big enough for them and their boat. Swimming is permitted anywhere in the lake and folks find an isolated cove and settle in.

I came to the official beach where hundreds had gathered and stood in the shade of the life guard tower. The guards agreed to watch my gear and I stripped as far as was prudent, given the fact that I did not have a swim suit.

Eva was sitting indolently in the shade of the awning, reading and looking like she was recharging her batteries when I got back. In contrast, I was a sweaty, gasping prune, needing to rehydrate.

Wild turkeys were grazing on the lawn around the museum and visitor center when we went to visit. We learned about Pleyto, the little community along El Camino Real that was organized by immigrants from the East Coast, England and Australia. The town had a livery stable, saloon, dance hall and post office. It sprang up in the 1880s and died 40 years later. The television series *Rawhide* was filmed there before the valley was inundated in 1959.

Pleyto means dispute, and there was a debate between the missions at Jolon and San Miguel regarding proper authority over Rancho Bartholeme, of which Pleyto was part.

We were curious about the north shore of Lake San Antonio so we drove over to take a look. It's a 25 mile drive through open country northwest towards Lockwood and Jolon. At about the time we crossed the San Antonio River, a mere trickle in summer, we spotted tanks on maneuver in the surrounding hills, part of Hunter Liggett Military Reservation. We turned right on G18, Jolon road, and entered the north shore campground on New Pleyto Road.

The north shore is barren. This land was ocean floor 12,000 -28,000 years ago, and shells of oysters, scallops, clams, whale vertebrae, etc. can be found here. The shallow sea bottom was sandy, which in time was compressed, uplifted, faulted and eroded to form the beach and lake bottom of San Antonio.

It's perfect for beach goers and boaters.

There were pickups, motor homes, trailers and tents along the edge of the lake. Campers and their boats were only separated by a few feet. Hot daytime temperatures and cool water for swimming and boating is the perfect combination of fire and ice.

There are cottages to rent here also. They're high on a hill and removed from the nomadic mob on the beach. They're modest, air conditioned mobile units with comfortable patios and decks. Lake San Antonio Resorts rents them, and boats from the single dock on the north shore, so you can go empty handed and pick up everything there.

Lake Nacimiento is another story. Although Lakes San Antonio and Nacimiento lie nearly side by side, they are fed by different rivers.

The San Antonio river is lazy and quiet, draining the slopes of the Ventana Wilderness, then meandering across the Jolon Valley, past the mission, and southward. When it was plugged in 1959 at a point close to where it joins the Salinas River, it spread out and covered the valley, leaving a lake shaped like a bath tub.

The Nacimiento river also arises out of the Santa Lucia Mountains, but it is rambunctious in winter rains, scouring and eroding the hillsides into deep canyons. When it was dammed, the deep canyons and side canyons filled and created a lake the shape of a dragon. It is by far the most glamorous waterway of the two with its coves, high stone walls and configured shoreline.

Lake Nacimiento is the first to fill in the winter, so it's the sacrificial lake during the summer to keep the Salinas river flowing and to satisfy the farmers in

Boater near the "Narrows" at Lake Nacimiento

NORTH

the valley who were the instigators in this whole development. Each of the lakes have plants and animals distinct to itself. Gray pines are numerous around Nacimiento; they are rarely seen at San Antonio. We observed western grebes, herds of deer and magpies at Lake San Antonio. There weren't any at Lake Nacimiento. Eagles are common at Lake San Antonio, rarer at Lake Nacimiento, although a nesting pair of golden eagles has stayed the summer at Lake Nacimiento, a first.

The facilities at Lake Nacimiento are managed by Lake Nacimiento Resorts, the same private company that operates most of Lake San Antonio's facilities, except for the campgrounds. The full hookup campgrounds at Nacimiento are more orderly, closer together and less natural than the campgrounds at San Antonio. There are no trails, save one 2 1/2 mile trail, no interpretive literature, no informed rangers who know the biota, and no attempt to interpret the striking features of this beautiful park to the public.

But, the cliff side lodges at Lake Nacimiento are outstanding. They are handsome cedar shingle two-story buildings high on a bluff overlooking the belly of the dragon. Modern kitchens, baths, fireplaces and outdoor decks make them ideal vacation homes. They sleep from 6-10 people. A loft on the second floor has bunk beds with full-size beds down, and singles up, accommodating up to 6 people. A steep staircase descends the cliff to a small beach where boats can be tied and passengers picked up for a day of skiing and tubing.

Nacimiento is even more popular with boaters than Lake San Antonio. With 165 miles of shoreline there are infinite opportunities for fishing and cruising.

We took a bass boat out from LNR Rentals. It was great to get on plane with a 60 hp Evinrude on the back and a growing rooster tail behind us. Eva begged me to slow down. After a year aboard our lubberly trawler doing 8 m.p.h., 30 m.p.h. in a bass boat is flying. So I tamed my *Water World* temperament and became the frumpy trawler-type again, working the shoreline and ending in Town Creek, a winding cove of steep rock walls. We putted at less than 5 m.p.h. and turned corners to surprises and close encounters with the plants and animals along the edge.

A few other boaters had preceded us and were swimming and having lunch far from the roaring boaters in the main channels who were whipping the lake into a froth.

But I got Eva to take the boat out of the cove and back toward the marina, timid at first, then more adventurous. I searched for expressions on her face that hinted of screaming delight, and I saw a glimmer. A couple more days in a speedy runabout and she could be a wild woman.

If you think everyone is out there just to ski and boat, let me tell you about the fisherman who was coming in with his son. He said that his twelve year old son could not help but get his limit of white bass because the fish were literally boiling the water and waiting their turn to bite the lure. Well, you know fishermen.

SIDEBAR
HIGHLIGHTS AND SPECIAL EVENTS

The two lakes are 55 miles from San Luis Obispo. Take G14 north out of Paso Robles. Follow the signs. Turn left at the dam to Lake Nacimiento Resorts, or continue northward across the dam of the Nacimiento River to the entrance to San Antonio Lake.

Lake San Antonio is one of the largest eagle winter habitats in Central California. Eagle Watch tours are on weekends, from January through mid-March.

The Wildflower Festival and Triathlon takes place each May at Lake San Antonio.

Lake San Antonio, South Shore, has 26 miles of walking and riding trails. Spring and fall are favorite times. This is the best walking and mountain biking park.

July 4 is celebrated each year with fireworks over Lake San Antonio

Lake Nacimiento has a large beach close to campsites. It's town center is a bustle of activity with a swimming pool, spa, restaurant, beach and marina.

Nacimiento Resorts reservation number—1-800-323-3839, or 1-800-323-3256. Nacimiento Resort Marina 805/238-1056

Lake San Antonio reservations—south shore—800-310-2313, north shore—805-472-2203;

Lake San Antonio boat and Jet Ski Rentals/Fishing information—805-472-2818.

Campgrounds and vacation rental homes are available year-round at both lakes.

Young boys walk from the cliff-side lodges of Lake Nacimiento

NORTH

29

REDWOOD GULCH

(An Afternoon In A Redwood Canyon)

Beyond Ragged Point the Big Sur Coast Highway begins in earnest. You soon approach the southernmost limit of coastal redwoods growing in the Salmon Creek water shed.

There are short hikes up Salmon Creek to the waterfalls, and extended hikes to Spruce Creek, Lion's Den and other back country campsites. The trails intertwine and intersect, eventually returning to the coast via the Cruikshank Trail or the Buckeye and Soda Springs Trail.

Several years ago we hiked from Salmon Creek to Cruikshank, but these wilderness trails are seldom maintained and are as obscure as deer runs.

A mile and a half north of Salmon Creek is Soda Springs Trail. It goes up to the Buckeye campground (3 miles) and from there ambles down to the highway on the Cruikshank Trail, or continues upward to the ridge and Lion's Den Campground.

A culvert on the creek shows the date of 1928, the middle years of construction of Highway One, which was completed in 1937.

The Soda Springs Trail head is also a marked drinking water spot and while we were there, 3 motorists stopped to fill their jugs from the spigot near the sign to the trail.

A couple of miles farther north is another gulch and another watering hole. Redwood Gulch, unmarked on the highway, has a short walk to a drinking fountain, and a creek bottom trail which follows the left bank to a series of pools and small waterfalls.

It's a steeply eroded gorge, typical of the redwood gorges along this section of the coast. A series of water pipes carries water from man-made impoundments along the creek. Getting off the trail, and rock-hopping upstream, we came to a point where it was difficult to continue; but then we saw a big redwood lying across the middle of the gorge which allowed us to climb to another level where picturesque chutes of mountain water dropped into tublike pools, perfect for summer respites from the heat.

Rock hopping is the only way to view some of the redwood gorges

Previous hikers had notched a fallen tree lying upstream, so we clambered up and walked the steeply inclining log along cleated makeshift steps to the next level, to see more funnel-shaped rocks carrying water to icy pools. It's a teetering walk with some peril, for there isn't a soft landing when you fall in a boulder-strewn gorge.

After twenty minutes of scrambling, the thickets closed across the creek and made our advances impossible.

On the way back to the highway we knelt on the ground to observe azure butterflies drinking from the moist ground. Sow bugs, as graceless as German tanks with their armor-plated bodies and tread-like motion of a myriad moving feet, swung their short antennae close to the bodies of the dainty butterflies, who were not the least distracted.

Before going up to our vehicle from the creek bottom Eva stepped inside the eight foot culvert that carries the creek to the other side of the highway. She called in a culvert voice, "Honey, I think we can walk all the way underneath the highway to the other side".

And so we did, our conversation echoing in the ribbed pipe while we tripped over objects in the dimming light to the other side.

Eva was intent on finding the water that had disappeared into the ground before we entered the culvert, and standing still we could faintly hear the trickle of water.

The ground in the flat places was moist, and horsetail rushes grew like trees in a miniature pine forest. The dripping-gurgling sound increased as we moved down stream. Soon we found the place where water surfaced again. The vegetation grew in wild and happy confusion, making the way difficult.

"I'm not going any farther," Eva proclaimed.

"OK, Toots. I'm going to go down to this next terrace and then I'll be right back.

I proceeded along huge rocks and then came to a cliff wall of dripping ferns and dense moss. "Oh, look at this. A hanging garden," I said to myself.

"What are you doing down there?" Eva called from above.

"Oh, just looking at a beautiful weeping wall with maidenhair fern and columbine," I said.

In a moment she scrambled down to this new view of mineralized canyon walls and dripping grottoes.

We thought we had ventured where few people had gone before until we found a ladies white shoe, stuck in the mud. How ever did she make it back to the road on one foot and one shoe? We wondered.

To find Redwood Gulch, look for the highway signs to Salmon Creek as you drive up the coast. Redwood Gulch is about three miles north of Salmon Creek.

THE ELEPHANT SEALS

(at Piedras Blancas Lighthouse)

A crowd formed, like people around a blue light special at K Mart. Kids and couples stood with hands over their mouths, witnessing something spectacular. When a person arrived at the scene, they excitedly called to members of their family still standing along the edge of the road above the beach.

There was a way the elephant seal moved and barked that made us realize she was in labor. She was round and full and we saw the outline of a pup within her.

The other seals didn't seem to be aware of her condition. The 5,000 pound male slept nearby, his elephantine proboscis inflating and fluttering like a snoring man. But she was not alone; her *Homo sapiens* friends had gathered round to witness the event.

The baby slid out, pulsing to the rhythms of its mother's contractions. And then it was there on the cold sand, a jet black pup the size of a small black lab. A bright red umbilicus trailed to the mother. She turned and in the twisting pulled more afterbirth from her body. Facing her baby, she barked nervously. The infant eyed his new world without emotion, almost without sign of life. The mother's incessant barking urged from it a responsive whimper. Finally a dialogue ensued, a screeching soprano cry responding to an alto bark.

The mother tossed sand onto her back in what appeared to be a nervous effort to cool herself or to vent her anxiety. The little pup caught the shower of cold sand until it looked frosted. There were no arms to hold it, no kindness shown and two inverted nipples were a world apart on a round white belly. Somehow, it had to grope along this surface by itself and find the promise of a warm meal.

December and January are dramatic times for elephant seals along the central California coast, and the beaches south of the Piedras Blancas Lighthouse, north of Cambria and San Simeon, are ringside seats for motorists. After months of swimming, fishing and getting blubbery fat, the elephant seals haul out, renew old friendships, have a baby, do a little (or a lot) of mating and go back to sea.

NORTH

The bulls hit the beaches before Christmas, making ready for seal nativity. Immature males may already be there, snorting and sparring in mock battles with other subadult males.

As the bulls with the elephantine noses arrive, the dynamics change. They intend to own the beach and garner a harem, so anyone who messes with them has to be ready for a little sumo wrestling. Their mere presence is intimidating, and shivers of fear run through the colony. Losers either fall to the ground with their snouts in the sand, gallop away (a kind of gelatinous gallop), or retreat to the salve of open ocean water and wait for another opportunity, maybe another year.

When two dominant bulls compete for the same section of beach, they become nearly erect and thunder resonant snorts through their fleshy flugelhorns. They throw their heads back and charge, heaving chests slap, and tusks slam into the opponent.

Some males try year after year to gather a harem, but never become the father of nations. Some bulls will mate with over 100 females, so only a small portion of adult males become the genetic model.

Pregnant females (cows) arrive around the end of the year. They give birth to skinny 75 pound babies and by the middle of January the beach looks like a nursery. Most have one pup, a few have two and I saw one cow trying to nurse three. One of those pups may have been adopted. They roll over and allow the babies to fill up on milk with a 55% fat composition. The wee ones grow and grow and achieve the look of a stuffed sausage within a month. After about 30 days of nursing her baby, who may gain as much as 10 pounds a day, she's torn between maternal and amorous instincts. One day she abruptly and unceremoniously abandons maternity: "Good-bye, baby, I'm going to do a little

"My beauty is in my nose!"

mating with the beachmaster and go to sea where I can find some time to myself eating squid, rat fish and small sharks. I may never see you again. I hope you have a good childhood and learn to swim and eat by yourself, because I'm outta here."

She will have lost a third of her weight giving birth, fasting, nursing and mating. She'll be pregnant again when she goes to sea but implantation of her fertilized egg will not take place for another three months, and with an eight month gestation, she will complete a cycle and be back at this spot within a year.

The abandoned babies are called *weaners*. They've had a straight diet of mother's milk, and now they must learn to eat, swim and fish. They assemble in pods to molt and shed the black baby fur for coarse, brown hair. During this time they toss sand onto their backs to protect themselves from the heat and the sun's ultraviolet light. Large waves and storms are a threat to them at this stage because they have no experience in the water; but gradually they explore puddles and shallow tidal areas, and by the final weeks of April are venturing out to sea.

Elephant seal life is a contradiction of solitary living interspersed with beach life that looks as together as Woodstock. Much of their life is spent at sea, fishing to depths of 3,000 feet. They sleep between dives and are isolated from other seals until it's time for shore leave again. They return to the beach of their birth and snuggle next to each other as if they are long-lost relatives.

Conditions haven't always been good for elephant seals. They were hunted to the brink of extinction in the last century. Their fat was rendered for oil, but with the advent of kerosene and other fuels, hunting stopped. Just in time. In 1907 a small colony of less than 100 was spotted on Guadalupe Island off the coast of Baja California and are the progenitors of the present population. In 1922 the Mexican government imposed conservation measures, followed by the United States a few years later. California elephant seals began to appear on the Farallon Islands west of San Francisco, and in 1955 came onto the mainland beaches of Año Nuevo State Reserve. Since then, the population has spread along the coast.

They were first spotted near the Piedras Blancas Lighthouse, north of Cambria and San Simeon in 1977, and the first pup was born on the beach in 1992. The population has been spilling southward into the narrow dunes that border Highway One.

So familiar is the sight of seals north of Cambria and San Simeon, that it has become a major tourist attraction. In the summer of 1997 there was a re-alignment of a section of Highway One with the construction of information signs and observation points.

The beaches always have seals on them. During the summer and fall months I saw animals of various sizes and sexes molting and resting. Groups of seals lay together in sweet somnolence. Others rest on the sand alone, their pussy-cat-faces sublime and innocent. Triple chins and long whiskers give them a cherubic appearance. During peak times of occupation, the beach is a cacophony of belches, snorts, sneezes and honks.

The bulls are territorial during the winter months of December and January. They look like tons of peristaltic blubber, but they move quickly. If by chance they attack people, their weight, if not their bite, could be fatal and the victim would be a mere imprint in the sand.

The marine terrace near the seal beaches closest to the Piedras Blancas Lighthouse, is land owned by the Hearst Corporation which allows public access by permissive use. The area is subject to their control, so be respectful when you go there.

The experience of seeing wild creatures free and uncaged, thriving in a world where habitat for animals is shrinking, is one of the thrills of visiting the beaches north of Cambria and San Simeon. This is not Disneyland; these are wild animals, untamed, trusting and unaccustomed to people. They don't have blue light specials out there, but it's a real spectacle. Keep your distance and witness a miracle.

Although elephant seals seem to tolerate human intrusion, be wary of mothers with pups and territorial adult males. The Mammal Protection Act forbids anyone from molesting, disturbing or harming mammals on the beaches. Observe them, but keep your distance. They deserve our respect and admiration.

VILLA CREEK:

(An Adventure in the Redwood Forest)

There wasn't a hint of calamity on that pleasant Saturday morning when six of us went hiking on the Cruikshank trail north of Salmon Creek, 80 miles north of San Luis Obispo on Highway One. The trail begins near the Forest Service buildings just north of Salmon Creek and quickly gets into the hills overlooking the ocean. Often this trail and these slopes are enshrouded in fog, and temperatures are moderate to cool. But this day was warm, and dry, and without the usual cool onshore breezes. We didn't know it then, but that became part of our problem.

Bill was there with his 12 year old son, Kelly. And Helen (76) came along, a veteran hiker who lost her husband recently and wanted to get back into walking the back country. Ben (52) our triathlete-hike leader had planned the itinerary, figured the distances and hauled us all up there in his big yellow Oldsmobile. Ernie, (73) was with us again. On previous, shorter hikes, he had proved himself wiry, tough and fast.

I overslept that morning after being out late so I drove myself up and caught the party on the trail about 2 miles up.

Helen (76), Ben and Bill had stopped to rest in a shady spot along the trail. Helen was taking her shoes off and straightening out her thin white socks. She said she thought her hiking days were over at 76, so she had given her sturdy hiking boots away to her granddaughter. She wasn't complaining about her feet, just the heat and being tired.

I wondered how long we might go on without getting Helen uncomfortably fatigued. There were two miles more to our destination, and then the return trip.

The four of us moved from our shady resting spot, and ambled the hills several thousand feet above the ocean. There were magnificent views up and down the coast, and for these moments we were glad we had come. Below us were the deep redwood canyons running in steep gorges to the ocean.

We were high above the tree line and only occasional black and blue oaks

NORTH

dotted the rolling landscape.

The exhaustion was growing and by 1 P.M. we stopped short of our destination to have lunch. The 45 minute respite was sufficient to restore our strength and we pushed on toward Buckeye Campground. Our trail-guide book promised us water, which by this time had become a necessity.

Ernie 73, and Kelly 12, had hiked on before us, too impatient with our leisurely pace and frequent breaks. We met them at the campground, 4 miles out from the trail head at Salmon Creek.

We all filled up on water that ran from a galvanized pipe to the horse trough, and talked about our return. Should we return the way we came—always the least interesting choice, or walk down toward Cruikshank Campground and follow the Cruikshank Trail on the southern side of Villa Creek down to Route 1?

It was four miles each way, so Ernie and I volunteered to precede the other four, getting down to Highway One as quickly as we could by way of the Cruikshank Trail on the southern side of Villa Creek. We then planned to hitchhike back to the cars at Salmon Creek and bring the cars up north where Cruikshank Trail hit the road.

Ernie and I studied the map, gave it back to Ben and took his car keys, promising we'd be at the trail by time they got down.

We followed a very obscure trail from Buckeye camp to Cruikshank, often wondering whether we were following animal trails or the designated foot trail. In an hour we came into Cruikshank campground and were reassured about our position. A clearly used trail ran down toward Villa Creek and we were soon hearing the babbling of water in the cool ambience of towering redwood trees.

The respite from the oppressive heat and dry of the upland trails was refreshing and we stopped to enjoy this great moment. I knew we were to catch the Cruikshank Trail on the south side of the creek, but we were already in the gorge and there wasn't a hint of a trail or a marker at Cruikshank Campground, or anywhere along the way.

Possibly it ran downstream for a ways and then crossed over. On the north facing slopes was the continuation of the trail we had been on but we remembered Ben's map showing that trail going further north over a series of slopes that would take us to another high mountain campground.

The usual starchy Ernie was showing fatigue. We had drunk nearly all the water I carried and we dug into our small reserve of nuts and granola for extra energy.

We had no map to refer to so we began walking downstream on a path to a picnic campground. Despite our best searching efforts we could find no easy trail down or along Villa Creek.

Climbing back out of the watershed meant to expose ourselves to the dry, hot hike out up the slopes in search of the obscure trail on the southern side of the creek. The rock hopping down stream was fast, always downhill and likely the shortest geographic distance to the highway we figured. This proved to be a

NORTH

Bridge crossing Villa Creek

serious miscalculation.

Our pace had slowed noticeably and for every 5 minutes of down stream movement there were several minutes of rest while Ernie gathered his strength. It was 3:30 when we entered the stream and by 5 p.m. we were encountering huge redwood trees that had fallen across the creek. The gorge had deepened and the walls had closed in on either side quickening the pace of the stream in narrow channels. I was getting concerned about time, even though we had more than a few hours of sunlight remaining.

Ernie was visibly faltering, slipping more and occasionally falling into the water. Once his boots were wet, his ability to balance and maintain his footing on rounded stones was impaired.

We climbed over huge trees, back down to the creek bed again, now walking the length of trees lying downstream - and back into the creek again. It was a great adventure that required good balance and a tremendous amount of climbing, scrambling and crouching.

The clock moved to 6:30 and I began to think we might get caught in the woods at dark, a devastating circumstance, inasmuch as our terrain was not the even predictability of a trail; in fact the course was getting steeper and the obstacles more numerous.

Our time walking was more frequently interrupted for periods of rest as Ernie found it difficult to go on. I waited impatiently for his strength to resume, at several places climbing out of the gorge toward the south looking for the elusive trail. Each foray was through impenetrable terrain of head-high thickets of poison oak, blackberry and nettle. The ground sloped so steeply that each step up sent rocks flying to the stream bed below. My exposed legs and arms were becoming scratched and bleeding, and getting back to the stream side where I could wash in the clean, cool water was great relief. Ernie was looking dejected and forlorn, not moving until I persuaded him we needed to keep walking.

He stumbled from rock to rock, most of the time now simply plowing through the water, no longer seeking the high ground.

It was 8 P.M.. The light had left the gorge. I heard the sounds of engines. The highway, I was sure.

It was a small plane. "They're out looking for us," I thought. I got in a clearing ready to wave. I never saw it.

I lapsed into and out of reality. We weren't really in this gorge stumbling downstream at 8 P.M.. The desire to be out on the road was so strong I was fantasizing. Then reality hit again.

"C'mon Ernie let's go. It's getting dark. We don't want to spend the night in the woods."

The sides of the gorge had narrowed and the stream sliced through a narrow channel with huge boulders on either side. I scouted the area thoroughly but there was no way down but to sit and ride the chute (waterfall) into the pool below. What was down there, and how deep, was unknown; but there was no time to wonder.

I sat in the cool water and tried to go slow, but like a minnow leaving the bucket I was down and into the pool. I hit the water and disappeared from sight, coming to the surface treading water in hiking boots, my pack with camera and recorder acting like a life preserver.

Ernie stood 15 feet above while I swam to one side of the pool and coaxed him down.

"You can swim, can't you Ern?" I called out. "This water is 10 feet deep."

"I can't." was his weak reply.

"Oh, God. Help us. If you get me out of this..."

We had reached a moment of deep despair, but this was no time to dawdle. I couldn't get back up that waterfall, and salvation only lie downstream. We had to risk it.

"Come as slowly as you can, Ern, and I'll catch you."

He came as quick as spit, and the two of us struggled in the water together, hiking boots pulling us down, arms struggling to swim against the surging water. I pushed him into the cliff sides where he hung like a bat onto the craggy ledges. Inching along the wall my boots eventually reached the bottom and I pulled him into my arms until we could both walk again.

Our thirst was assuaged, but now we dealt with cold.

For the most part we were walking in the water, looking for the flat ground between the boulders.

The cool-blue light of evening penetrated the woods. We could still see but it was becoming more difficult. No more breaks now. I cajoled, I scolded, I persuaded and extolled. I goaded and pushed poor ol' Ern and myself—under thickets that blocked our way and through more waist-high pools. One more corner in the creek.

And there it was—the highway—high above us riding on its spindly legs on the creek bridge.

"The highway, Ern. We made it." I cried out. He stopped and looked. Oh, how he wanted to be up on the highway, sitting on a soft car seat with the guarantee of home and bed, and water and rest.

But the only way out of the creek side was up a nearly vertical wall of scrambling, grappling, thorny, barbed and poisonous thickets.

No time for careful consideration. Things would only get worse as the night grew darker.

I could see the barest sliver of a new moon rising over the ocean, emitting the stingiest possible light. A cruel circumstance.

One foot a minute, up and over. The exertion was more than I thought possible for Ernie, but he found the last measure of courage and strength, and came up behind , uncomplaining, pushing onward, coughing and gasping in the dust generated from our thrashing and slashing,

My bare arms and legs strained against the vines and thistles that attempted to hold me. I could feel them tearing my skin, but there was fifty yards to go before we reached the side of the highway.

By 9:15 we had reached the edge, but being forced high because of obstacles and deep ravines, the highway was now 40 feet below us . The way down was steep and clear - no brush. From passing cars we could see only a ledge wall.

I lowered myself over the edge, using finger holds and occasional roots and plants for handholds...and then felt that moment of relaxation as I fell backward and drifted weightlessly through space. I was falling 20 feet down the slope, with my eyes to the stars...and then the shuddering halt as my vertebrae came into massive realignment.

I think my fanny pack and the water bottle on my belt softened the way and I was quickly on my feet assessing my hurts. I seemed to be all right.

Ernie had reached the edge and as another car drove by I saw him teetering on the edge.

"Over to your left, Ern. It's too steep here. You'll fall. Come down over here where it's more gradual and hang onto whatever you can reach."

I stood below him. He came slowly, but suddenly in a fury of rolling stones and uprooted plants Ernie was falling backwards towards me. I caught him—or at least broke his fall—and the two of us crumpled into the ground.

He was okay and apologized for being so much trouble. Trouble? He was no trouble. I was just glad he was alive and talking to me. He had done an incredible feat at age 73 and was still alive.

The lights from a car from the north appeared and I quickly jumped the guard rail and stood on the yellow line waving my arms.

I didn't wait for good will. In my condition no one was going to volunteer to pick me up. I stood squarely in the middle of the road. The vehicle would either hit me, or stop.

I think it was Jesus in a Nissan pickup that night. At least the driver was one of His; a person who took us in and gave us drink and a ride to our cars.

We met Ben along the way. He was walking along the highway looking for us, thinking the worst.

On the way home we stopped in the late night gas station in Cambria for something to eat and drink. Two state troopers had stopped in for coffee and one of them sauntered over to me and said, "Are you all right?"

"Yeah, I'm OK," I said.

"Where have you been?"

"Oh, my old friend and I got lost in the woods," I replied.

"Well, you look like a victim of violent crime. I thought I'd ask. You're sure you're OK?"

Incidentally, Ben came off the elusive Cruikshank Trail with Helen at 8:30 p.m. They also had difficulty finding the unmarked trail but found it eventually, nursing Helen who had increasing immobility, but succeeded nonetheless by leaning mightily upon Ben—who established a new endurance feat for triathletes, carrying a 76 year old woman three miles down a rough mountain trail in two hours.

Bill told me that son Kelly, sensing there was trouble as the night deepened, had fallen to his knees on the side of the road and said in a pleading voice "Oh Lord, I don't like this. It's really dark and Ron and Ernie are still not here. Make them come out soon."

In fifteen minutes Ern and I fell out of the sky and appeared among them in the pickup. Kelly knew he had been heard.

When my kids were growing up and they'd get into trouble I'd invariably say to them "Well, what did you learn from that?"

This is the wisdom I gained from this episode:

1. Don't hike the creek beds of the Big Sur country unless you're prepared for lots of surprises and herculean athletic challenges. Know how to swim.
2. Start early and bring lots of water.
3. Pack emergency provisions.
4. If it's hot and dry, shorten your time on the trail.
5. Don't hike without a trail map.
6. Match your age and physical condition with the trail. Trail maps are always out of date and conditions change from the time the guides are printed. Allow for mishaps and error.
7. Triathletes don't have a realistic notion of what is tough and what is not. Don't believe them when they say it's easy. They run some courses that are difficult for most of us walkers. Multiply distance and difficulty by 3.14 to approach reality. This is the "easy as pie" formula.

TRAVELS TO LA PANZA SUMMIT

(Wildflowers And Mountain Passes)

I came upon a bouquet of women having a picnic in a field of Goldfield flowers, their wide brimmed hats flapping and scarves furling in the wind. They looked like giant sunflowers on a flowered carpet. I think they were having a powwow, maybe a close circle of friends giving a bride-to-be advice on love and marriage the second time around.

The junction of Shell Creek Road and Highway 58, 15 miles east of Santa Margarita, is always a favorite wildflower viewing area and across the road is a perfect lunch spot, so I pulled off and had lunch on the banks of a wandering stream and under the canopy of a pride of old cotton wood trees.

My wife and fellow campers came later in the day and we took our motor homes up Highway 58 to Navajo Road and traveled towards La Panza Summit. La Panza was an area of gold exploration and mining around 1878-79. Numerous quartz veins produced gold for about fifty miners who used the scarce water resources for placer and sluice operations. No heavy equipment was ever brought in and gold mining existed only in small camps of men, mostly Mexican, who worked the creeks leading down to the San Juan River.

Navajo Road, marked 29S15 on Forest Service maps, is an improved dirt road, if there is such a thing. We did a number of creek crossings in our 24 foot motorhomes, probably uncovering nuggets for gold diggers but not stopping to find out. We were not deep in the water, but deep enough to cause some concern because a motorhome is not a nimble creature and getting stuck could mean a name change from motorhome to land-based yacht.

We pulled into a large clearing along the road which was a rendezvous for dirt bikers, their trailers and their camping rigs. We considered spending the night there, but the probability of being surrounded by whining motorcycles and late night revelers who would probably go full throttle on beer and chili, dimmed our enthusiasm and we headed toward La Panza Station, an abandoned fire station that was used in the '60s and '70s.

More "improved" creek crossings. You never know the nature of creek bottoms, and some have been known to suck-up lesser things than motor homes; but these were "nice" and we wound up and over hills, scratching the side of Ben and Barbara's newly painted motorhome as they followed, cursing us, I'm sure, for taking them into the La Panza wilderness with only the faintest notion of where to spend the night.

Our vintage motorhome does not sport a new paint job so we tipped and wobbled through ruts, and scraped overhanging trees in carefree abandon as we ventured toward the center of the La Panza and Pozo Summits. I had checked with the Los Padres National Forest Rangers before we entered off of Highway 58 and they assured me the road was safe for motor homes and campers, and said that they travel this road frequently with big fire trucks.

Gray pines were in the hills, the buckwheat was in bloom and patches of gold with glimpses of violet shooting stars filled small meadows.

The road climbed steep hills with chunky rock and was somewhat rutted, which made its reputation as an improved dirt road questionable, but it was passable at low speeds.

We pulled into La Panza Station. A staircase to a phantom building, a few stone walls and a drinking fountain are all that remain. We circled around like a dog before it lies down and threw out the anchor. It was time to settle down, explore our temporary home, take a ride in the jeep and get ready to spot the comet Hyakutake as it streaked across the sky. This is a delicious place to study the heavens; civilization is far away and the dark is penetrating and deep.

In the morning we discovered an Indian grinding rock near a two-foot square cement slab in the campsite, and additional bedrock mortars farther up-hill. This was undoubtedly a seasonal Chumash camp.

An abandoned Jeep trail crosses the creek and heads upstream, becoming a lane of waving grass and spring flowers. Sky rockets were everywhere interspersed with owl's clover and goldfields. The trail crosses the creek several times and ends in a thicket, a quarter of a mile beyond the campsite.

There were no gold nuggets that gleamed from the clear pools, but gold is still here and after a good rain gold dust and small nuggets could probably still be found along Manzana, Navajo and Placer Creeks.

Ben and Barbara, finicky about their new paint job and less than jubilant about any more creek crossings, decided to exit via the La Panza Summit on 29S01 in the morning, so we followed them, heading eastward toward Highway 58 and the Carrizo Plains

The La Panza Campground is only .3 miles from our overnight stay at La Panza Station. It's an organized campground with water, toilets, fire pits and picnic tables. There are good pull-inns for motor homes and trailers and at the end of the campground is a turn-'round so you don't have to spend the rest of

NORTH

NORTH

Barbara Horner takes the jeep for a spin through the creeks

your life there or have a helicopter pick up your motorhome and turn it around. Numerous jeep and motorcycle trails are nearby and these camps are popular with motorcyclists. Not to worry. These are not your Hell's Angels types, just ordinary guys who like to fly.

The road climbs out of the canyon and reaches the 2,947 foot summit. Queen Bee camp is a mile from here. This road is pleasant and uncluttered, with no creek crossings. At the place along the drive where the pavement begins there is a village of mountain homes that have been brought in from the wilderness like stray sheep. They're corralled together like someone is preparing to make an old west movie set.

The paved road is pastoral and beautiful as it winds through the foothills of rolling grasslands and oaks. An old stone barn of the Bowman Ranch alongside the road marks the place of the La Panza Post Office from the last century. It was named after the La Panza Gold Mine and served the small population of miners and ranchers.

When Hi Mountain Road, also known as Pozo Road or the New Road to Pozo, was completed from Pozo to Arroyo Grande in 1896, a flood of traffic was expected over this road. It was the choice of many travelers coming from the valley, and was shorter than the route that ran from Pozo to Santa Margarita and down the grade. Because of the severe terrain of both the Pozo Road and the road to La Panza, and frequent washouts from winter rains, these routes barely survived and now are used only as back country recreational roads.

The name La Panza is translated as *belly* or *paunch*, from a time when cattle were slaughtered and the stomachs and viscera were poisoned and set out to kill grizzly bears. The Chumash and Salinan Indians feared bears, as did early settlers. The word La Panza may date back to 1828 when the area was referred to as *Parije La Panza.*

In the distance we saw the Temblor Range which forms the eastern wall of the Carrizo Plains, then turned left and made our way home along Highway 58.

I don't know if Ben and Barbara will ever go back to La Panza again in their motorhome, but I promised my wife I'd take her back again on our anniversary. She said she wanted me to take her to some place special.

The distance from SLO to La Panza is about 55 miles.

NORTH

TOP TEN ATTRACTIONS FOR NEW POLY STUDENTS

I'll bet that when you first considered coming to Cal Poly you and your parents sized up the university and the town and concluded that San Luis Obispo is a good place to go to college. The climate is agreeable, the mountain environment within the city limits is pleasant and the ocean is nearby. The town has a reputation for being well-mannered and untainted by the big megalopolises of San Francisco and Los Angeles.

You're right. This is a good place to live. And to further our reputation I've thought about ten special places that will provide relief from the tomb-quiet of the library and the endless stress of papers and exams.

By now you've been to Farmer's Market, the town meeting featuring vegetables and sidewalk performers and everybody's idea of a cheap date; and you've been to Linnaea's and the Palm Theater and all the other night places. And of course you've found the churches. You have been to church, haven't you?

Here are some activities when your body yearns to be stretched and your mind is on vacation.

THE HILLS BEHIND THE CAMPUS

The hills behind the campus are a pastoral world of hiking, biking and equestrian trails. Take Poly Canyon Road—by Fischer Science Hall off Perimeter Road - through the eucalyptus grove alongside Brizziolari Creek until you come to the gate to the university ranch.

On the left is a path to the architectural monuments of students of the past who designed futuristic things that may either humor, amuse you or amaze you. To the right, by the redwood tree, is a path that winds around the hill and ends up by the letter P on the side of the hill above the residence halls. You may wish to paint it another color while you're there. Many have.

Straight over the gate is the wide open spaces, with trails that run to the railroad tracks and beyond. You can take trails all the way to the Cuesta Ridge or through the ranch lands to Stenner Creek Road, which ties in with the dairy and poultry road beyond the railroad trestle. From there walk by the cattle barns and the chicken coops to Highland Drive. Highland becomes Perimeter Road near the library.

The hills are sepia soft in fall and vibrant green with carpets of blue lupine in the spring. They give you a feeling you are miles from campus and town.

CERRO SAN LUIS

Cerro San Luis Obispo (elevation 1292 ft.), misnamed Mount San Luis or Madonna Peak, looms over the city and the Madonna Shopping Center. In the Christmas season it wears a star on its crown and is the focal point for the city,

You can hike to the top of the peak by catching a well-worn tail from Laguna Lake on the mountain's southern slope. Alex Madonna owns this land and you are his guests while you're there, so be respectful. Don't bring your dog who will spook the cattle, and close gates behind you. Cows in town are not allowed.

This is a particularly pretty hike (walk) at sunset. The last time I did this the fog rolled into the Los Osos Valley and totally covered the city while the setting sun shone above the clouds in scene straight from heaven.

Across Foothill Boulevard is another beaut. Bishop's Peak (elevation 1,559 feet) is a craggy outcropping of granite that boiled to the surface once upon a time to form an intrusive plug (just like Cerro San Luis), but Bishop's Peak is higher. Along Foothill Boulevard, near the Calvary Baptist Church, is a turnout on the road where hikers walk the trail to the Bishop's crown . The hike is a scramble over rounded boulders to the top. From the pinnacles you get great aerial pictures of the campus. "Look, Mom, this is the campus from Bishop's Peak. My dorm is here."

AVILA BEACH

Avila Beach is unofficially Sand Box U. where undergraduate courses in anatomy are conducted in an open laboratory. Maidenforms and incredible hunks lie about for close analysis and many students are seen taking notes - or is it names and numbers? Take Highway 101 to the Avila Beach Road exit to the end. Actually the Port San Luis pier is the end; also a fascinating place to visit.

Even more incredible, but suggested almost shamed-facedly, is NUDEE Beach, near Pirate's Cave, an area of gorgeous views, no pun intended, rounded hills, no pun intended, foaming breakers and thunderous claps akin to magnificent heartbeats.

Take Highway 101 to the Avila Beach Road, to Cave Landing Road, across from the Avila Beach Resort golf course. Drive by the Unocal tank farm on the top and park in the helter-skelter tipsy-turvy parking lot. The cave is straight ahead or right, the beach is to the left. WARNING. Prudes (like me, and maybe you) feel very uncomfortable approaching the beach, but if you brave it I guarantee you'll have a topic for the next psychology paper you have to write - "AN EXAMINATION OF VESTIGIAL CALVINISTIC ATTITUDES THAT IMPINGE ON THE PSYCHE WHEN DISROBING IN PUBLIC", something like that.

Other access points to hidden beaches off Highway 101 going south are the staircases at the Cliff Hotel (along north side); the end of Spyglass Drive to the seaside park (great surfing point); end of Montecito Avenue in Shell Beach; end of Cliff drive to Margo Dodd Park; and the staircase at the Shorecliff Hotel (north side). Of course for the ultimate beach go to Pismo. There's 18 miles of beach from there to Mussel Rock.

More? Take Highway One into Nipomo toward Guadalupe. Get off Oso Flaco Road to the end; or Main Street Guadalupe to the ocean; or farther along Highway One to Brown Road to Point Sal State Beach. Gorgeous and lonely.

SYCAMORE HOT SPRINGS

Sycamore Hot Springs along Avila Beach Road is a good place come— with your friends. It's an age-old place with a modern twist.

In the early 1900s it was a health resort complete with formal gardens, a fine restaurant, mineral baths and attendants in white coats; but now it's strictly in the pleasure business .

Most of the people I know go to Sycamore Springs for the Avila Gardens Restaurant, but the appeal of the resort has always been the water and the redwood tubs situated on ledges above the main building. The tubs all have names— Rendezvous, Twilight, Enchantment, Tubby, Hideaway, Shangri-La, and many others. Tubby is great for total privacy, Shangri-La for quiet and openness, and Enchantment for a deep woods environment.

For a reasonable fee you can enjoy tubbing under the oaks and squander a week's spending money. You can bring munchies and drinks with you and make a tub-side smorgasbord. You'll never be the same. This could even be a more significant life-changing event than taking philosophy.

The tubs are used frequently during the day and afternoon, but there is a particularly enchanting time at sunset when the fog rolls in and the sun peers through an apricot sky laced with the craggy limbs of the oaks overhead. Get credit for Poetry 201.

Then there is OASIS SPA, a serpentine ceramic spa ideal for a fraternity or for an intellectual seminar in the restorative powers of mineral baths.

AVILA HOT SPRINGS

Closer to Highway 101 on Avila Beach road is Avila Hot Springs. Avila Hot Springs began in 1909 when the first owners drilled for oil, but at 900 feet hit hot water. A row of mineral baths was built around the well head in a building that you can see today. A few years later the pool was added, with a kiddies' pool off to the side. The kiddies' pool has been converted to a hot bath where on a cool night prostrate bodies cook in a sulfurous inferno. Get religion credit. No, this is not a substitute for church!

The emphasis at Avila Hot Springs is on swimming in their giant tepid pool, although they also have mineral baths with masseuses and masseurs on duty. A snack bar and grill serves the campers who stay overnight in their campground.

In the evening around 8:30 p.m. they show black & white cartoons on the wall above the hot pool. After a few months of philosophy, economics and math, you may be ready for this.

They are open daily at 8 a.m. and remain open for night swimming through the winter until 10 p.m. Passes for multiple swims are available at a good savings...which will make your father happy because you will have saved him so much money.

Avila Hot Springs is just off Highway 101 at the Avila Beach exit.

MONTAÑA DE ORO

If you can get your hands on a bike or a car get down toward Morro Bay. There are a number of interesting things to see and do.

Take Los Osos Valley Road into the burg of Los Osos and continue to Montaña De Oro State Park on Pecho Road. Los Osos Valley Road has wide shoulders for bikers.

The park includes eight thousand acres, extending from Coon Creek at the south all the way to Morro Bay. There are over fifty miles of trails, including equestrian trails. Bicycling is possible on some of the trails including the Islay Creek Trail, which runs alongside the creek to a waterfall and historic barn.

It's a park of wild things including mountain lions, raccoons and feral pigs. There is natural chaparral, wildflowers and of course the ancient rocks.

Ah, those ancient rocks! They really are something. Faulted, twisted, and convulsed into distorted and painful forms, this land has been pushed from below and from all sides. At one time it was the sedimentary bottom of the ocean, but it was thrust upward and the evidence of these convulsive movements is seen graphically along the headlands of Montaña de Oro. Long chutes have developed as the sea wears away the softer fragments, and at the far end of the two-mile bluff walk are doorways and arches cut into the rock by the sea.

Stop at the old Spooner Ranch house which is now an interpretive center. Maps and information will give you enough to see and do for many visits.

KAYAK OR CANOE MORRO BAY

Go to the Natural History Museum in Morro Bay on State Park Road across from the state park golf course. Situated on the edge of the Morro Bay (estuary) it's an excellent place to get an overview of the bay. Take the walk to the top of the rock above the museum where you can see teeming birds on the estuarian mud flats at low tide feeding on the tons of invertebrate animals that burrow in the mud and the small fishes that get caught in the shallows.

From the frenzy of feeding birds you'll see great blue herons rise off the surface, slowly beating their huge wings, their long legs stretched straight behind and their necks bent into an S curve. The herons nest in the grove of eucalyptus east of the museum. Walk the short distance to the heron rookery viewing area.

The birds begin their mating rituals around January and nesting pairs are busy fledging their young all the way into August.

By far the best place to view the estuary is in a canoe or kayak. There are a number of places where you can rent these. One is Morro Bay State Park Marina south of the museum (ph. 772-8796). Others include Kayaks of Morro Bay at 699 Embarcadero, (ph. 772-1119), and Kayak Horizons at 551 Embarcadero (ph. 772-6444).

Get out at low tide and paddle the canals through the eel grass. About 70 percent of the estuary is exposed at low tide and you'll be in the midst of all those creatures who suck slimy little creatures out of the ooze. As the tide comes in you'll be able to canoe anywhere. If you go out at high tide and get stuck in this sea of muck you'll have another topic for another paper like - MORRO BAY AT NIGHT AS SEEN FROM A CANOE AT LOW TIDE IN THE MIDDLE OF THE MUD FLATS.

RIDE THROUGH THE IRISH HILLS

The winter and spring are ideal months to visit the Irish Hills. Take Foothill Boulevard to Los Osos Valley Road, left (east) to Prefumo Canyon Road, then right into the hills. The road winds in and out of the rising canyon, past little ranchos and along picket fences of rustic homes with smoke curling from their fireplaces. The road has many idyllic spots where runners, bikers and motorists stop.

Be careful. The altitude, bright sunlight and showy springtime flowers can make a person giddy. If you're with the person you love you may do something silly—or wonderful. I know of a number of families that began with this ride.

You'll see why they are called the Irish Hills—they're as green as Ireland and were named by the McHenrys, McArdles and the McAndees, early Irish settlers.

The Barres raised dairy cows in these hills around the turn of the century and brought their milk and cream to the L.A. Creamery (now Foster's Freeze) by horse and wagon. Later Albert Barre milked 40 head and made daily trips to the Golden State Creamery on Higuera, now the Creamery Shopping Center. Today the farm is the home of "Tex", the Cal Poly-raised longhorn steer, and 99 of his fellow kind that roam the open range on top.

Montaña de Oro is off to the seaward side of the high road and across the green hills are the seven sisters, or morros, volcanic peaks that run between the Los Osos Valley and the Chorro Valley. These are magmatic plugs which have never erupted, but rather just bulged to the surface to make this row of majestic mountains, beginning with Morro Rock in the sea and ending with Bishop's Peak, Cerro San Luis and Islay Peak (by the airport).

At night the blinking light of Piedras Blancas Lighthouse can be seen from atop Prefumo Canyon road.

Take the road all the way across the hills to See Canyon. In the fall the road is lined with apple stands selling the varieties that grow in this cool canyon. Exit on San Luis Bay Drive. Then left back to Highway 101.

Note: The lands on all sides of the public road are privately owned. Be respectful and don't leave evidence of your visit.

DRIVE HIGHWAY ONE TO THE REDWOODS

In San Luis Obispo we are close to the southernmost extension of coastal redwoods, trees which at one time grew extensively across the world. Their range has diminished but we can still see them just beyond the San Luis Obispo County border at Salmon Creek, 60 miles from town, and in all the gorges north toward Big Sur.

Salmon Creek falls are a spectacle in the spring. A million gallons a minute hit the rocks and spray fresh mountain water over the entire landscape. There is a great commotion of rushing water and wind that typifies the rutting season of nature.

A trail leads from the highway to the falls among boulders the size of VWs. Alders and laurel overhang the creek, and streamside vegetation grows luxuriantly.

Beyond the falls the trail continues uphill for two miles into landscapes of firs and the babbling stream environment of Spruce Creek (the guys who named this creek didn't know the difference between firs and spruce. It's really Fir Creek). Spruce Creek has small sandy beaches and cool water pools. Its the perfect place to lunch and take an afternoon nap.

In the summer and fall the water continues to run at Salmon Creek, but quietly, almost contemplatively. The pools are deep and quiet, and water striders glide across the surface.

On the way to Salmon Creek you'll pass the elephant seal beaches just south of the Piedras Blancas Lighthouse. Mating and calving takes place in December and January and the spectacle of warring males over territory and females is dramatic. Get biology and psychology credit.

Northward is Ragged Point, one of the last scenic points before you leave the county. Stop at the restaurant and walk the grassy lawn to their descending staircase. It's outstanding. Ragged Point is the beginning of the rugged Big Sur coastline and from that picture point you can see why the Big Sur coast is one of the central coast's main attractions. Get PE credit.

A DRIVE IN THE COUNTRY TO POZO

I never stop being amused, surprised and delighted by visits to Pozo, the little country saloon and restaurant in the middle of nowhere. It's a united nations gathering of cowboys, bikers, yuppies and families, assembled to celebrate the good life.

Archie Johnson punishes a honky-tonk piano that is the equivalent of a chopped Harley and everybody sings along with the freedom of being country miles from anyone who might complain about the rowdy carryings-on.

Even though there is an olive in the beer glass, which is served in a Mason jar, (no you can't have any. You're not old enough. Don't even ask for a sip) nobody has their pinkie up.

Outside they're throwing horseshoes in the side yard or slouching in the shade with a cool drink in their hand. At the Pozo Country Club everybody is equal, the tri-tip is rare, dollar bills stick to the ceiling and the waitresses are good looking.

Pozo can be reached from San Luis Obispo by two scenic routes. One is via the Cuesta Grade and Santa Margarita to Route 58, then to Pozo Road— about 25 miles and a half hour driving time. The road has recently been paved and is a perfectly civilized way to get to Pozo.

The other way is about the same distance once you get to Arroyo Grande but the approach is entirely different. You go through the town of Arroyo Grande, or take Orcutt Road out of SLO, and catch Lopez Lake Road. Before you enter the Lopez Lake Recreation Area turn right on High Mountain Road. Pozo is 16 miles away on a partially paved, but mostly dirt road which crosses the 2076 foot summit.

The road is paradise to four-wheel drive vehicles in the wet season when the clay berms and gumbo ruts become taffy, but in the dry season most sedans can make it, albeit they'll look like they've aged 10 years by the time they reach Pozo.

There are creek crossings, steep grades and idyllic ranchland landscapes of giant oaks in broad valleys. It'll be a trip that you'll write home about...

"Hey dad, I was on this rough road and...could you send me some money for some new tires...and new shocks...and the paint job got really scratched and..."

I love you,

Brad

JUMP IN THE LAKE

Lopez Lake is one of our prize possessions. We drink from it, swim in it, boat in it and look at it a lot. Through an anomaly of nature this man-made lake filled in several months during a memorable deluge in 1969 that brought 49 inches of rain during January and February.

In a short time old ranches, a park, Indian ruins and miles of country road were lost from sight. The only way you can see these things now is by diving 160 feet to the bottom.

Fortunately for you and me, old buildings, privies and chicken coops were removed, so there's little chance you'll hit one of these if you're out there on the surface water skiing.

Even the old Santa Manuela Schoolhouse was moved, and you'll go by it as you leave Arroyo Grande to pick up Lopez Lake Road. It's on the corner of Branch and Highway 227.

Besides sunning, swimming and hiking there are many things for rent at the marina to make a full day—paddle boats, canoes, ski boats and skis, pontoon boats, fishing boats, fishing poles and long pink worms, just like the ones they use in the zoology lab. Actually you can't rent the worms, you have to buy them.

There is also the Mustang Water Slide which will run on weekends into October.

Admission into the park is only $5 per car, so if you have 10 people that would be only 50 cents a piece. If you want more information or want to reserve anything call 489-1122.

The source of Lopez Lake is the water shed behind the lake (east). There is a road that runs around the back side of the lake that leads to several canyons and a set of falls and pools.

To get there take High Mountain Road east into the hills toward Pozo. Pick up this road just before you reach the entrance gate to the recreational area. Follow it around to the left. It will climb high, then descend eventually to the drainage creeks that feed the lake. When the pavement ends the fun begins because the "road" ambles in and out of the creeks and at times cannot be distinguished from the creek.

In the dry season it's a piece of cake, but in the wet season it's snorkeling in a Toyota. Take friends to help pull you out. Rope and a little cash to buy help never hurt anyone either. Really, it's not that tricky. We did it in a Buick station wagon with eight people (they got out at each creek crossing), but we made it fine and only lost the exhaust system and two tires.

After the seventh creek crossing and 1.5 miles from the end of the pavement, the road broadens. A rusty sign on the right marks the trail to Little Falls. Hike up the trail for a half mile, past the idyllic streamside pools, until you're climbing up. There in the shade of the maples and bay trees are a number of romantic, naturally-sculpted tubs, just right for soaking, lounging and lunching on a hot summer day. Incidentally, there's a lot of poison oak about, so take a biology major with you to point out the stuff or you'll be in big trouble.

Big Falls is another two miles up the creek. There will be a small falls on the left side and parking for a number of cars. Take the trail right, into the hills. The layout is similar to Little Falls with a trail going up very steeply to the pools and grottoes above.

A rope hangs from a tree above the first pool, inviting swingers to take off for a plunge into the water. Some jumpers leap from the 50 foot cliffs and never touch the bottom of those pools.

Don't show your mother this stuff. Our reputation for a safe and reasonable place to go to school may be in question and you'll end up going to some dreadful place like Fresno State or Bakersfield.

Have fun.

SOUTH

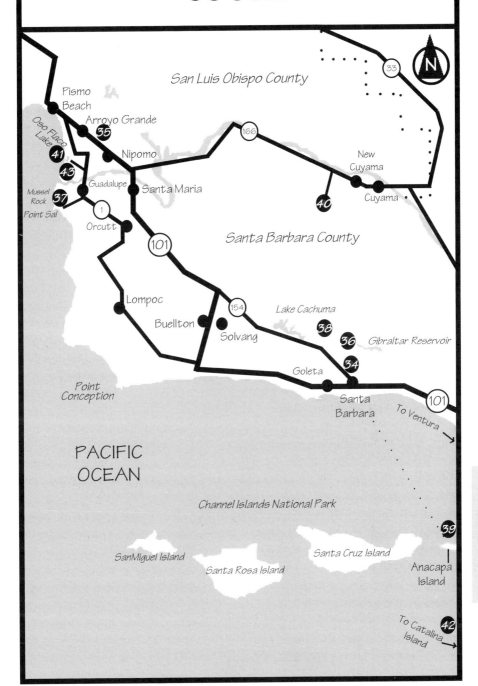

San Luis Obispo County

Pismo Beach
Arroyo Grande
35
Oso Flaco Lake
41
43
Nipomo
Guadalupe
Santa Maria
Mussel Rock
37
Point Sal
1
Orcutt

166

New Cuyama
40
Cuyama

33

Santa Barbara County

101

Lompoc
Buellton
154
Solvang
Lake Cachuma
38
36
Gibraltar Reservoir
34
Goleta
Point Conception
Santa Barbara
To Ventura
101

PACIFIC OCEAN

Channel Islands National Park

SanMiguel Island
Santa Rosa Island
Santa Cruz Island
39
Anacapa Island

To Catalina Island
42

A 24 HOUR HOLIDAY BY TRAIN

(To Santa Barbara)

Every time we get near a train station or an airline terminal we feel excitement and envy; all those people going to far away places.

We stood at the San Luis Obispo train station ready to board the train for a twenty-four hour anniversary-holiday to Santa Barbara. We picked up brochures about what to see and do in Santa Barbara and began to think seriously about how we would spend the night. We already had reservations at the Villa Rosa Inn, a few blocks from the train station but the evening was uncharted.

"Train Number 11, the Coach Starlight, southbound for Santa Barbara, Simi Valley, Glendale and Los Angeles is currently estimated to arrive the station at 2:32 p.m.," the stationmaster said over the loudspeaker.

"Train number 14, northbound, is running on time and will be available for boarding as soon as the southbound train has departed the station." The two trains meet here in San Luis Obispo, so you see travelers going north to Seattle as well as those going south.

We boarded the train and moved toward the lounge car which has a glass dome and extra large windows. The seats pivot so you can look out either side of the train. Soon we were gliding out of the city, setting our mood to the clicking of the rails.

Islay Hill came up on our left, fields of ripening grain on our right. Picking up speed we passed under Highway 227, then through Price Canyon near the historic home of John M. Price.

We crossed Grand Ave in Grover Beach with the whistle wailing, picking up speed as we flew across the Oceano produce fields—slowing again as we climbed the Nipomo Mesa. From our seats the whole Oceano Mesopotamia lay before us, flat as a table, green as a salad, a picture of life and abundance. Let's hope we never allow this to become housing tracts. The train snaked around the bends, contorting itself so we could see the engine and the forward sleeping cars.

The dunes lakes came into view, then groves of eucalyptus planted like corn and onto the Guadalupe produce fields, a mosaic of garden greens.

In and out of the city of Guadalupe we rode, through the Casmalia hills and up a long valley that leads to the sea.

For thirty minutes we moved through the Vandenberg Air force Base and the Strategic Air Command's Western missile test range. The space launch pad had a huge flag hanging on it.

A million skeletons of the dune coreopsis dot the dunes. This ride is spectacular in March when they're in bloom.

The oil derricks in the Santa Barbara Channel came to view. We're running on the edge of the sea now. All the dull-eyed travelers are on their feet. The endless trail of food gatherers who come to the lounge cars for snacks has stopped. The sights are incredible; it seems as if the surf is licking the rails.

Point Arguello Lighthouse was right out our window. In 1923 there was a horrendous naval accident here when nine destroyers plowed into the reef, ripping open the hulls and sending sailors into the turbulent sea in the deep of night. Seven of the nine ships sank and 23 sailors died trying to get to shore. We rolled by Jalama Beach to the Point Conception Lighthouse, then a 90 degree turn east into the Santa Barbara Channel.

We skirted the ocean again and cameras were clicking. At the Elwood oil field my wife read to me from Amtrak's travel log about a Japanese attack on the oil fields on February 25, 1942. A Japanese submarine surfaced offshore and lobbed 17 rounds from its 140 mm guns. "It was probably the only direct enemy attack on the continental U.S. in the past century," the report said.

The train came to a slow stop near the Moreton Fig tree along Highway 101 in Santa Barbara. We gathered our things and walked down Chapala Street toward the ocean. The Villa Rosa is a few blocks down on a quiet street of charming 1930s apartment villas.

It's a civilized sanctuary offering serenity and coddling service. The muted canyon colors, deep cushioned chairs, plantation shuttered windows that overlook the pool, and a romantic fireplace for cool evenings let me fantasize that I was a famous writer that had come to stay for two years while I worked on my next book.

In the evening wine and champagne were served with melted cheeses and fruit; and in the morning relaxed guests lingered at small tables eating Texas size muffins, croissants, juice, coffee and fresh fruits.

The concierge coached us on where to go for dinner and soon we were out again and situated at the Bay Cafe, a few blocks away at 131 Anacapa. This small sophisticated restaurant-market is run by Bryn Martin, fisherman and chef. For thirteen years he has been stealing the critic's awards for exceptional dining in Santa Barbara.

Then it was into a cab for a ride across town to the Arlington Theater for

SOUTH

a movie. To our surprise and delight there was a musical interlude at 7 p.m., between shows that was better than the movie.

Out of the stage rose a colossus, gilded theater organ, built in 1928 by the Robert Morton organ company in Van Nuys, California. The organ was installed in a theater in Jersey City and in 1988 came back to California. Its 1800 pipes, are hidden in the Spanish houses located behind the balconies. The sound is thundering, gushy and whopping enough to blow out a match.

After the show we taxied over to the Biltmore Hotel for a late night what-

The historic Santa Barbara train station

ever. It was a quiet and sophisticated, "over the hill" audience listening to the trills and arpeggios of a pianist in a mideastern gown and headdress.

The Biltmore is a quietly ostentatious hotel in Reaganesque style, with elegant tapestries underfoot and outrageous floral arrangements the size of bathtubs. Chandeliers drip with silver dollars and sinful pastries are out on the table to tempt the weak and self-indulgent.

By 11:30 we arrived back at the Villa Rosa. The attentive staff had pulled back the bedding and placed a long stem rose on the pillow with several chocolate kisses. My wife said she hoped I would continue this treatment when we got back home.

Too soon the morning came and with it the prospect of a lazy morning along the waterfront. Bicycling sounded perfect, so we walked around the corner to Beach Rentals, on Cabrillo Blvd., and rented a four-wheeled bicycle surrey.

We wheeled down the waterfront on the 12 foot wide bike trail in the company of athletic bodies walking, jogging and roller skating. We passed the zoo and pedaled alongside the freshwater lagoon to the Andree bird refuge.

By the time we got back to Beach Rentals it was time to pick up our bags from the Villa Rosa and walk the three short blocks to the train. We boarded the train and ordered some relaxing drinks from the bar in the lounge car, savoring our whirlwind stay in Santa Barbara. I'm glad anniversaries come only once a year.

For information:
Amtrak 1-800-872-7245
The Villa Rosa, 15 Chapala Street, Santa Barbara, 93101. Ph. 966-0851

SOUTH

35

FINDING THE MAGIC OF CHRISTMAS

(In Arroyo Grande)

We were Christmas shopping in the village of Arroyo Grande a while ago when the temperature was 80 degrees and people were milling about in the warm afternoon sun in front of Burnardoz, rolling melting ice cream cones over their tongues. A couple kids on skate boards rolled by...yellow hair, cinematic shirts and flowered shorts.

It made me think back to snowy Christmases in Chicago and Irving Berlin's wishful lyrics :

"The sun is shining,
the grass is green,
the orange and palm trees sway...
There's never been such a day in Beverly Hills, LA.
But it's December 24th and I'm longing to be up north.
I'm dreaming of a white Christmas"

On those snowy Christmases in the midwest, the grime of the city was blanketed in white. The brittle clatter of streetcars and machines was muffled, the blatancy subdued , the rough places made smooth, and in the morning after a night of snowfall the city was transformed into a new world of light.

Shoppers shuffled along in the mounting snow, kneading it under a thousand galoshes until it became pedestrian hash. Stores with golden lights displayed the insatiable riches of Christmas – rhinestone necklaces, electric trains and animated animals whirling and smiling in an elfin forest. Survival of the fittest gave way to peace on earth and unnatural good will.

Back in Arroyo Grande we stepped across Branch street and bought an ice cream cone, joining the Christmas shoppers who realized heaven's answer to a bleak midwinter was licking the cold atop a cone and searching for the magic of Christmas right in town.

We headed over to Amanda's Interiors to see how preparations were com-

Historic church in Arroyo Grande - now Amanda's Interiors

SOUTH

ing for the Christmas tea. She has converted the old gingerbread church into a cozy parlor, filling its nooks and crannies with ferns, copper bowls, carved geese, and brass candles.

In the "sanctuary" is a forest of twinkling trees garlanded with handmade ornaments and a host of gold angels. On the altar a ten foot angel spreads her wings, her gown a gauzy tapestry of gilded linen and lace.

When Amanda bought the church she inherited all its various buildings, including the parsonage in the rear. Now the parsonage functions as a retreat from the bustle of Branch street.

Peace, rest and freshly ground coffee is served with sinful pleasures like tortes, and petits fours on the front porch and upstairs in a secret room for lovers. Baskets of dried flowers, water color paintings and furnishings of unusual styles and quality decorate the home, the kind that draw short gasps and light sighs from hopeless romantics.

At the end of the parking lot by the parsonage is a break in the pavement and in the surrounding hedges. Beyond the hedges, and under the utility lines, is one of the county's shortest back roads.

Grown over with weeds, but still discernible is the old road to the Methodist Camp and tabernacle. Some of the old timers call this lovers' lane, a place where moonbeams, the Spirit and the flesh all worked together to change lives forever.

The road climbs the hill, and after a short jump up a mud bank, joins the new camp road that runs alongside the swimming pool.

Atop the hill is the old tabernacle, built around 1896, a simple frame structure resembling a giant Big Top.

In October of each year the tabernacle throws its doors open and old time gospel music rolls down the hill. There's eating and horse shoe throwing and lots of people celebrating the tabernacle's place in Arroyo Grande's history, the site of Chautauqua meetings that brought culture, education, politics and entertainment to the county until the early 1930s.

From the parsonage our walk continued to Hart Lane, a short street opposite the parsonage, where we stopped to admire the 1850s Guest House. It's an old fashioned bed and breakfast home hidden behind the trees with an idiosyncratic garden at the front door.

Mark Miller welcomed us in for a glimpse of how the old place is going to be decorated for his open house on Sunday afternoon, from 4-8 p.m.

We continued our walk to Nevada St., then left to Le Point. On the left side is the Hoosgow (sic) where there is not going to be an open house, nor flowers at the front door. As the city jail in 1905 it was one of the saddest places in town, especially at Christmas, but now it's just another pleasant interlude in a walk around town.

We walked Le Point to Mason, then right, past a few early homes to Branch Street, then right again to the white frame home past 221 Branch where Matthias Swall raised 12 kids, including Romie (Swall) Ritchey, a personal friend who died recently. She was born in this house in 1893 and married here in 1919. Mr. Swall became the president of the bank on the corner of Branch and Bridge Streets .

A few doors down (west) is Santa's Little Red House, next to the old Union Hotel, where kids submit preposterous budget-wrecking lists of wants to Santa. This makes Santa laugh very hard and his ho ho ho's can be heard all over town.

Across the street, Arroyo Grande Meat Company (built by Matt Swall) advertises geese, ducks and smoked turkeys just like it did years ago.

If you can get by Burnardoz ice cream emporium, turn left on Bridge Street, and past the old IOOF Hall, then left on Nelson to Short Street, left again to the swinging bridge at the (dead) end. Swing over to the city park and join the carolers who will be making merry at the gazebo.

The Chamber of Commerce office can provide you with a schedule of Christmas entertainment and activities; there'll be barbecues, fiddle music and dancing, photos with Santa and Mrs. Claus, square dancing, a chili and hot-dog supper, choral music, puppet shows and, by special arrangement, a sleigh loaded with toys and gifts for everyone will descend out of the clouds, pulled by a team of ten tiny reindeer.

You know, dreaming about a white Christmas is not a bad idea. Sometimes dreams are better than the real thing.

SOUTH

The Swinging Bridge spans Arroyo Grande Creek

36

A HIKE TO GIBRALTAR DAM

One trail guide referred to the hike to Gibraltar Dam as "moderate", a 6.47 mile round trip via the high road and returning on the low road. Another trail guide was equally non-disclosing, simply calling it a popular place to hike..."numerous swimming holes abound along the river," and ...(you can) "leisurely follow the river bed back to the car."

Leisurely? Well, the high road to the dam was leisurely but the low road back...well, that's something else.

We stayed overnight in the Santa Ynez Valley at the campground of Lake Cachuma, and in the morning drove to Paradise Road at the base of San Marcos Pass, 7 miles south. Paradise Road winds into the back country, through the Santa Ynez River, and comes to the fee station for the Los Padres National Forest where they collect a small fee for each vehicle.

The road snakes through hills and valleys and wooded canyons. It appeared that we were going straight to the top of the mountains.

Paradise is a good name for this road. It's scenic and travels through many different habitats. Scotch broom, prickly phlox and baby blue eyes covered the roadside slopes. Picnic day use areas alongside the river are ideal for groups enjoying a day in the water and sun.

We crossed the river again. The water was shallow and easy to navigate in late spring, even in our lubberly motorhome, although in some years these crossings, even in late spring, are deep and treacherous. Crossing a shallow tributary to the river, we came to the Live Oak Campground where kids were playing in the middle of the crossing.

At the end of the road we parked the motorhome, gathered our lunch, water bottles and camera gear, and set out for a walk we thought would be scenic and simple—take the high road up and the low road back, just like the trail guides said.

The high road rose gently from the parking area until we were hundreds of feet above the parked vehicles. Brodeia, ceanothus and sage were blooming and the air was heavy with the spicy scent of sage and drying grasses.

The road wandered across the hills on a fairly even plain. It was pleasant, and the sky-blue profusion of ceanothus made it showy. Two bikers passed us and stopped in the middle of the road to give a big rattlesnake the right-of-way.

In 45 minutes we were at a vantage point overlooking the dam. The road became patches of blacktop again as it circled around and dipped to the base of the dam.

I was ready to break out lunch, but Eva wanted to look across Gibraltar Reservoir, so we hiked to the top and found a picnic area on a gravel pad.

The dam was built in 1920, and in 1949 was raised 23 feet. It's owned by the city of Santa Barbara, but the land surrounding it is owned by the U.S. Forest Service. No swimming or boating is allowed.

After lunch we returned to the base of the dam and looked for the low road that would take us along and through the Santa Ynez River back to the parking area.

The low road was rough and weedy and it was obvious that vehicles hadn't been along it recently. We walked 200 yards and the road ended abruptly in a hedge of poison oak. We looked above us for evidence of another road, then back tracked and peered across the river. A path led to the brink, and on the other side we saw a road. We got ready to do our first river crossing.

I was resigned to getting wet so I wore shorts and planned to wear my hiking boots and carry Eva across to the other side, but the river was flowing too fast and there were lots of boulders and small pools. She took off her vintage Nike boots and stepped into the water. I'd never be able to walk barefoot across a creek, but as a child she and her sisters spent the summer months in Arkansas without shoes.

She twisted and slipped on the boulders but didn't complain; in fact she was giggling with the stimulation of cold water and slimy green algae. The water was up to her knees. We walked hand in hand and got to the other side where she dried her feet on a towel we had taken along. Crossing one was behind us.

We were now on the right side of the river but not at all sure this was the right road. It was a stream bed/road of rounded boulders that soon turned into a dirt trail. No longer were there two tracks.

After several hundred yards the path led back to the water. I helped Eva rock hop around fallen trees, swinging her from rock to rock, but it became evident that the trail was crossing the river in earnest, so it was time for Eva to take off her shoes again.

Her feet were getting a bit sore with the second crossing. She was still giggling over the adventure, but the water was deeper and her long pants were insufficiently rolled up and were wicking water to her thighs. I waited for the time when laughter would turn to anger or disgust. I usually oversell these adventures and I was eager to have this come out positively, or I would be doing future hikes by myself.

When we reached the shore I suggested she take her pants off and get down to her Victoria's Secrets. She gave me a startled look. "Look, Hon," I said, "there's nobody out here. We are obviously lost and by ourselves, and who would see?"

Off came the pants. She fashioned an oversize flannel shirt as a skirt and became more natural with every crossing.

But a sock was missing. We looked back in the river where it was taking a ride. I splashed back into the river and retrieved it. I had one wet sock, a towel and one pair of wet pants hanging from my pack. Anyone looking at my drying laundry could have figured out that Eva was half-dressed.

We met three bikers at the next river crossing which was more than 200 yards long. They came upstream against the current, carrying their bikes on their shoulders. A young woman stumbled through the shallow pools and over slippery rocks while her spotted dog frolicked in the water. This was the 7th crossing from the parking lot for them and they were wet, slimy with algae and stumbling over the glossy rocks in a state of exhaustion/exhilaration.

We slipped off huge boulders into deeper water and Eva was up to her groin. She squealed with surprise as cold water reached warm areas as yet untouched. Each step in the river was uncertain. I worried about my camera and lenses in my pack, and I was dragging so much algae with the toes of my hiking boots I felt like I had hooked a green carpet.

"It seems like miles of thigh-high water," I called out to Eva as we slogged along. "It's crotch high," she shouted back. She vowed this was the last crossing she was carrying her shoes. From that point forward, her classic Nikes went swimming with her.

Each creek crossing took us about ten minutes, and we had six more to go.

We met another biking couple on the trail. Everyone was in high spirits, and we were too, because we got information from them on upcoming river crossings and estimates of time to the parking lot. The sun was bright, the water was cool, the algae was green and everyone was like a family on an outing.

We came upon a couple who found a cozy rock ledge above a blue lagoon. This is the appeal of this walk. There are numerous places where families and couples can spend a day swimming and picnicking along the Santa Ynez River.

Close to the end of the trail are some really fine pools and the traffic is heavy. We saw people with dry shoes and socks and deduced that the crossings from that point downstream were dry, dull and hardly any fun at all.

Eva went on ahead to the motorhome and showered before I got there. I lingered for a while to photograph and to enjoy the last moments along the river.

"How did you like the hike, Toots?" I asked.

"Well, the high road is just a road. You've got vistas but there's nothing exciting or adventurous at all about it. The low road isn't a road at all, but it was fun."

This from a woman who wet her pants, soaked her shoes and really didn't want to go in the first place. Am I lucky or what?

SOUTH

37

AN ADVENTUROUS TREK

(To Mussel Rock And Point Sal)

We didn't intend it to be perilous and risky. We simply planned a hike to Mussel Rock and Point Sal because of their remoteness and beauty. Their landscapes of bizarre colors and extraordinary geologic formations are so inaccessible that hardly anyone gets to see them; yet they're only an hour from San Luis Obispo.

While the whole distance from the beach at Guadalupe to the beach at Point Sal, across the two points, is only five miles or so, it is virtually uncharted territory. High walls run down to the sea and the uncertainty of tide and swells makes crossing at the points perilous.

The trails are nebulous and uncertain in places, but there is a path to follow, and our group, ages 11 to 73, did it, but with some very tense moments.

Ben and I left two vehicles at Point Sal State Beach the night before our hike, riding our bicycles back to Arroyo Grande. The next morning the chosen 12, full of faith and anticipation, gathered at the Methodist Church and headed over to Guadalupe State Beach, driving Main Street west from Guadalupe, past the Union Oil guard station.

Coincidental with our hike was a celebration of National Coast Week. A large group of us hiked the dunes a half mile down the beach, past surf fishermen and through dunes formerly used by off- road vehicles.

Bill Deneen pointed out beach morning glory growing in the exposed sand where dune vehicles used to run, and dune thistle, a rare plant whose habitat range is in this narrow stretch of dunes from Mussel Rock to Oso Flaco.

Our trek went through the haystacks of the foredunes, crossing an old Coast Guard road that was built during World War II in anticipation of a Japanese landing. The Coast Guard had created artificial embattlements made from blackened telephone poles that stuck out from the sand toward the sea like heavy artillery.

At a traditional Indian midden, where broken white shells from thousands of Chumash Indian meals created a mound, we squatted in the sand and listened to Pacifica and Mike Zarate, representatives of the Bear Clan of the Chumash, talk about the sacredness of land, sea and air. The presence of two Native Americans, whose long line of ancestors were company to these meals, gave the moment poignancy.

Within a half mile the beach thins and the headlands of Mussel Rock begin. The trail winds into the first canyon where water weeps from the sand-covered rocks. Cattails and calla lilies grow luxuriantly, a strange paradox in an environment otherwise exhausted from the late summer lack of rain and water in late summer.

The rock cliffs are bent into deep folds like bread dough. The rock is subtle shades of green, gray and brown. Some of it is black, with brittle structure, and what appears to be gas bubbles formed when it was magmatic.

We approached the first prominent point of Mussel Rock and created a temporary midden spreading our lunch on the ground.

Greg & Tracy Stob repelling down at Point Sal State Beach

Ahead of us a quarter mile to the south lay another point, and between the points was a beautiful crescent beach.

"If that's Point Sal," I thought, "we're in good shape. It's only a one-and-a-half hour walk from the point to the vehicles by the state beach." But it turned out that wasn't the point.

The tide was high and waves were washing up across the beach to the vertical rock face. Forty feet above the waves and the beach is a thin trail that Pat ventured out onto while we continued our lunch. We watched him go, picking his way precariously along the edge of a 40-foot wall. At one point the trail descends 20 feet down a slide. There wasn't a handhold anywhere and Pat had to ski this section in a straight line or end up on the rocks below. We followed, sliding down the sand chute on our fannies, until we came to the beach at the base of the next Mussel Rock prominence.

At an eroded gully, sculpted into stony needles and multicolored pagodas, Eva said excitedly, "Look, a miniature Bryce Canyon."

SOUTH

Phil and Janice went down to the water's edge to poke around in the tide pools, finding tubs of sea anemones and sea stars, and Eva and I joined them.

We spotted a blue nylon rope tied around a huge boulder that goes up to the second Mussel Rock point. We set our feet against the rock, and with cooperative pushes between the crashing waves reached the top. Standing in the mist and wind we were smitten with the beauty of the mile-long beach between Mussel Rock and Point Sal.

It was 1 p.m. and we had to be back to our cars before 6 p.m. when the guard locks the Main Street gate, so there was an urgency to get to the vehicles parked at Point Sal State Beach.

From that second point we ambled over a treacherous trail barely etched into the steeply sloping hillside. Soon we met the gang that had taken the high ridge trail and together descended down a 40-foot wall along toe holds and finger ledges.

To our surprise there were several surf fisherman on the beach, standing like figurines in the surf, mesmerized by the seductive dance of their poles. We approached them, peeked into their buckets and saw large catches of sea perch.

Halfway down the beach is Kon Tiki South, a flotsam shack that is somebody's Shangri-La. An old surf board hangs from the roof, turning in the breeze like a weather vane.

The walk was long and the sand was soft, and the faithful began to sag and sigh. Kelly, our youngest hiker, asked his mom, Tina, the inevitable kid question, "Mom, are we almost there?"

Eventually the beach withers and the headlands of Point Sal take over. We crossed black rock fields streaming with iridescent green algae and vertical cliffs of gray-green rock with unusual ball-like accretions. The odor of the sea was like the musty breath of a million sea creatures.

Tina, Bill and Kelly were the first ones up Point Sal and Kelly soon forgot his tiredness when he faced a herd of deer grazing near the point.

Seal Rock, just off the point on the southern side, was alive with barking seals lolling in the water and a group of aggressive characters pushing cormorants around near the top of the rock.

The trail to Point Sal Beach is a continuation of small beaches, rocky prominences and perilously thin trails. Mount Lospe (1640 feet) and the Casmalia Hills form a magnificent backdrop.

Two formidable rocks jut into the ocean blocking the way to the beach. The last one can be surmounted by following a steep and tiring trail that winds high above it, or you can scale it by climbing a rope left by previous adventurers. At the end of our seven hour hike this challenge was more than some could handle, so they pulled up their pants and took off around the rock in the churning sea.

The tide was out but it was still treacherous. Pat went first, gingerly step-

Phil and Janis Stob overlooking the ocean near Point Sal State Beach

ping into the surging water, carrying his photo bag on his head. The surprise is the hole in the sand at the tip of the point, where, according to wave size and surge, you can be in water from your thighs to your arm pits or more.

Pat made it okay, then Barbara; but Allyson hit this spot when a wave struck and she came to shore using the Australian crawl.

It was a motley crew that dragged their weary bones over that last long stretch of beach to the waiting vehicles. Most were wet, some were scratched and bleeding, and all were dirty and muddy on their back sides.

What is adventure to one person is life-risking mania to others. I sure hope my friends talk to me again.

For decades many federal, state, county and private conservation groups have sought to preserve the extensive sand hills of the Nipomo Dunes for their exceptional beauty and the extraordinary community of rare and unusual plants they support.

Now under the central administration of the Nature Conservancy, these lands are assured the sanctity befitting a wild area of unexcelled scenic diversity.

In 1991 a visitor's center was constructed at the Main Street, Guadalupe Beach, offering interpretation and information to visitors. For information contact the Nature Conservancy at 672 Higuera Street, San Luis Obispo, CA 93401. Ph. (805) 343-2455.

ALISO CANYON NATURE TRAIL

The Santa Barbara County ceanothus (California Lilac) are gorgeous in spring. The hills are resplendent with puffs of white to midnight blue the last weeks of March and the beginning of April. In many places it appears that ceanothus is the only species in the chaparral.

We took a ride up Highway 154 toward San Marcos Pass in early April, exiting at Paradise Road, beyond the turnoff to Bradbury Dam on Lake Cachuma.

Paradise Road winds off the highway and meanders along and through the Santa Ynez River, past shady campgrounds to popular river-front picnic and day use areas.

A few miles down Paradise Road is the Fremont Campground situated in an oak grove, then Paradise Campground, equally woodsy and peaceful. A walkway leaves the grounds of Paradise Campground through a stone tunnel under the roadway to the edge of the Santa Ynez River.

The river is usually a shallow stream bed and it's an ideal playground for children on warm sunny days, but on the fourth day of April when we were there the river was flowing fast and small children had to be held lest they tumble downstream. At the rate of flow of the river, Lake Cachuma was going to fill, although the experts said another 3 inches of rain was needed before the water crested Bradbury Dam where the water level had crept to within 6 feet of the spillway.

Beyond the Paradise Campground is the White Rock River access day use area, then the Los Prietos Campground.

A few miles further is the Sage Hill Group Campground and the Los Prietos Ranger Station, an information office with maps and brochures to the back country camps and trails. The road into Sage Hill runs alongside the ranger station then heads across the river to day use areas and the trail head to Aliso (Spanish for Alder) Canyon, the focus of our attention.

The road across the river was at least 6 inches under water, and it gave us a moment to consider, but a little compact car came across from the other side plowing a wave as high as its headlights and proceeded out of the water dripping wet but running good, so we gingerly entered with the pickup, taking our time and wondering if the current was strong enough to push us off the roadway into the stream and its boulder strewn bed.

The road on the other side of the river runs past picnic grounds shaded by towering valley oaks, and alongside sunny playing fields ideal for soft ball. At the far end, past the single lane bridge, was the trail head to Aliso Canyon.

Aliso Canyon nature trail is a three-mile interpretive loop which parallels Aliso Creek, then climbs the ridge and circles back again to the parking lot. (Pick up the trail guide at the ranger station before you begin this hike).

The trail begins at the end of the parking lot and ambles along the stream in a contemplative atmosphere ideal for blooming things and positive human experiences. After the fourth sign post there was a junction of the trail to Upper Osos camp, but we continued straight ahead on the Aliso Canyon trail, following the stream. This is a well marked, broad trail with interpretive sign posts along the way.

Forget-me-nots spattered the sunny hillsides and swallow tail butterflies flitted about brodeia, fuchsia, flowering gooseberry and shooting stars.

At station 10 the trail ascended, leaving the creek side. We tasted the fruit of the wild cucumber, a soft spiny green ball with white foamy flesh that puckers the mouth and inclines one to spit a lot.

Cascades of flowers draped the hillsides creating spectacles—carpets of poppies amongst the yucca, full bunches of fiesta flowers and vividly bright prickly phlox. In an hour we had removed ourselves from the maddening crowds along the river and were isolated in the back country, seemingly miles away, yet an easy one-mile walk for any able-bodied person.

After station 13 we came to a small creek and were tempted to go right (which simply goes up the creek for a ways), but continued across the creek to the left and circled around the hill.

We stopped alongside the trail where my friend, Guilbert, counted seven kinds of showy flowers growing in a three foot radius. We all stooped and gushed—California poppies, zygadene-star flower, Indian warrior, blue dicks, fiesta flower, yellow violets, and blue-eyed grass. Guilbert broke out into song, his Irish tenor voice ringing out across the canyons...The Hills Are Alive With The Sound Of Music.

Lelia, catching the moment, began to warble...We SHALE Overcome...as we picked our way along the broken shale trail. And then her sister joined her for a duet in verses from The Happy Wanderer:

SOUTH

"Take my hand Lelia"

I love to go awandering
Along the mountain track
And as I go, I love to sing
My knapsack on my back

There was no stopping them.

Prickly phlox were blooming on the south face of the canyon near a place where we caught sight of pillows of molten rock, evidence of a period of volcanism.

The trail went up-hill along a deeply eroded gully. We straddled the chasm coming along pools wriggling with tadpoles. It's going to be a good season for the songs of frogs and toads. Better than Guilbert.

We came to a ridge saddle where we pondered the direction of the Aliso Canyon loop trail. A white-faced mountain of matilija sandstone was to our left. One trail continued over the ridge, going down the other side to join the trails to Upper and Lower Oso. Guilbert climbed the hill to our right, beckoning for us to come when he had reached the top.

At the top was a trail sign which left little doubt that we were to follow this high ridge trail back to the parking lot alongside the river. At several points we had magnificent views of the Santa Ynez River Valley below where children romped and horseback riders stood belly deep in the middle of the stream.

This is a three hour trip of three miles...which some will do in an hour or less. Some come to hike and sweat, some come to smell the flowers and sing.

Oh, may I go awandering
Until the day I die
Oh, may I always laugh and sing
Beneath God's clear blue sky.

ON THE WAY HOME: Stop at Bradbury Dam which was built in 1953 to impound the Santa Ynez River. Across the expanse of water are the San Rafael Mountains and the San Rafael Wilderness.

Paradise Road is 80 miles from San Luis Obispo.

SOUTH

ANACAPA ISLAND DAY TRIP

We pulled out of the Ventura Harbor at 9:30 a.m. under sodden skies. The skipper of the boat eased the boat out of the slip and began a prattle of useful information about Forster's terns, brown pelicans and western gulls.

We could barely see the obscure silhouette of Anacapa Island, lying like a monster across the seamless sea. The three sections of Anacapa looked like it had been broken into three parts, but joined at the water's edge by a thin bridge of land.

Anacapa is a unique place in the Santa Barbara Channel, 18 miles from Ventura. In 1938 President Roosevelt entered Anacapa and Santa Barbara Island into the National Park system. Since then five of the eight Channel Islands have been included to comprise our 40th National Park.

Rising from the south, and contiguous with the Santa Monica Mountains in Los Angeles, the Channel Islands are an underwater mountain range that show themselves only briefly in a series of peaks we call islands.

What makes them particularly attractive and distinct is their isolation from the mainland, and their situation in the warm and cold currents that surge up and down the Santa Barbara coast. Their position is far enough south to include sub-tropical species, and far enough north to include visitors and residents of northern climes.

Many plants and animals show variations from mainland species because of thousands of years of separation. Along their shores seals, sea lions and walruses live. West Anacapa's slopes are the primary nesting sites for brown pelicans, and East Anacapa is a principle breeding ground for western gulls.

Giant kelp beds around the islands are nurseries for thousands of colorful species of abalone, sea urchins, and sea anemones. The National Marine Sanctuary extends a mile to sea on all sides of the islands, insuring the survival of species threatened by mainland traffic.

Our boat ride was pleasant and interspersed with sightings of oil platforms and more natural things. We encountered a school of Risso's dolphins and the skipper obligingly slowed the boat and circled 'round the pod while we leaned to catch the eye of one of these marvelous beasts. In the calm of the sea the dolphins heaved and rocked to the rhythm of their breathing, exhaling in loud, steamy breaths, so that we could nearly smell them. It was a rare opportunity for intimacy with the creatures of the sea.

As we approached closer to the island we caught more of the detail of this volcanic rock, jutting out of the water with its sheer cliff walls and hidden grottoes. Cormorants, gulls and pelicans nest and feed here, covering the rocks with their guano and filling the air with their presence. The sea washed into black volcanic caverns, compressing and churning into white hissing spouts and explosive back charges. We motored close to the cliffs, finally rounding the corner into the protected cove. It's a place unusually bizarre and beautiful.

Six people at a time donned life jackets for the short ride in the motorized launch to the ladder at the base of the dock. Grasping the ladder from the launch that was riding the swells required spider-like qualities, but we all scampered up the rungs safely.

Expeditiously the crew loaded the launch again and again, until we were all safely on the dock platform.

A metal staircase of 100 steps rises up the sides of the cove to the top of the treeless island. We looked back to the deep blue lagoon where our ship rode the swells. Huge strands of kelp swayed gracefully in the clear water.

We were met by a National Park Service Ranger. She gave us good information, and warnings about getting too close to the edge of the cliffs. She announced that we had come on a lucky day. The Coast Guard was ashore to service the lighthouse and we would be able to see up-close the historic light which was installed in 1932 and is still shining through its French Fresnel lenses. It was automated in 1966 and the lonely tour of duty for Coast Guard men and their families ended in 1969.

The National Park Service has taken over the former Coast Guard residence (three were destroyed before the National Park Service intervened). Fortunately one has been saved, along with the engine and generator room, the communications center, pump house, workshops and garage.

Today a National Park Service Ranger resides on the island ready to interpret the fascinating features of Anacapa.

Anacapa is not much more than a square mile of flat walking surface so it wasn't difficult to see most of the island's features.

Ascending the steps of the lighthouse gave us a panorama of the island. Its entirety can be viewed from there—the residence and workshops, the water tanks, now respectfully housed in a Gothic structure, the treeless terrace, Middle Anacapa Island and beyond to West Anacapa.

The story the rangers tell is that there was a time when the two 55,000

SOUTH

gallon redwood tanks became targets for sharpshooters in passing boats. To stop the tanks from becoming sieves they built a Gothic building over it and immediately the shooting stopped. The sanctified water is provided by a Coast Guard ship, for there is no natural water source on Anacapa.

There was time for lunch on the picnic tables near the information building and a walk along the interpretive trail. The western gulls were not nesting when we were there, but sites are neatly staked out by individual birds. Everywhere you walk there are gulls and the deposits thereof, a virtual rain of fertilizer to nourish the plants of the island.

In springtime Anacapa is a riot of activity. The giant coreopsis are as numerous as the birds and for a short time Anacapa teems with color and life.

Our walk to the end of East Anacapa gave us views of the isthmus between the east and middle sections where the remains of the side paddler, *The Winfield Scott*, can still be found. It was this 1853 tragedy , and others to follow, that dramatized the need for a light on Anacapa.

Our three hours on the island were up and we straggled back to the dock for the shuttle to the ship.

It took us two hours to drive from Arroyo Grande to Ventura and two

Eva Stob wanders through a field of coreopsis on Anacapa

SOUTH

hours to travel by boat to Anacapa. It was a full day but not one of our party of thirty had any regrets. Gray skies gave way to sunshine, and the surprises of this natural wonderland were a stimulating experience.

To get there: Take Highway 101 to Ventura, exit at Seaward and turn left on Harbor Boulevard. Follow the brown and white information signs along the way that will direct you to the Channel Islands National Park Information Center.

Who does it: Island Packers, adjacent to the Channel Islands National Park Visitor's Center, provides charter boat service to all five of the National Park islands - Anacapa, Santa Barbara, Santa Rosa, San Miguel and Santa Cruz.

For information call Island Packers 805 642-1393. Note: Island Packer's trips are an adventure. Island landings may be wet and the trips are not for the faint, weak or timid.

SOUTH

40

MCPHERSON PEAK

(A Window To The Cuyama Badlands)

Ben sounded speculative and apprehensive as we started up the trail, pointing to a trail on a hill to our right which he thought would be our return route.

The small congregation jabbered like a covey of quail as they ambled up the dusty road. The buckwheat was a deep russet color and the ornamental Scotchbroom was glowing with iridescent plumes. It was almost as pretty in seed as it is in bloom. Likewise, the wild clematis with its flower heads of down, shimmered against the laser beams of the winter sun.

The yucca on the side of the hill were spent, their gray spindly stalks arising from bases that were totally exhausted from flowering. Other nubile yucca, veritable virgins with unborn flowers, looked maiden fresh with smooth complexion and green leaves.

We had driven 66 miles from Arroyo Grande on Highway 166 and turned right on Aliso Canyon Road, which is a few miles west of New Cuyama, and drove through the chaparral oil fields into the wooded canyon.

We parked the cars under the canopy of the oaks at Aliso Campground and started up a jeep trail toward Hog Pen Camp. McPherson Peak towered above us, the sight of our attention and a goal for some of us.

After an hour we were still on the Jeep trail leading up to Hog Pen Camp, a base camp before the climb to the top. We could have driven this distance and Eva and I quibbled about whether I should recommend you drive your cars on this rutted road. If you follow her advice you walk the two miles from Aliso Camp to Hog Pen and save your exhaust system. Take my advice and ride, for there is plenty of walking yet to do after you reach Hog Pen.

The pioneering McPherson families homesteaded these parts in the 1890s and ran cattle in the Cuyama Valley. They used the well at the base of the hill for their hogs, thus the name Hog Pen. Pieces of fence, a few foundations and sections of asphalt road are remnants of their efforts to settle on the land.

H.M. McPherson hunted quail in the Cuyama Valley and harvested sufficient numbers of birds to send to market in San Francisco. In 1896 he was shot

McPherson Peak overlooks the Cuyama Badlands

in the back accidentally by Mike Newsom, and Dr. Paulding from Arroyo Grande, was summoned. By the time Dr. Paulding arrived on a buckboard pulled by a team of horses over trails steep and treacherous following heavy rains, the patient was dead.

At Hog Pen campground we assembled at trail marker 27W01 and read the signs to distant places. Ben spoke excitedly about fascinating views, grand panoramas and the exhilaration of seeing a new world when we got to the top. He didn't say a thing about sweat, blood, tears and aching joints. Whenever he gets spiritual and emotional like that we suspect he is preparing us for an experience that may become an ordeal.

"When we get to the ridge we should be able to see all the way to Carissa Plains. We've got a day that's just gorgeous...and then in the other direction we should be able to see into the Sisquoc area and the Cuyama Badlands." Some people in the group actually believed this hype and jumped- off like they were afraid these fabulous sights might disappear before they got there.

The trail ascends to the left of Hog Pen campground, running along a steep canyon wall. It was nice. The day was as clear as gin and the countryside of scrub oak, sage, manzanita and the swaying heads of golden grasses back lit by the long rays of the sun, was beautiful. The chaparral is a profusion of natural dried flower arrangements without a hint of contrivance, yet is artistically arrayed. At a point along the trail we looked back and caught views to the north of the Caliente Mountains, a system of treeless convoluted ridges that separates the Carissa Plains from the broad valley of Cuyama.

The climb is relentless, but not particularly steep or difficult. Faye Lehman was feeling the miles and the stair-step workout as he joked - "Either this slope is getting steeper or I'm getting older...fast."

Someone might look at this land and wonder, "What is this land good for?"

It's good for butterflies and snakes and scrub oak, and the birds of the bush...and it's good for us and anyone who wants to walk among the wild creatures of the earth.

I'm grateful to the visionaries of the early 1900s who thought we needed this experience. They persuaded Congress and the President of the United States to set aside these lands as natural preserves.

President McKinley signed into existence the first million and a half acres as the Zaca Lake and Pine Mountain Reserves in 1898, and in 1938 President Roosevelt renamed these lands the Los Padres National Forest, which now occupies more than a 1.7 million acres in five different counties. In 1932, 75,000 acres were set aside as the San Rafael Primitive Area and in 1968, 110,000 acres were designated the San Rafael Wilderness.

After 4.5 miles of uphill trudging we came to the Sierra Madre road, 32S13, and gained the long views into the San Rafael Wilderness with the pine covered ridges of Figueroa Mountain to the southwest, beyond the Sisquoc River Valley. Ben was right. The views were magnificent.

Across the expanse of wilderness and the spine of Hurricane Deck we looked into the Manzana Creek and the Sisquoc River Valleys. These canyons are the site of an old schoolhouse and remains of the homes and barns of a settlement of 100 people who joined the charismatic Hiram Preserved Wheat in the 1880s. After repeated floods, and then the drought of 1897, the community broke up and moved to Santa Maria and other places.

Our hiking group split here, some going back down the way we came, the rest of us going on toward McPherson Peak.

The walk along the high ridge of the Sierra Madre Road was pleasant, but the starch was out of this gang and some complained of aching knee and hip joints. When a little red pickup truck appeared, the idea of mooching a ride to McPherson Peak was on my mind.

At first mention a few stalwarts demurred and said, "No we're all right. We don't need to ride. We can walk it. We want to walk it. We love to walk it. We want to see more rocks and trees and dust and road."

But I had had enough, so when the driver turned around at Lamar Johnson's corral, which blocks the road, and came back our way, I flagged him down and asked if we could ride in the back of his little red truck to McPherson Peak. "Sure," he said, "hop in."

I'll tell you, I've never seen such a flurry of dust as the principled ones pivoted, spun and skidded in the dust in their haste to get in the back of this little red truck for the 1.5 mile ride to McPherson Peak.

We learned that he had driven from Tepusquet, off Foxen Canyon Road (about 10 miles from Santa Maria) , taking 11N04 through Colson Canyon by the Colson Forest Service Station, then 11N03 north toward Miranda Pine Mountain, turning east on Sierra Madre Road 32S13 to McPherson Peak.

If you want to come up here by road take Highway 166 east toward Cuyama and turn right on 32S13, Sierra Madre Road near the Rock Front Ranch off Highway 166, a distance of about 26 miles from Santa Maria and Highway 101.

McPherson peak at 5,747 feet is one of the tallest peaks in the Sierra Madre Mountain Range and formerly supported a fire tower. Now it has a number of transmission towers on it. A twelve foot diameter, six foot high empty cement water tank is used by hikers to get out of the wind and to take shelter during rain.

The down trail (27W01) takes off to the east of the peak and is clear and discernible for a quarter mile, then gets absolutely gnarly. It's overgrown so badly in places that the trail is not visible a few feet away. Our feet were on the trail but our bodies were bushwhacking. Two hikers in short pants who joined us at McPherson Peak were cut and bruised as they thrashed downward.

Suddenly the trail would be clear again and the edges trimmed and we would have ten minutes of freeway...until the next savage section of pygmy forest.

The last section of the trail was excellent and I suspect in time trail crews will finish grading and bushwhacking their way to McPherson Peak.

You were right, Ben. It was a grand experience in the great outdoors with fascinating views, grand panoramas...and a bit of an ordeal. Fun though.

SOUTH

41

OSO FLACO

(It's All About Bears)

One of the first places named by the Spanish in our county is Oso Flaco, and it's one of the reasons why San Luis Obispo Mission was the fourth of 21 California Spanish Missions established before missions like La Purisima at Lompoc, Santa Barbara and San Francisco.

The early Spanish galleons were looking for a good harbor along the California coast. After repeated failures, the Spanish monarchy decided a land party was necessary to thoroughly explore the California coastline.

In 1769 Gaspar de Portolá and the Franciscan Padres Junípero Serra and Juan Crespi teamed up for a winning combination of aggressive politics and religious fervor. They landed at La Paz, Mexico for a cross country trek of discovery.

On August 30, 1769 de Portolá and Father Crespi crossed the Santa Maria River, slogged across the dunes and came to an inland lake where a small bear was bagged. They named the lake *Oso* (bear) *Flaco* (meager or thin), more commonly translated *Skinny Bear*. They had a bear barbecue and discovered the following morning that they had difficulty standing. Apparently, the bear had been poisoned by the Indians who often set out poisonous meat for the bears. Bears were a threat to the native Chumash and without guns and bullets, they had limited ways of dealing with them. The alkaloid poison paralyzed the bears and made them easier to kill.

The troupe moved on when their temporary paralysis wore off and discovered many bears in the Chorro Valley. This was an important observation for a bunch of guys living off the land because when they ran out of food in Monterey, they came down and bagged over 100 grizzly bears near the Laguna (lagoon), returning to Monterey with 9000 pounds of jerked bear meat.

While they were here, the soldiers fell in love with the Chumash girls and the officers saw that the mouth of the "Valley of the Bears" near two creeks (Stenner and Chorro) was a good place for a mission.

The mission became the soul of San Luis Obispo and the center of our lives, but what about Oso Flaco, the place where bears were first sighted?

It's been celebrated, too, or desecrated. For years it was playground to anybody with a motorized vehicle that didn't get stuck in sand, and with the advent of a*ll terrain vehicles*, nothing was off limits. It was fun, and it was destructive. The back dune lake of Oso Flaco, one of 12 lakes in the dunes, was threatened unless the bare dunes, stripped of their vegetation, could be reclothed in their natural flora. Some active dunes move 20 feet a year, and under the worst conditions, 75 feet a year. Oso Flaco Lake was in danger.

The 18 miles of dunes that extends uninterrupted for 18 miles, from Pismo Beach to the north to Point Sal State Beach to the south, have been given three designations. The Pismo Dunes State Vehicle Recreation Area south of Grand Avenue remains a motorist's dream. To the south of that, around the *skinny bear* lake, is the Guadalupe-Nipomo Dunes Preserve, a quiet place that has put the dunes and its associated biota back together again. Far to the south is Point Sal State Beach.

We walked the causeway into the Guadalupe-Nipomo Dunes Preserve, a quarter mile lane that catches fleeting images of animals that live in the dunes. Bobcats, cougars and raccoons have been observed here. All we saw were fishermen and families with kids, but early and late in the day the wildlife play.

The State Vehicle Recreation Area authorities reseeded the area blown out by vehicles and the hills are making a recovery. When wind blows over 11 m.p.h. it moves sand, so tufts of straws were plugged into the sand to stop the movement. A hydro-sprayer blew a mix of water, wood pulp, fertilizer and seed before the winter rains.

Beach evening primrose was ideally suited for this kind of planting, a pioneer plant that breaks up wind. Other plants followed. To protect the vegetation, boardwalks strike out across the lake and over the dunes making it wheel chair accessible and a pleasant hard surface for walkers.

The entire project was completed with volunteer labor. Money for material came from Proposition 70. Plastic "lumber", recycled from waste plastic and beverage bottles, was used for rails and floor. Pilings made of treated wood were driven through 6-12 feet *of duck butter* at the bottom of the lake and into firm holding sand.

The dune plants don't seem to be on the same calendar as the rest of California and Hooker's primrose is still in bright yellow and beach yarrow and Blockman's groundsel look colorful and cheery in late summer.

Wooden platforms in the lake are left over from the days when they were used as duck blinds for hunting. They're now used by cormorants who dry their wings in the sun. Dabbling ducks with their derrieres in the air grub for food and a mother with too many babies glided across the pond with her wee ones snipping at duck weed and insects.

SOUTH

We spotted a big old gold fish, indolently wasting the day. One day he was bait, the next he was free and had the pond to himself. Pennywort grows along the edge of the lake giving it an artistic frame.

The raccoons are out there too, their excrement in the corners where they had their last meal—maybe someone's lunch. They have been known to snitch snacks from unaware visitors and workers.

Jack Beigle, a docent with the Nature Conservancy, spotted a ruddy duck, a bird that Peterson's Field Guide describes as "a chubby duck". It's one of the few ducks that cannot walk on land. Its nest is attached to reeds and holds 6-10 large eggs.

Wild strawberries saved the strawberry industry when fungal diseases destroyed the domestic crops. Agriculture professors looked for strawberry plants that had resistance to mildew. This plant endures foggy days and dewy nights in the dunes but doesn't get mildew fungus. Cross pollination resulted in a resis-

Hikers walk through the dunes at Oso Flaco

SOUTH

tant strain. This is only one reason for maintaining wild populations of plants and animals.

Wax myrtle and arroyo willow grow side by side near the water. Wax myrtle is shiny green with a serrated edge, willows are dull green; together they're an impenetrable thicket.

Near the ocean we had lunch on a knob over a scenic view of the Pacific and the wandering stream from Oso Flaco Lake.

Open sand sheets to the south at times cover, then expose Chumash middens, places where the Indians disposed of their kitchen wastes, mostly shells of mollusks. They preceded the Spanish by 8,000 years and had numerous camps along the coast.

The least tern, an endangered bird, nests in open sand and chooses sites where walkers and cyclists are. Their 3 speckled eggs are laid in a slight depression in the sand and are easily destroyed unless enclosures are constructed around the nests. .

So how is this place of the bears doing? Very well, thank you. And if you haven't been out there for some time, get in the Volvo and take a ride out. Take Highway One south from Grover Beach and cross the Nipomo Mesa until you come to the produce fields and Oso Flaco Road, a few miles north of Guadalupe. Turn (right) toward the ocean.

There's not an age group that can't do this walk, and the climb over the last hill to the ocean is as wild and beautiful as that day in 1769 when the Spaniards bagged a skinny bear.

SIDEBAR

Eleven other dune lakes are north of Oso Flaco Lake. The private sporting club that own these lakes have agreed with the Coastal Conservancy to sell two of the lakes and put a conservation easement on the other nine. The northern most would go to the State Park, the southernmost lake (Black Lake) would go to the Nature Conservancy. The nine in the middle would still be owned by the Dunes Lake Club but they could build three homes and one B&B. Negotiations are nearing completion.

SOUTH

SAILING THROUGH THE NIGHT TO CATALINA

Eva and Dave took the first watch. The rest of us were supposed to catch some sleep below deck, but we were too excited about the midnight passage to Santa Catalina Island under a new moon. All five crew members crowded the cockpit of the 37 foot sloop "Classy Lady" as we left Santa Barbara Harbor. Beyond the last lighted buoy, Dave hoisted the main sail for stability and set a southeast course (hard to comprehend, but true) for Anacapa Island. From there we would set a more easterly course for Catalina.

The Pacific Ocean was living up to its name, being gentle and even with minor swells that rocked us gently. Under a new moon, which I learned was no moon at all, the passage to Catalina Island at midnight was dreamily beautiful. The lighted oil derricks winked from the near distance and the absence of fog gave us an intimate look at them. They are tubular cities with three-hundred foot legs that extend to the ocean floor.

We star-gazed and floated through the universe, lost in the vastness of a black sea and a sky skewered with lights. Crew member Bob amused himself and us with stories of Orion and the bear and the hunter and fantasy images derived from patterns of stars and constellations. We were exercising the ancient heritage of star-gazing and story-telling. Seldom do we have a lap full of stars and time to wonder.

White-sided dolphins, who don't sleep either on moonless nights, raced beside us, playing in the bow wave. With only the lights of stars for illumination, their visages were luminescent zephyrs racing through our dreams.

Eventually three us retreated to below deck for sleep while Dave and Eva scanned the horizon for obstacles and cargo laden vessels in the shipping lanes. My night watch was from 4 a.m. to 7 a.m. I needed the sleep.

At about the time sleep finally took me, the engine slowed and I heard the unfurling of the jib. The engine stopped and I heard Dave exclaim to Eva, "I think I've gone to heaven. It's the middle of the night and we have enough wind to sail. I can't believe it."

So this is what makes sailors happy, I mused.

The behavior of the 37 foot sloop changed. No longer was she slipping through the water; now she was bucking and weaving, heaving herself onto the following sea and racing down the waves. She wallowed and twisted and pitched me to the hardwood floor before I could comprehend my situation. I apologized to my fellow crew members for the indiscretion of smacking the floor in the middle of the night, and returned to my sack splayed-out like a spider and gripping the bedding.

The heaving ship cast me to the floor a second time, but this time I was prepared. I simply dribbled off the bed like a cat grapples onto bed linens when it gets kicked off.

I don't get it. Sailors yearn for the wind to come up, they hoist their sails, the seas get high, everybody gets sick, nobody can eat or sleep and this constitutes a marvelous experience.

The morning was gray with clouds soulfully dull and baggy, the sea a confusion of pudding pewter. Classy Lady rode the waves like a porpoise. Most of the crew was top side, looking grim and green. Only the captain went below deck to sleep.

By noon we brushed the coastline of Catalina, and soon we were at our mooring at the Isthmus. The island of Catalina is shaped like an hour glass, with a slim band of land tying the west and the east end. The city of Avalon on the east side is the usual tourist destination for visitors, but the Isthmus (also called Two Harbors) is like the Pozo Saloon of Cold Spring Tavern. Herein resides a handful of natives who run a bed and breakfast, a general store, a few primitive cabins, a gas facility for boats and a restaurant/bar.

Eva and I needed to get our legs under us again, and we quickly set off for the public showers and a nap on the beach under the palm trees. There was time that first day for the half-mile walk across the Isthmus to Catalina Harbor on the south side. It's a peaceful little enclave where boats find refuge from the long fetch of the Pacific Ocean. California brown pelicans were creating a spectacle by dive bombing for fish, corralling the school around the bay, taking to the air again and transforming themselves from improbable flying machines to live spears.

We had dinner on the beach that night, making a fire in the grill and enjoying the sunset. Dave's wife Marcie came in on the San Pedro shuttle around 8 p.m. with at least a hundred other souls who were spending the weekend at the Isthmus—at the Banning House Bed & Breakfast on the hill and the many campgrounds nearby.

Catalina Island is a small world of 2,000 foot peaks, picturesque coves, ironwood canyons, grassy plains, coastal chaparral and isolated beaches. Beneath the clear waters is a preserve of beautiful sea life that attracts scuba divers

SOUTH

A visitor gazes down to the harbor at the Isthmus

to the island from around the world. A dive shop rents gear and tanks at Two Harbors.

Many of us know the Wrigley era on the island. William Wrigley, the chewing gum millionaire, made Catalina Island the winter training grounds for the Chicago Cubs as well as his private retreat. In 1975 Wrigley decided to will 86% of the island to the Catalina Conservancy who would control development on the island.

The Conservancy has set aside vast areas of the island for wilderness camping and as a preserve for the island's native plants and animals. An extensive trail system provides hikers access to remote areas. The Catalina Safari Bus provides transportation around the island - to the Catalina Conservancy Nature Center, picnic spots, hiking trails, secluded beaches, and all the campgrounds along the way.

But at the Isthmus, it's the bar and dance floor scene that brings the moths to the light. Every boater jumps into his/her dinghy in the early evening for a night of stompin', singin' and swingin' on the Isthmus' dance floor. That old wooden dance floor resounds with the thuds of a thousand pounding hooves and there isn't a sad or gloomy face anywhere. Gone are the clouds "soulfully dull and baggy, and the sea a confusion of sculpted pewter." This is really what makes sailors happy. I think I've got it.

The dinghy dock is like a swarm of whirligig beetles. It is so crowded that dinghies had to ram and squirm between the flotsam of inflatables for a tie-up. And at night following the festivities, everyone had to find their dinghy in the dark and ply the harbor waters for the precarious ride home. Buttocks on bladders a few inches off the water makes for an eventful passage.

An ideal way of visiting if you don't own a boat is to take the ferry from San Pedro or Long Beach. It's only about $36 (round trip) and 45 minutes and you're there. Stay at the Banning House B&B, a 1910 historic renovated lodge with 11 rooms overlooking Isthmus and Catalina Coves. Or...try camping. There are three types—Camp sites for tent campers with their own gear; tent cabins, which include cots, camp stoves, lanterns, picnic tables; and teepee tents which are ideal for groups. Each teepee sleeps 8 to 10 on foam pads along with camp stove, fire ring, BBQ and lantern.

Or...stay for a day and take your mountain bike. There are bike trails over all of the island. A shuttle boat runs between Two Harbors (Isthmus) and Avalon daily. If you ferry in to Avalon, arrange for the boat shuttle or the island Safari Bus to get you around. And if you can talk the driver into stopping at Doug's Harbor Reef Restaurant, Snack Bar and Saloon at the Isthmus in the evening, you'll understand why all those boats are moored in the Isthmus Coves.

Here are some important numbers:
Two Harbors (Isthmus) Visitor's Services (310) 510-0303 will give you information and reservation numbers for camping, the Banning House Bed & Breakfast, Catalina Express Cruise Ships from San Pedro and Long Beach, Catalina Cruises from Long Beach , and the Catalina Conservancy Bicycle Program.

SOUTH

Banning House Bed & Breakfast

HIDDEN WILLOW VALLEY

Most of us have a beautiful place in the world where we often go, and when friends come into town this is the place we take them. For some its Hearst Castle and Route One up the coast, for others it's the beaches or the back road to Pozo, but for those looking for the remote and the beautiful its the Nipomo Dunes and a secret place called Hidden Willow Valley.

You have to have a guide to get there, and those who see it don't often tell others where it is. If I fail to divulge all the details...well, there is a part of me that doesn't want you to find it either. But it's too good to keep for just a few, and I think that those who follow will find a walk in the back dunes as enjoyable as we did.

We began by taking Highway One out of Arroyo Grande, across the Nipomo Mesa, to Oso Flaco Lake Road, several miles north of the town of Guadalupe, then west (right) toward the ocean. Coreopsis Hill, a conspicuous green hill spotted with showy coreopsis in March and April, came to view across the produce fields to the left (south) just before we reached the dead end.

We hiked the causeway from the parking lot to the boardwalk that spans Oso Flaco Lake, then ambled through low dunes until we approached a high dune that separated us from the ocean.

From the top of the dune we eyed the creek that had to be crossed. We crossed the creek and headed southward, back into the dunes toward the big green hill with the yellow flowers.

From atop a nearby dune, we viewed the series of lakes that comprises the Oso Lake complex. At one time an extensive marsh protruded into the fields, but drainage tiles in the fields and the moving dunes have eliminated most of the marsh and only two remnants of wetlands remain.

Far to the north we spotted the Diablo roundhouses, then the old San Luis Lighthouse and the villages of Avila, Shell Beach and Pismo Beach along the rim of this wide bay. From Pismo Beach the Nipomo dunes run uninterrupted for 13 miles to Mussel Rock.

We climbed Coreopsis Hill and Bill Deneen, our guide, identified the myriad of flowers that carpet the hill. Besides the elephantine coreopsis with their brightly beaming bouquets of cheerful yellow flowers, there were gardens of carnival poppies, owl's clover, sedum, prickly phlox, fiddle head, phacelia and mounds of dune heather.

To the southwest Bill pointed in the direction of Hidden Willow Valley, near a dune with parallel striations created by dune buggies and ATVs that tore up and down the hills in the past and created scars that still show.

Our migrant group set off across a desert of bright light and shifting sand where nothing grows, then headed down a slope where the ground is damp and a mama beach primrose has scattered her seeds, and babies have spread over the sand like stars in the sky.

Still far away was the hill with the three scars.

The European beach grass invades from the west running long the ridges, holding the sand with gauzy roots that make a network the grains cannot escape. This imported beach stabilizer has such an appetite for running dunes that it threatens to totally annihilate the native California plants.

After several hours of walking, with frequent stops, we trudged into the protected quiet of Hidden Willow Valley. Horse tail rushes and cattails grew on the moist valley floor. Inside a thicket of willow was a clearing and a fire ring. A log provided seating, and in the grassy clearings our group spread out lunches for a late morning snack.

Bill pulled a chair out of the thickets and looked like Dr. Livingston in Africa with his tribe all around. A diary was taken from a cabinet on a post and Bill read some of the inspirational verses of earlier dunites who came to be away from the anxieties of life.

Kent didn't know it, but he was sitting on the jaw bone of a large blue whale. Someone had found remnants of the beast along the beach and had hauled it into camp.

The walk out from Hidden Willow Valley was across the dunes toward the ocean. No prescribed way of going. That's mostly the way you go in the dunes, because paths and trails are soon covered with the random sorting of sand and the spontaneous growth of plants across the surface.

The beach, in contrast to the back dunes, is a turbulent place of sharp winds and flying sand. Millions of By-The-Wind-Sailors, a relative of Portuguese man-of-war, were driven onto the beach by the wind, making windrows of grayish-blue forms according to the shape and height of the last wave. Their vertical sails set them on courses dictated by the wind, and thus unguided were whipped into the surf and onto the beach.

Phil was waiting for this moment where wind, blue sky and a lack of obstructions makes for perfect kite flying. Soon three of us were having dog

SOUTH

fights in the air with heavy duty kites flown by steerable strings.

We walked north for 45 minutes, flying the kites as we went, until we came to Oso Flaco Creek. Climbing the dune beyond the creek we caught sight of the trail markers and proceeded toward the cars parked at the end of Oso Flaco Road.

As we came back into the quiet of the dunes, we thought about Thoreau's statements on the need to escape our desperate enterprises and enter into a world of unhurried beauty.

SOUTH

WHAT TO DO WITH HOUSE GUESTS

(During The Holidays)

It's wonderful to have the house full of visiting family during the holidays, isn't it. ISN'T IT? Or is having a houseful of guests a mix of dread, fear and mirth? You're not alone. Many of us begin to lay plans for escape after a few days of everyone hanging around the house, eating figgy pudding and ham sandwiches, occupying our favorite chair and watching television shows we think are corrupt or tasteless. For you and Christmas grumps around the county, here's a list of things that will keep those days merry and bright, and your guests out of the house enjoying the best of the Central Coast. Problem is, they may have such a good time, they'll plan every Christmas at your place.

Here's a selection of outings to rejuvenate those Santa Claus-size bodies that have grown round with ham and nuts and fruit cake washed down with egg nog.

A. *SOUTH*

Walk The Dunes at Pismo Beach.

There are a couple of neat walks that will make them tired...and quiet. Unfortunately, they may get hungry again. Park the station wagon (or the motorhome if everybody is going to ride together) at the end of Grand Avenue in Grover Beach. There are two ways to go.

Walk the beach north, throw the frisbee, dig some clams (they must be legal size, license required), build sand castles, lay in the sun, get burnt. Walk to the Pismo Pier and beyond until you get to the last staircase at the far end where the rugged headlands of tuff and alluvial terrace deposits come down to the water's edge. The very last staircase belongs to the Cottage Inns By The Sea, and you can get to it if the tide is out, but it's around the sea mounts that protrude into the water.

The next-to-last staircase, just before the huge protruding rocks, is the

Sea Crest Motel staircase. Climb the steps and walk through their lobby and you will be at the back door of Marie Callender's where you can stop for pie and coffee. Walk back to your car, following Shell Beach Road to Dolliver Street, past Old West Cinnamon Rolls (good luck), then right on Pomeroy, past the Eclair Bakery (try their Dutch Marzipan, filo pastry filled with almond paste. Better than figgy pudding) to the beach and back to your car.

Or...go south from the Grand Avenue parking lot by the beach. Cars are allowed on the beach from Grand Avenue south, so you'll be out there with traffic, and there are some yahoos out there with poor manners, so take the way less traveled, the way of rolling back dunes with swales of mock heather, silver lupine and dune verbena on the Grand Dune Trail. The trail is directly across the street from the kiosk at the parking lot and saunters south a mile to the Oceano Campground of Pismo State Beach. Many of the things you've been seeing in the dunes are identified in a native plant collection in a triangle of road near the hiking and biking camp area.

Also at the Oceano Campground is a natural history museum. Ask someone at the campground entrance station for information. They are open Saturday, and Sunday. Times will vary during the holidays, depending on interest.

If you still have legs, walk the Loop Trail Around the Oceano Lagoon. This lagoon is not to be confused with the Oceano Park lagoon you see from Pier Avenue as you approach the beach, the one with the hybrid ducks full of crackerjacks. People love to come here and feed the ducks and it's a zoo out there. Those ducks even eat figgy pudding.

The lagoon I'm talking about is out of sight until you get inside the Oceano Campground. At the entrance on your right will be the trail head. It's very pretty with still life views of spiny rushes, ferns and horsetails thriving in quiet pools, and coots and grebes feeding along the shore. It's a level walk with many places to sit along the way. Even picnic tables if you have to eat again. The puny ones in your group may opt for this walk alone. As for me and my mother-in-law who has just had a couple of new knees installed, I'll try this one with her. If we can't get all the way around I can bring a car through the campground and drag her out. It'll be my Christmas gift to her. Talk about cheap.

While you're in this area, you must stop to see the Monarch butterflies at the Pismo State Beach Monarch Butterfly Grove. There are naturalist-led walks Saturday and Sunday. Walks last about 45 minutes. To get there: take Highway One north from Grand Avenue in Grover Beach a quarter mile. Pull off on the side of the road near the eucalyptus grove. Free parking is also available in the North Beach State Campground off Highway One.

Be careful where you step if you're there early in the day. Butterflies may fall from the trees in the wind and the cold and be on the path. When the day warms, they'll move slowly, then quiver and finally become airborne. There are thousands hanging in orange and black draperies in the eucalyptus, pine and cedar trees. Viewers sit in silence along the walkways with field glasses, reverentially observing this natural phenomenon. Some of these little fellows have traveled six hundred miles to spend Christmas in Pismo. (An aside...from the butterfly grove on Highway One, take the short scenic walk to the beach. It's a breathtaking approach. Follow the boardwalk across the creek and through the Pismo Beach State North Campground.)

The Nipomo Dunes at Osos Flaco have new boardwalks that makes walking easy and enjoyable for anyone, and for those with a yen for climbing dunes and rolling down the back side, there is that too. I took my mother-in-law (who was in her seventies at the time) here once and she amazed us by not only climbing to the top of the highest dune, but by rolling up like a sow bug and hitting the slopes in a great flurry of flying sand that had us all amazed. We of course could not be intimidated by the old lady, so each of us made the descent, laying ourselves across the slope of the hill like a Tootsie Roll and rolling to the bottom.

To get there: Take Highway One from Arroyo Grande at the end of Grand Avenue south, across the Nipomo Mesa (10,000 year old dunes) to Oso Flaco Road in the Santa Maria River basin. Take the road all the way (west) to the end. The Nature Conservancy now operates this facility and charges a small fee for using the park, but it's worth it.

There are several things to do in the Lopez Lake Recreation Area. One of them is to hike the Blackberry Springs Trail. The trail winds into the hills where you have spectacular vistas south and eastward. The trail brings you back to the entrance station, a distance of 1.8 miles.

If you time it right, you'll see the daily free-fall of turkeys from the ridge that separates Squirrel from Eagle Campgrounds. Find a place to sit quietly and look and listen. They assemble on the ridge to the north at dusk and soar into Squirrel Campground with the grace of a heavy bomber that has just lost power...landing gear down, pedal like crazy and screech to a halt. Then it's scratch a little, peck a little, peck, peck, scratch a little as they make their way up the hill and fly into the trees, cracking limbs as they go, until they're settled for the night. They're wonderful to watch and a piece of American natural history.

They were transplanted from east of the Rocky Mountain Divide by the U.S. Fish and Game to the foothills of California where they have established themselves very nicely. There are more than twenty in this flock and during the day they make their rounds of the campgrounds and the parking lots eating cracked (smashed) acorns, seeds, insects and spiders. They'll even eat figgy pudding. The admission to Lopez Lake is $5/car.

A Half-Day Hike in the Lopez Lake Recreation Area

Drive out of Arroyo Grande on Lopez Drive to the park, pay your entrance fee, and proceed to the end where there is a locked gate. Park the car by the side of the road and walk the dirt road along the Wittenberg Arm of the lake to Camp French. Pick up the Tuouski Trail at the south end of the camp and hike through oak groves and sunny slopes until it bisects with the Two Water's Trail. Distance is 1.25 miles to this point.

The trail name changes to the Two Water's Trail as it crests the ridge, where you have a choice. Over the top and down the other side takes you to the Lopez Arm of the lake, distance 1.3 miles; but if you catch the Duna Vista Trail on the ridge and walk south, you'll dead-end at a great vista point with long views to the Oceano Dunes and into the Santa Lucia Wilderness.

Another approach is to drive around the recreation area and park your car at Camp French. Turn right on High Mountain Road before you enter Lopez Lake. Turn left on Lopez Canyon Road in a mile (good fossil pickin's at this junction) which winds up and down and over and beyond and eventually comes to Camp French. It's a beautiful ride on paved roads. Maybe I'll take my mother-in-law there, too. Two Christmas presents.

Great American Melodrama features Christmas plays and silly vaudeville presentations. Ask them about their all-natural menu of hot dogs, polish sausage, barbecue beef, pretzels, beer and cakes. No, they do not serve figgy pudding. You won't have to cook the night you go to the Melodrama but you may be up with your company all night unless you have the medicine cabinet stocked with Alka Seltzer and antacids. GAM is located on Highway One in beautiful downtown Oceano. Call 489-2499 for ticket information.

Nature Conservancy Lighthouse Tours of the San Luis Lighthouse are available for tour. Call the Pecho Trail reservation line—541-8735. The walk is exceptionally beautiful and docents give the history of the lighthouse and information on the local flora and fauna. The Nature Conservancy also conducts walks in the Guadalupe-Nipomo Dunes from Oso Flaco Lake. Call 545-9925.

Nojoqui Falls is 4.5 south of Buellton on Highway 101. Get off when you see the sign to the falls, or look for the exit to Alisal Road.

It's a 10 minute walk to the falls along well maintained trails. In the dry season the falls are a disappointment, but in wet winters and springs it becomes a gusher, cascading 100 feet down a marbleized rock face.

Continue down Alisal Road to Solvang for some ableskivers and coffee with heavy cream. It's important to maintain your weight, you know.

B. CENTRAL

Bishop's Peak Hike.

Now this is a hike. Start on Foothill Boulevard in San Luis Obispo halfway (about) between Santa Rosa and Los Osos Valley Road (.4 miles south of Patricia Drive or 1.3 miles north of O'Connor Way). Bishop's Peak was named by the mission padres who thought the three peaks resembled a bishop's headpiece. The peak is one of the Seven Sisters (peaks) running between Los Osos Valley and Chorro Valley. The hike is easy for a while, then climbs through the rocks to the top. Wear appropriate footwear, preferably hard-soled hiking shoes. Sneakers will do, but the boulders are slippery. Total round-trip time, depending on fitness, is about three hours. Bishop's Peak is the highest peak in the chain at 1559 feet. Mount San Luis, across the road is 1292 feet. From the top you can see the entire chain of mountains, from Islay Peak near the airport (elevation 775), to Morro Rock in the misty far away.

Montaña De Oro and Valencia Peak.

It almost goes without saying that Montaña De Oro is a spectacle you have to share with your visiting friends and relatives. If you want to sweat and grunt, take the trail to Valencia Peak, but the terrace walk is the most tame and visually spectacular. To get there take Los Osos Valley Road to the end. It becomes Pecho Road and enters the park. Turn right on Monarch Lane, near the entrance to the park to view large numbers of butterflies in the grove of eucalyptus trees.

Elfin Forest.

Elfin oak trees, stunted by salt wind, sandy soil, and winds are the miniaturization of our coastal live oaks (Quercus agrifolia). Some of them are over 500 years old. Hummocks of tiny oak trees no taller than ten feet, are clustered together, surrounded by thickets of coastal chaparral. Take South Bay Boulevard to Santa Ysabel Street, turn toward the bay (west) and right again on either 13th, 14th or 15th streets. Park at the end (but not in front of driveways or mail boxes). No, there will not be any signs or Lilliputians beckoning...*Welcome To The Elfin Forest*. Walk in and follow your whim. Be sure you walk to the edge of the preserve that faces the bay. It's particularly breathtaking at sunset. Bring field glasses for observing waterfowl.

Children's Museum

Children's Museum in San Luis Obispo at 1010 Nipomo is open daily during the holidays to entertain the kids in your clan. I may bring my mother-in-law. They feature interactive displays and hands-on experiences for kids of all ages. I loved it. I was playing with the bubble ring and some kid came along and said I had to share. I didn't want to share. They've got a cockpit of a plane, a Chumash Indian cave crawl through experience where kids end up sliding down the throat of the mystical *Coyote* (they call him Freckles), and many other clever experiences and displays. Call 544-5437 for information.

Whale Watching

The holidays are the time of year when California gray whales go to Mexico for a vacation, skirting our coast as they wend their way southward.

They parallel the 250 foot depth of the coastal ocean floor, taking short cuts across the points, which bring them close to shore where we can see them. In the north county there is good viewing from Leffingwell Landing and from Moonstone Beach (north of Cambria); or from the Cayucos Pier as they cross Point Estero. Point Buchon is another place where they come close to shore with good viewing from Montaña De Oro State Park.

In the south county, you can often see them from the cliffs along Shell Beach. But the best way to see them is to take a charter boat that can just about guarantee you sights and sounds of these magnificent sea monsters. Here's a listing of who to call.

AVILA BEACH SPORT FISHING CHARTER SERVICE, AVILA BEACH. 595-7200. Offers daily excursions at 1 p.m. and 3:15 p.m. Bring binoculars. Galley aboard ship, or bring your own snacks.

VIRG'S DEEP SEA FISHING, MORRO BAY. 772-1222 RATES - $15 adults, $ 9 for kids under 12. Wednesday, Saturday and Sunday trips, but they will go anytime on a private charter basis if your party is over 10. They will be running whale excursions the weekend following Christmas, weather permitting.

C. NORTH

Painted Rock is eighty miles away from San Luis Obispo on Highway 58 but it's a nice day's excursion. At Soda Lake Road take a right and follow the signs to Painted Rock. Soda Lake appears in 13 miles, then the Painted Rock

Visitor Center. The interpretive center is open from December to June. In 1994, over 2,000 birds wintered here, but there has to be water in Soda Lake. Call (805) 475-2131 or 391-6000 for information and condition of the road to the rock, because if there's water in the lake, there's water in the mud road and you may not be able to drive to the rock. You can still hoof it, however.

Along Highway 58, about 26 miles out of Santa Margarita on Highway 58 is Lazy Arrow Outdoor Adventures, a 32,000 acre cattle and exotic animal ranch. They've got an interesting program including hay rides where visitors feed the animals, walks through fossil beds and observe bison, water buffalo, elands, Barbary sheep and assorted indigenous species. They work with the Department of Fish and Game and may have various wildlife in residence requiring asylum and care. They also provide an afternoon or evening cookout. Call them for information and rates (805) 238-7324

Charles Paddock Zoo on Highway 41 in Atascadero is more than what you think. I've spent enjoyable hours at this well-maintained zoo that features wild cats, primates, birds, alligators and bears. They're open 10 - 5 Friday, Saturday and Sunday; 10-4 other days. For information, call 461-5080

Templeton Livestock Market has a cattle auction every Friday beginning at 1 p.m. This is a fascinating scene for kids as well as adults. There are bleachers for observers and the song of the auctioneer fills the arena as animals are brought in and sold. Equally interesting is watching the horsemen move the cattle in the back corrals. Find a place where you can safely sit while they pen the cattle and get them ready to move to the auction arena. Call 434-1866 for information. The livestock barn is at the east end of Main Street, where all the cattle trucks, pickups and horse trailers are parked,

Ragged Point and Salmon Creek Trails are on the edge of the county and slightly beyond. These are good places to see waterfalls in the winter. The views along the Big Sur coastline are always spectacular.

D. THE MISSIONS OF CALIFORNIA

Within 50 miles of San Luis Obispo are five restored missions, including our own San Luis Obispo Mission. North is Mission San Miguel along Highway 101 north of Paso Robles; and Mission San Antonio in the Jolon Valley. To the south is La Purisima State Historical Monument in Lompoc, the most extensively restored mission in this area, and Mission Santa Ines in Solvang. Most are open daily for tours.

SIDEBAR

Figgy Pudding? Some of you are saying. What the hey is Figgy Pudding? Figgy pudding is a Christmas delicacy mentioned in the lines of a traditional English carol that go something like:

> *Good tidings we bring*
> *to you and your kin*
> *We wish you a merry (or, meddy) Christmas and a happy new year (or, yeah)*
> *For we all like figgy pudding (or, pooding...said with a pucker)*
> *for we all like figgy pudding*
> *for we all like figgy pudding*
> *so bring some out here (or heah)*

Should you have the faintest curiosity what it is or how to make it, here's my best shot. Nowhere in the literature, not in cookbooks covering the long tradition of the British since the time of Peter Rabbit, nor in festive holiday recipes from merry old England, did a recipe, or even a mention, of "figgy pudding" appear. This is the best (and only) recipe I found, from a 1961 New York Times cookbook (since revised and the recipe deleted). Good luck. And may all yaw days be meddy and brrright.

Stob's Steamed Figgy Pudding (an interpretation)
From a 1961 New York Times Cookbook

1 cup dried black figs, (fresh figs work fine)
1/3 cup finely chopped citron (not to be confused with Citroen, the French car)
1/3 cup finely chopped candied lemon peel (I'm sure you have this in the cupboard)
1 cup chopped walnuts
1 3/4 cups sifted flour
1 tsp soda
1/2 tsp salt
1/4 cup shortening (butter)
1 tsp cinnamon
1/2 tsp ground cloves
1 cup brown sugar (dark for more character)
2 eggs
1 cup grated raw carrot (don't challenge the recipe)
1 cup grated raw potato (go ahead, do it.)

COOKING INSTRUCTIONS:

Chop and boil dried figs, unless you're using fresh figs. Mix with citron, lemon peel and nuts. Sift the flour with the soda and salt. Add one-half cup to the fruits and nuts, and mix.

Cream shortening with spices and sugar, beat in eggs, one at a time until fluffy. Add the grated vegetables. Gradually stir in the remaining flour, beating until smooth. Mix in the fruits and nuts.

Fill a greased 1 1/2 quart mold 2/3 full of mixture (the mixture will rise) and cover with lid or foil. Stand on a rack in an inch of boiling water in a pot with tight cover. Steam two hours, take a nap. Add more water as necessary. Serve hot with hard sauce.

HARD SAUCE

1 cup butter, softened. Please, no margarine, olive oil or butter substitutes.
1 cup confectioners sugar
1/4 cup brandy (plus what goes into the cook). Or use rum or sherry.
Nutmeg, some

Cream butter and sugar. Swig the brandy. Add brandy to the recipe a few drops at a time and beat until fluffy. Swig more brandy until *you're* fluffy. Add the nutmeg to taste and chill. Serve the figgy pudding warm with a dollop of hard sauce. Wait until the hard sauce dissolves partially into the pudding and there is an orgiastic melange of colors and textures. Eat, roll your eyes, lose control, play Bolero. Kiss someone.

Meddy Christmas,

Ron

INDEX